READING CULTURES

READING CULTURES

▼ THE CONSTRUCTION OF READERS
IN THE TWENTIETH CENTURY

Molly Abel Travis

SOUTHERN ILLINOIS UNIVERSITY PRESS

Carbondale and Edwardsville

Library of Congress Cataloging-in-Publication Data

Travis, Molly Abel, 1951–
    Reading cultures : the construction of readers in the twentieth
century / Molly Abel Travis.
        p. cm.
    Includes bibliographical references (p.   ) and index.
    1. American fiction—20th century—History and criticism—Theory,
etc. 2. English fiction—20th century—History and criticism—
Theory, etc. 3. Fiction—Appreciation—United States—
History—20th century. 4. Fiction—Appreciation—Great Britain—
History—20th century. 5. Authors and readers—History—20th
century. 6. Books and reading—History—20th century. 7. Reader-
response criticism. I. Title.
PS379.T72 1998
808.3—dc21   97-10063
ISBN 0-8093-2146-7 (cloth : alk. paper).   CIP
ISBN 0-8093-2147-5 (pbk. : alk. paper)

CONTENTS

ACKNOWLEDGMENTS

I want to express my gratitude to a number of friends and colleagues who have influenced and read this manuscript over the course of its evolution. Thanks to Krista Ratcliffe, Jeanne Colleran, Jamie Barlowe, Cheryl Glenn, Rebecca Rickly, and Merry Pawlowski for years of generous friendship and intellectual conversation. I thank those colleagues in the English department at Tulane who have provided community and intellectual intensity, including Amy Koritz, Rebecca Mark, Theresa Toulouse, Cynthia Lowenthal, and Supriya Nair. I was fortunate to participate in two splendid NEH seminars with Paula Treichler and Anthony Appiah that directly influenced the subject matter of this book. I benefited from Richard Lanham's considerable knowledge of and expertise in hypertextuality and digital literacy and from his insightful comments on chapters of this text. I am forever grateful to James Phelan for his searching questions and carefully considered commentary on my work, beginning in graduate school and continuing through this project. To my colleague Molly Rothenberg goes my deepest gratitude for her meticulous reading and valuable criticism—and for the patience she displayed in responding to the early, rough draft of this manuscript. Her generosity and intelligence have immeasurably improved this book.

Tracey Sobol has been the most wonderful of editors: unendingly supportive, wise, candid, and an incisive reader. Also, I extend my appreciation to Carol Burns for her good advice and direction in shepherding this project through its final stages.

A grant from the Committee on Research at Tulane University (summer 1990) enabled me to begin this project.

I dedicate this book to my husband, Paul, and my sons, Austen and Joshua, who keep me honest and sane by constantly returning me to what is important in life.

Two sections of this book have been previously published and are reprinted with the permission of the publishers. Chapter 3 is based on work that was first published in *Narrative*, Vol. 2, No. 3 (October 1994). Copyright 1994 Ohio State University Press. All rights reserved. An earlier version of chapter 4 originally appeared in *Mosaic*, Volume 29, Number 4.

READING CULTURES

INTRODUCTION
Readers
in and out
of Texts

■ Why is the writerly our value? Because the goal of literary work (of literature as work) is to make the reader no longer a consumer, but a producer of the text.

—Roland Barthes, *S/Z*

E lizabeth Freund in *The Return of the Reader* argues that reader theory has reached an impasse, with the determinant text and the constitutive reader locked into an irresolvable opposition. Rather than seeing this point as an impasse, I perceive it as a juncture in the development of the theory. As a result of the influence of a variety of cultural analyses, including feminist, queer, ethnic, and postcolonial theories—reader-response and reader-reception studies have begun to contemplate audience response in terms of specific political and historical situations. To prove adequate to the theoretical moment, reader theories should acknowledge the resistant and creative reader, theorize differences among readers and audiences, place reception within the wider field of cultural production, and begin to consider the vast changes in reading that will occur with the transition from print technology to electronic/digital technology.

This study moves beyond such provisional conclusions as "the text produces

the reader" or "the reader produces the text" and reflects on the ways twentieth-
century readers and texts attempt to constitute and appropriate each other at
particular cultural moments and according to specific psychosocial exigencies. I
use the overarching concept of the reader in and out of the text not only to differentiate the textual reader from the actual reader (which are both constructions), but to discuss various in-and-out movements that occur in the process of
reading—the alternations between consumption and production, immersion and
interactivity, role-playing and unmasking.[1] Most reader theorists have fixed on the
product of reading to the exclusion of the process, which means that they necessarily return to the text. Even those theorists who have argued for the reader's
resistance have made the text determinant, such that text and reader are conceived
as discrete entities in a closed universe, mechanically exerting force and counterforce respectively. Missing from these accounts are "wave" and "field" theories
concerned with dynamic and contrastive effects, such as transformations in the
act of reading over historical periods and changes in readers during the course of
reading as well as differences among readers in the context of a cultural field. This
study seeks to fill in gaps in current theories of the reader by focusing on process
and difference.

To examine changes in the literary reader's role over the course of the century,
I begin with the reading of modernist texts, then take up postmodernist texts and
finally interactive hypertexts. In this trajectory, the pleasure of realist immersion
gives way to increasing metafictional interactivity for the reader, while on the horizon lies the very different immersion offered by virtual reality technologies in
which readers exercise instrumental creativity as role-players in a virtual world.
I agree with James Naremore and Patrick Brantlinger's claim that Romanticism,
modernism, and postmodernism have all been responses to the intertwined processes of democracy and technology at particular historical moments (2). I would
add that informatics/cybernetics has reconfigured yet again the democracy and
technology nexus. To historicize the reception and appropriation of texts, one
must understand the effects produced by their material—or, in the case of hypertexts, immaterial—forms.

In identifying the theories that underpin this study, I want to indicate some
of the important stages in the evolution of reader-reception theory. The traditional model of literary reading stems from idealist aesthetics and has been shaped
most notably by the theories of Immanuel Kant, Friedrich Schiller, William
Wordsworth, Samuel Taylor Coleridge, Matthew Arnold, I. A. Richards, T. S.
Eliot, and Cleanth Brooks. The idealism of these aesthetic theories was a response

to the material conditions of textual production. In the second half of the eigh-teenth century, a "reading revolution" occurred in England, France, and Germany that was marked by a vast expansion in the publication of books and newspa-pers, a decrease in book prices, and the proliferation of lending libraries and read-ing societies (Chartier 17). Martha Woodmansee points out that once eighteenth-century German readers began reading nonspiritual literature, many people worried about the effects of such unpoliced, promiscuous reading: "Nothing so vexed the German ideologues as the habit their contemporaries had supposedly acquired of devouring greedily one after another of these new titles," with this extensive mode of reading compared with "cruising or philandering" (90). The extensive style of reading contrasted with an intensive style that required one to read, recite, and memorize a narrow body of sacred texts (Chartier 17). The "rightists" in the ensuing reading debate proposed to solve the problem of indis-criminate reading by controlling the supply of books to the market (Woodmansee 91–92). The "leftists," however, sought to correct the problem in terms of de-mand, by attempting "to influence the *way* people read" (93). The correct method of reading, which derived from the secularization of hermeneutic practice, was prescribed in 1799 by the popular philosopher Johann Bergk. It bears a striking resemblance to the New Critical method of close reading as it was resystematized a century and a half later: first, find the work's main unifying effect, then divide the work into components to see how they contribute to the whole, and finally reassemble the parts into the whole. Only difficult texts could repay this reflective mode of reading (Woodmansee 99). Thus, ascetic arduousness would check the threat of promiscuous wandering.

Under the New Critical mandate, this model of literary reading resulted in effacement of the reader before the ontological primacy of the text. New Criticism also ignored the differences among material forms of various modes of literary discourse. By the mid-1950s, New Criticism was under siege, with one of the most damning critiques coming from the inner circle: R. P. Blackmur took the move-ment to task for its refusal to be self-reflective about its early insights into the rhetoric and psychology of poetic language.

Along with numerous other theories still ascendant, reader-response and -re-ception theories developed in the early 1970s as a reaction against New Critical formalism. Although reader theory was touted as revolutionary in breaking the stranglehold of the New Critics, it maintained closer ties to formalism than was recognized at the time. All forms of reader theory claimed to reject the primacy of the text and the concomitant assumption of a passive reader acted upon by the text, but throughout the 1970s theoretical explanations focused almost exclusively on the reader implied by the text, making questions about active reading and the constitutive reader beside the point. The influential reception theorists at the University of Constance, including Wolfgang Iser and Hans Robert Jauss, sought to avoid the pitfalls of excessive psychologizing and formalist objectification of the text. But when Iser in *The Implied Reader* (translated into English in 1974) and *The Act of Reading* (translated in 1978) focused on the reader, it was to posit an ideal reader whose expectations are contradicted and whose responses are corrected by the authoritative text.

Stanley Fish's early work, *Surprised by Sin* (1971) and *Self-Consuming Artifacts* (1972), also attempted to dispense with the notion that the literary text fully determines meaning by claiming that the meaning emerges from the process of reading. But Fish explained the similarities among individual interpretations of a text by pointing to the text as a ground—a concession that positioned him closer to New Criticism than he wished. Proceeding to the next phase of his theory, in *Is There a Text in This Class?* (1980) he removed the text as the ground of meaning, arguing that interpretive communities provide readers with strategies that determine texts. In this scheme, there is no text prior to interpretation, and the individual's reading is predetermined by the conventions of the interpretive convention. The problem with Fish's notion of the interpretive community is that it does not adequately account for changes in interpretive conventions and differences among interpretations, and it also ignores questions of agency in reading. Both Iser's and Fish's theories imply competent but compliant readers.

With the poststructuralist work of Roland Barthes came claims for a resistant and constitutive reader, demonstrated in Barthes's own reading performance in *S/Z* (translated in 1974) and further elaborated in *The Pleasure of the Text* (translated in 1975). Refusing the compliant and self-negating position imposed on female readers of misogynist texts, Judith Fetterley's *The Resisting Reader: A Feminist Approach to American Literature* (1978) uncovered a monolithic patriarchal paradigm in American literature and criticism. Barthes's and Fetterley's insistence on oppositional reading moved beyond the theoretical impasse of the cooperative reader who defers either to the text or to the conventions of an interpretive community and initiated the next phase of reading theory, which focused on reading and subjectivity as well as on the sociology and the politics of reading. Susan Rubin Suleiman and Inge Crossman's edited work, *The Reader in the Text* (1980), was pivotal in this respect. Although, as its title indicates, this collection of essays deals with the textual reader, it does move toward a recognition of reader agency, specifically in Norman Holland's essay on the constitutive role of subjective responses in creating a text and Jacques Leenhardt's analysis of empirical studies of five hundred readers from different social origins in Hungary and France.

Hans Robert Jauss's historical emphasis extended reception theory well beyond the textual constraint of Iser's early work. In *Toward an Aesthetic of Reception* (1982), Jauss addressed the antagonism between Marxism and formalism by interposing reception, which mediates between history and literature, as part of cultural production. Jauss focused on the historical process of reception, a process defined by the difference between a work's meaning and significance at the time of its construction and at the time(s) of its reception as well as by the distance between the reader's expectations and the writer's production. His reception theory is thus a kind of "thick" formalism in that it accounts for the historical standpoint of the interpreter. Jauss's connections to formalism are most evident in his discussion of the potential of new and difficult literary texts to change a reader's interpretive expectations.

Like Jauss, Barthes, Iser, and Fish, I am interested in the disruptive effects of texts and want to claim that the transgressions achieved in literary form not only affect conventions of reading but influence the cultural construction of subjectivity and identity in general, helping to shape an emergent episteme and to reconfigure the cultural imaginary. But unlike Jauss, Iser, and Fish, I am concerned also with the agency of the reader. To conceptualize an agency of reading, one must look closely at the structural determinism that characterizes the marxist and marxian theories that have influenced much poststructuralist literary criticism and cultural critique. Theorists as diverse as Louis Althusser, Pierre Macherey, Julia Kristeva, Fredric Jameson, and Colin MacCabe reach the same theoretical end point of making the reader subject to the ideological effect of a powerful text. But none of these theories acknowledges the fact that texts do not necessarily succeed in interpellating subjects. These theories forget one of the central insights of poststructuralism: texts do not perfectly reproduce ideology, for language is not univocal, centered, and fixed. Resistance to ideology is inherent in every ideological stance. By describing the reading subject as an agent who, though never free of an ideology, can resist various ideological determinisms, I mean to differentiate this agent from the autonomous individual of bourgeois humanism and the subject interpellated by ideology.

In attempting to describe agency, I join an ever-growing throng of theorists and critics in the hunt. We are looking desperately for agency, but I wonder if we are not looking in all the wrong places. What does it mean to be an agent? The

compelling psychoanalytic arguments about split subjectivity—conveyed suc-
cinctly in Joan Copjec's reminders that "sex does not budge," that freedom cannot
be wrenched from compulsion, and that the signifier cannot account for the subject, which is unknowable in language (22, 24)—convince me that agency cannot
mean a voluntarist, fully realized choice as it is construed in the libertarian political scheme or in the vulgar version of deconstructive interpretation. Agency, as
defined in terms of individual performance, is not an intention but an *effect* that
is always read in a social milieu—and there is no guarantee that the effect will be
received as intended. From a communitarian perspective, one conceives of agency
strictly in terms of collective action, complicating the task of locating it. A third
conception of agency posits it as derivable only from social norms, which are
themselves unstable effects.[2]

I conceive of agency in reading as compulsive, reiterative role-playing in
which individuals attempt to find themselves by going outside the self, engaging
in literary performance in the hope of fully and finally identifying the self through
self-differentiation. Such finality is never achieved, for the self is perpetually in
process. Furthermore, readers never escape a social context; they are both constructed and constructing in that they read as part of interpretive communities
and are involved in collective cultural imagining and reimagining. The postmodern feminist concept of political agency that I make a case for in this study is an
ironic agency that requires one to engage constantly in self-questioning, never for-
getting that values are contingent and that knowledge and belief systems are situated historically and culturally.

Almost all of the groundbreaking work in audience/reader agency in the past
fifteen years has involved studies of mass culture, in particular television, and has
been influenced by the Media Group at Birmingham University's Centre for Contemporary Cultural Studies.[3] The Birmingham group has been concerned with a
"social theory of subjectivity, power and meaning construction" (Moores 7). The
most influential of these projects in the late 1970s and early 1980s included Stuart
Hall's work on the audience's ability to decode encoded meanings and to refuse
the positions offered to it by texts, and David Morley's study of the dialogic relationship between the audience implied by television programming and the actual
audience members. Hall's and Morley's studies offered critiques of and alternatives
to the model of readers and spectators constructed by the journal *Screen* that had
been in the theoretical vanguard in the 1970s. Contributors to *Screen*, under the
editorship of Colin MacCabe, combined semiotics with Althusserian Marxism

and Lacanian psychoanalytic theory, producing a hybrid theory that reduced readers to a set of textually inscribed "subject positions."

The chief problem with *Screen*'s positioning theories was that they failed to explore the relationship between a film viewer's background and the ideological effects of films. These theories overlooked interpretation in their stress on the perpetuation of ideology. Cultural studies critics arguing for an ethnographic approach claim that because an audience generally decides on a meaning not through resistance in the form of decoding but through inference, a reception theory concerned with variations among interpretations requires a methodology drawn from relevance theory and an inferential model of communication (Christie 64).[4] Theories that assign readers to fixed subject positions elide questions of interpretive variation. Cultural studies critics have been sharply critical of film theorists' universalism and ahistoricism in constructing a reader positioning that overlooks the experiences of actual audiences (Mills 6).[5] Cultural studies' ethnography counterposes empirically oriented theories to the formal theories of film.

One of the rare empirical studies of literary reading is Janice Radway's *Reading the Romance: Women, Patriarchy, and Popular Literature* (1984). Though the study began as an analysis of the way romances are interpreted, it gradually evolved into "the way romance reading as a form of behavior operate[s] as a complex intervention in the ongoing social life of actual social subjects" (7). The habits of actual readers, who "appropriate the texts for their own purposes . . . suggest that the commercial mass-production process is not entirely successful at structuring individuals' cultural lives" (16). Radway opposes her study to the work of literary critics such as Tania Modleski and Ann Douglas, who privilege their own readings and explanations for why romance is read while rejecting the explanations of romance readers themselves. These critics apparently assume that only the trained literary scholar can discover "the text's true core of significance," and that untrained readers are "passive, purely receptive individuals who can only consume the meanings embodied within cultural texts . . . [,] powerless in the face of ideology" (5–6). Although Radway admits the validity of theories that use the consumption analogy to account for the role of the individual in industrialization and mass production, she warns of the overextension of this analogy: "The condensing treatment of mass-culture audience is, in the end, the final, logical consequence of a theoretical position that reifies human activity, ignores the complexities of sign production or semiosis, and transforms interactive social process into a confrontation between discrete objects [text and reader]" (8). Radway's work implies that an adequate account of reader response and reception involves both empirical and formal theories. I would add that empirically oriented and formal theories, although generally construed as antagonistic theoretical perspectives and methodologies, need each other, with each questioning the other's warrants and conclusions.[6]

When Radway concludes that pockets exist within the social fabric where people engage in oppositional appropriation, she expresses ideas similar to those of Michel de Certeau in *The Practice of Everyday Life* (1984), whose theories allow for individual creativity in a way in which the more structurally determinist theories of his contemporaries (such as Michel Foucault and Pierre Bourdieu) do not.[7] And it is in the move from printed texts to electronic texts that systems theories and theories of postmodernity and posthumanist subjectivity, such as those of de Certeau, become absolutely necessary for retheorizing reading. While Michel Foucault's panopticon can serve as an analogue of the dark side of cybernetics, signifying totalitarian surveillance and control, de Certeau finds limits to totalization in the very vastness of the postmodern cybernetic system (Bukatman 212). De Certeau's theory explores the possibilities of creativity and agency in the face of constraint, with subordinate groups devising tactics of empowerment in everyday living (Moores 138)—for example, the secretary, underpaid and isolated in a windowless cubicle, who uses the corporation's stationery and computer to compose letters to a lover on company time. Because de Certeau is concerned with microfields of power within a vast macrofield and with the constitutive effects of wandering and randomness, his work is especially suited to theories of cybernetics and hypertext. His is a theory that sees wandering/promiscuous reading as creative agency.[8] Reading, for de Certeau, is an act of jouissance (here defined as sexual bliss and usufruct): "[The reader] insinuates into another person's text the ruses of pleasure and appropriation: he poaches on it, is transported into it, pluralizes himself in it" (xxi).

Gilles Deleuze and Félix Guattari's posthumanist political theories are also important to any attempt to theorize reading in the context of information technologies. In *A Thousand Plateaus* (1987), Deleuze and Guattari dream of a new culture in which *nomos*, the designation of places or occasions, rather than *logos* is constitutive. The recurring tropes of this text are the nomad and the rhizome, and the dream is of the nomad's random movement in a chaotically distributed/ rhizomic network (such as cyberspace)—a resistance to the omnipresent State through contingency and temporary autonomy at the site of gaps in the State network (Moulthrop, "Rhizome" 301). In this dream, contingency is all-important. Valorized in the postmodern theories of Deleuze, Guattari, and de Certeau (who in turn were influenced by Friedrich Nietzsche and Henri Bergson), contingency becomes the necessary condition for life in physical systems, creativity in intellectual systems, and autonomy in political systems (Rosenberg 294).

Contingency is central to hypertext theory and its application and has given rise to a new set of questions about reading. Once literary hermeneutics became systematized in the twentieth century, the method involved grasping the whole, dismembering it, naming the parts, and then re-membering it. This notion of hermeneutics is organicist, with the text conceived as a body. But hypertext requires a different description of reading pleasures and a reconception of hermeneutic activity, for one cannot grasp the whole of a hypertext and there is no systematic parts-to-whole relationship or equation. In hypertext a part can be a node (on one screen), and the information on this one screen can serve as a conduit or switching center through which ten (or twenty, thirty . . .) narrative paths move. Thus, the parts are constantly changing, and the shape of the narrative "whole" is always in flux. A hermeneutics based on an organicist model will not work for volatile, unfixed electronic texts.

As nonsequential writing with reader-determined links, hypertextual fiction is more concerned with linking, routing, and mapping than with plot or character development. The goal of hypertext is to provide the reader with the most complex and intricate ways of organizing the textual strands or pieces and inventing structure. Proponents of hypertext argue that the linking and combining of discrete chunks of text—a bricolage effect—can result in perceptual and conceptual breakthroughs. I concur with Gregory Ulmer's claim that we live in a period in which the new logic of pattern is operating coterminously with the older logics of expositional argument and narrative. The logic of pattern, whose essential form is collage, is conductive, whereas the logic of argument is inductive and deductive and the logic of narrative is abductive (Ulmer 161, 163); each of these logics establishes a different kind of reading response and style of reading. In collage, the principles of construction are appropriation, fragmentation, and juxtaposition and the primary principle of reading collage is association or linking (Ulmer 160). The writer and the reader do not discover or recognize a preexisting pattern; rather, they make patterns possible.[9] Hypertext provides a structure for what has not yet come into being, a structure for becoming.

Critics of hypertext bemoan the trading of lateral and multilinear movement for depth (rhizome structure versus tap root). Sven Birkerts in his popular *The*

Gutenberg Elegies argues that electronic mediation robs us of "deep time," and that the consequences are dire: "No deep time, no resonance; no resonance, no wisdom" (76). He feels that in contemporary culture, depth survives only in "true aesthetic experience. For this experience is vertical; it transpires in deep time, and, in a sense secures that time for us" (76). "[S]erious reading" also helps us to "resist the skimming tendency and delve; we can restore, if only for a time, the vanishing assumption of coherence" (76). Birkerts's lament includes a litany of phrases such as "*authentic* work of art," "*true* aesthetic experience," and "*serious* reading" (my emphasis). He calls interactive media "powerful grazing tool[s]" that allow readers to cross "borders that were once closely guarded" (137–38). Thus, the electronic reader is errant, foraging, and transgressive.[10]

Birkerts's elegy completely ignores the history of reading. He makes it sound as if solitary, deep, and intensive reading were the only kind of reading that could be classified as true aesthetic experience. But he overlooks the importance of reading aloud, reading as declamation, and reading as group performance. The practice of reading aloud for oneself or for others, common in ancient civilizations, continued to be the most pervasive kind of aesthetic reading until silent reading became the accepted practice among educated readers, beginning in the sixteenth century (Chartier 16). This change from reading aloud to silent reading occurred only after Irish and Anglo-Saxon scribes separated words in manuscripts, allowing readers to read much more quickly and to process more complex texts (Chartier 15–16). Silent reading was first monastic and then scholastic, interiorizing works of the imagination and privatizing intellectual property. Oral reading was and is public and phatic. The technological move from printed text to electronic text has resulted in a synthesis of oral and silent/visual reading, allowing for the exteriorizing of the imagination in collaborative creativity with other readers in a public space.

Birkerts and other critics of virtual reality technologies who fear the onset of a posthuman era characterized by the repression of interiority not only fail to historicize but also fail to psychologize adequately the concept of interiority. My concerns with process and difference in reading, with the reader in and out of the text, and with the communal aspects of reading require that I focus on the dyads of self/other and I/not-I. In this respect, psychoanalytic relational model theories are helpful. Like the field and systems theories I mentioned earlier, these psychoanalytic theories represent a model of reality in which dynamic and interactive processes and relationships are constitutive. D. W. Winnicott's object-relations theory has offered arguably the most plausible psychoanalytic account of aesthetic experience. Departing from the Freudian explanation of art as sublimation, Winnicott claims aesthetic creation as the bridging of an intermediate space between the self and other, inner reality and the external world. His concepts of the "potential space" and the "transitional object" describe this process as transactional, beginning with the infant's occupying a realm between its body and the outside world and using transitional objects (a stuffed animal, a blanket) to overcome the anxiety of individuation and separation from the mother (*Playing and Reality* 2). This task of relating inner and outer realities—the acceptance of reality—is an ongoing, never completed psychic process. Aesthetic experience provides an intermediate space between the subjective and objective in which creative symbol-formation occurs, not defensive instinctual sublimation as in the early Freudian view, but the reader's exploration of his or her relationship to the world, to life, to death.

Synthesizing object-relations theory with sociological theories of the imagination, Wolfgang Iser's recent projects concerned with "literary anthropology" analyze the complexity of aesthetic experience to derive the fundamental reasons why humans need the form of make-believe that literature provides. He adapts Roger Caillois's sociological theory of game-playing to the reader's involvement in literary fictionality. Caillois distinguishes four game types—*agon, alea, mimicry,* and *ilinx*—that, in turn, represent specific attitudes toward the game: the desire to be tested and win by one's merit (agon), the submission of one's will to the experience of chance (alea), the desire to assume a strange persona (mimicry), and the desire for vertigo, which Caillois describes as a "voluptuous panic upon an otherwise lucid mind" (288–89). Literary experience "permits limitless patternings of human plasticity," indicating "the inveterate urge of human beings to become present to themselves; this urge, however, will never issue into a definitive shape, because self-grasping arises out of overstepping limitations" (Iser xi). The masking/staging that occurs in literary reading makes possible "an ecstatic condition" whereby the reader is both herself and standing outside herself (76); thus, interiority involves the reader's in-and-out movement. Through this ecstatic staging we "attempt to confront ourselves with ourselves," which can be achieved only through performing ourselves (303).[11]

Most theories of reading are humanist, focusing on the extension of the reader's emotional range and the enhancement of self-knowledge. Although I find Winnicott's and Iser's theories to be helpful, they still focus heavily on the individual reader. My own interest is in reading communities/cultures, interactive reading, and collaborative creativity. Thus, I would want to stipulate that Iser's reader moving outside herself merges with the other in Winnicott's transitional/potential space. All textual reading-interpretation (including psychoanalysis) is empathic in that it involves a temporary fusion with the other, followed by separation/ differentiation and active interpretation. But if the merging leaves the interpreter unchanged, then the radical potential of such fusion is lost—both in aesthetic terms and in interpersonal terms.

In terms of narrative theory, the reader's in-and-out movement corresponds to the oscillation between the conditions of immersion and interactivity. Marie-Laure Ryan points out that in literature, immersion and interactivity exist in conflict with each other; one cannot be in and out simultaneously (par. 37).[12] This alternation between immersion in the fictional world and the engagement of one's self-reflective, critical faculties is most pronounced in the reading of postmodern literature. Although postmodern readers are invited to become interactive producers of the open text from the outside, with the interactivity most pronounced in constructive hypertext as the reader contributes text to the network, this interactive role results in a distancing from the fictional world. Ryan perceives a positive aspect of computer-generated virtual reality in its ability to reconcile the processes of immersion and interactivity through the body's mediation (par. 39). She suggests that the particular kind of immersion that virtual reality offers—the experience of a fictional world from the inside through the body as well as an interactive role of instrumental creativity from within that world—will transcend the opposition between the two perspectives and "turn language into dramatic performance" (par. 39).

The more interactive that hypertextual literature becomes and the closer it moves to virtual reality, the more the reader becomes a role-player in "real-time" dramatic performance with other readers. This kind of performance features the same game-playing that Iser describes as fundamental to literary make-believe, but with the addition of textual others who talk back. One is involved in a dialogue not only with one's "othered" self but with real others. Although reader theory has convincingly argued that all literary reading requires performance, the performance mandated by the immersive experience of representational realism contrasts with the performance of the interactive reader as role-player in a virtual world. In this respect, I argue that the most significant difference for reader-reception theory does not occur between nineteenth-century realism and the formal experimentation of modernism, or between modern and postmodern literature, but between representational realism and virtual realism. Modernist and postmodernist texts differ only in the degree of interactivity provided, whereas the two realisms differ in kind, with classic representational realism characterized by a hyperrational paranoia (an attempt to prevent contingencies) and virtual realism characterized by paralogy (nothing but contingencies).

In this study of various twentieth-century reading cultures, I have synthesized theories of subjectivity (psychoanalytic, marxian, gender, and race theories) with narrative, performance, and systems theories. Along with the synthetic theoretical perspective, my method is syncretic as I alternate between theoretical/textual and empirical/historical analyses, oscillating between texts and contexts. Individual chapters discuss the construction of twentieth-century readers in the contexts of class, gender, race, technology, and teaching. These discussions derive from theoretical questions related to the complex of discourse-bodies-spaces, specifically in the interanimation of such topics as aesthetics and politics, identity formation and cultural construction, textuality and cybernetic technology. Although the chapters work together to construct a cultural field of literary production and reception in the twentieth century, each chapter can function independently in examining a specific aspect of the field.

Chapter 1, "Two Cultures of Reading in the Modernist Period," empirical in its method and influenced by Radway's scholarship, compares the construction of the highbrow reader and the middlebrow reader in U.S. culture of the 1920s and 1930s. Using James Joyce's *Ulysses* as a paradigmatic literary text of, and the *Little Review* as creative vehicle for, high modernism, I analyze the considerable gap between the readers implied by high modernist texts and the actual/historical readers at the time of the literary production. In one of the most sustained dramas of twentieth-century literary production, the initial reception of *Ulysses* extended through censorship and trials, interrupted serialization, and the tireless efforts of the publishers and exegetes who attempted to distribute and interpret a novel that waged war on a reading public (Schiller's metaphor) trained in the conventions of nineteenth-century fiction. I am interested in the cultural effort that went into making *Ulysses* readable.

Though Joyce acquired exegetes, Virginia Woolf instructed actual readers in an attempt to construct an audience for experimental modernist literature. Woolf clung to a belief in the absolute necessity for a community of rational individuals—specifically, common readers—engaged in critical judgment that was threatened by totalitarianism, by an all-consuming marketplace, and by the homogenizing effects of mass media. Her arguments for the agency of individual readers echo the fierce debates that occurred in the United States in the 1920s and 1930s concerning book clubs and the cultivation of middlebrow readers. I analyze the Book-of-the-Month Club's efforts to provide individuals with the information they needed to make themselves into cultured performers and distinguish themselves as au courant. Some of the most vociferous critics of national book clubs accused the editors of capitulating to the forces of "moral and intellectual goose-stepping" in trying to impose standardized notions of literary value and thus robbing individuals of their autonomous rationality (Radway, "Scandal" 726). Supporters of book clubs voiced arguments similar to Matthew Arnold's: cultural knowledge and critical sensibility would uplift the philistine masses by providing a center and substance for a population increasingly given over to frivolous and shallow stimuli and completely alienated by the excesses of a dehumanizing literary modernism. Though the constructs of highbrow and middlebrow defined themselves in opposition to each other, they shared anxieties characteristic of the modernist period: anxieties about massification, standardization, and authoritarianism.

In chapter 2, "Sexing the Text: Postmodern Reading, Feminist Theory, and Ironic Agency," I dispel the notion that postmodern reading necessarily means reading like Roland Barthes, playfully but aggressively having one's way with a text that invites such an approach. Instead, postmodern reading often involves a complex performance of learned responses, including those required by the political imperatives of feminist and multicultural texts. It is in this discussion that I develop the idea of a postmodern agency of reading inflected by feminist theory. I critique the postmodern reading lessons offered in the fiction of Vladimir Nabokov and Italo Calvino, in the process assuming the persona of Kathy Acker—punk, pirate, and plagiarist—to reread *Lolita*. The chapter concludes with a discussion of Angela Carter's fiction, which uses postmodern parody, carnivalesque excess, and feminine masquerade to undermine master narratives of Western culture. Unlike the postmodern fiction of Nabokov, Calvino, and Acker, Carter's texts construct a space for the subject of postmodern feminism, a discursive subject that oscillates between the site of the Woman of normative, masculinist gender construction and the feminist utopic space outside; thus, Carter's reader is an agent who moves back and forth between these two positions, in and out of discursive spaces, deconstructing the gender ideologies of both. I have chosen to focus on Acker's and Carter's texts because they are unsettling to many feminist readers, with my larger point being that there is not one right way to read (or write) as a feminist; rather, significant differences exist even among allied readers' responses. This recognition of the contingency and partiality of one's own perspective makes for an ironic agency; as such, the postmodern feminist reader is an ironist.

Chapter 3, "*Beloved* and *Middle Passage*: Race, Narrative, and the Critic's Essentialism," takes up the question of identity politics in reading and argues that such an inquiry is necessary to construct an adequate social model of reading response. The chapter begins by establishing a historical and cultural context for the reading of these two novels and then proceeds to analyze the opposing positions of Toni Morrison and Charles Johnson in terms of race and aesthetics. Morrison's novel *Beloved* establishes the narrative experience of otherness for those readers culturally distant from slavery, requiring them to understand the experiences of the characters while resisting the shallow sympathy that is characteristic of the reader as colonizer. The reader is drawn close enough to the main character Sethe to discourage rejection or abjection of her as an object of unthinkable, absolute otherness but is kept at enough distance to prevent the introjection or assimilation of Sethe into the reader's own identity; thus, *Beloved* provides the occasion for a less defensive way of responding to otherness than by introjection and rejection. Johnson attempts to transcend racial difference in his narrative by creating a middle passage where intercultural conversation and communication can occur. His narrative middle passage enacts D. W. Winnicott's notion of the "intermediate area" in object-relations theory, the site of the production and reception of literary and other texts that provides a safe space to acknowledge difference in the process of dissolving and transforming the boundaries of our selves. Read in Winnicottian terms, Johnson's narrative method overcomes cultural difference by allowing otherness to be transformed temporarily into sameness. Morrison wants to hold on to differences, while Johnson wants to deconstruct them. In the final section of the chapter, I attempt to explain my valorization of Morrison's aesthetic choices and my suspicions of Johnson's, yet I end by interrogating the critical essentialism that underlies my demand for cultural *difference* in the fiction of African American writers, an unacknowledged essentialism that appears widespread in current academic criticism.

The fourth chapter, "Reading (in) Cyberspace: Cybernetic Aesthetics, Hypertext, and the Virtual Public Space," offers a detailed construction of the evolving culture of electronic reading. The discussion begins with an analysis of various cultural responses to cybernetics, responses characterized by the techno-sublime and ranging from fear to rapture. Focusing on the hypertextual fiction of Michael Joyce, Carolyn Guyer, and Stuart Moulthrop, I describe a cybernetic aesthetics of hypertextual literature and consider the ways that hypermedia transform the task and process of literary reading. Cybernetics instantiates a habit of reading predicted by the theories of M. M. Bakhtin, Roland Barthes, Michel Foucault, and Jacques Derrida. Whereas high modern and postmodern literature engaged in the teaching of readers, hypertext arrives for an audience that is prepared for it. The reader implied by hypertext has been/is being constructed through sustained exposure to the virtual realities of mass media and information technologies. In order to compete with full-immersion forms of virtual reality experience in the near future, hypertextual literature must offer the pleasures of virtual immediacy, intricate movement, a rich web of hypermedia texts (enhanced graphics, video, audio), and interactive connection between readers and writers. *Interactivity* is the current buzzword in mass media. And, according to research on computer networking in this country, people do not use the computer net primarily to access data but to engage interactively with other users. Conceiving of the public sphere as dynamic and diffuse rather than concrete or locatable, I argue that the dialogue in the public computer network constructs a postmodern public space, allowing for communication and community without attempting to impose an impossible commonality.

Although there are too many variables for anyone to predict with much assurance the future of the vast public cyberspace, I am optimistic about the use of computer conferencing in university teaching. The final chapter, "Cultural Production and the Teaching of Reading," makes a case for a new pedagogy that combines curricular multiculturalism—with all the attendant friction of bodies occupying the same space, bodies rubbing against other bodies—and computer conferencing, the friction-reducing technology of informatics. The benefit of this approach derives from the facility (lack of friction) with which students can read and reflectively respond to each other's and the instructor's texts, sustaining the conversation in and out of the class over the course of a semester and even communicating through e-mail with students from other cultures and countries. Also, encountering cultural "others" who talk back and reading contestatory multicultural literature would likely effect the self-interrogation and cultural discomfort (friction) necessary for the reader to perceive her subject position in relation to others. The long-range goal of such experience would be the reader's ability to avoid responding to cultural difference as a threat.

In this pedagogical model, the computer does not replace the instructor; rather, computer conferencing supplements the traditional lecture-discussion format, a format that, though long-lived, is far from perfect. The lecture format has been the cornerstone of a traditional, top-down instructional method, the same method as reflected in the model of literary reading constructed in idealist aesthetics from Kant through the twentieth-century formalists. Convinced that the teaching of reading should help to construct a reading culture or a community of readers, I am proposing a model with extensive lateral connections to allow for more collaborative deliberation, a model that seeks to reverse the tendency to conceive of the student reader as a monad.

As Katha Pollitt has argued in *The Nation*, it is precisely because we are not a nation of readers that the battles over the canon have occurred. Those of us involved in the debates enact a belief in the importance of literary reading and the recognition that the only place that students are likely to encounter challenging literary texts is the classroom, which Mary Louise Pratt has described as a cultural "contact zone . . . where cultures meet, clash, and grapple with each other" (34). This study attempts to describe fully the contact—of discourse, bodies, and spaces—that has occurred in twentieth-century reading cultures, and speculates about the construction of readers and literary reading in the electronic culture of the near future. But my intentions go beyond description and critical analysis. This study is also exhortatory, an extended appeal to readers to help theorize and put into practice an ethics of reading based on what Drucilla Cornell describes as "a nonviolent relation to the Other," a way of reading cultures that assumes the ethical responsibility of avoiding "the appropriation of the Other into any system of meaning that would deny her difference and singularity" (78). My hope is that we will use the connection and collaboration that information technologies make possible to facilitate this kind of reading.

CHAPTER ONE

Two Cultures of Reading in the Modernist Period

■ The true battle in my opinion lies not between highbrow and lowbrow, but between highbrows and lowbrows joined together in blood brotherhood against the bloodless and pernicious pest who comes between.
                    —Virginia Woolf, "Middlebrow"

The decades between 1880 and 1920 witnessed a tremendous proliferation in book publishing as a result of technological advances that created an advertising industry and improved book distribution. An essay in the *New Republic* in 1925 complained about the effects of such a publishing glut:

> [T]he dear reader is a maverick, and nobody can ever count on locking him up in the stable again. The dear reader, from having been a feeder, is now a nibbler, and the reason is because there is so much more fodder and so many more extraordinary varieties of it for him to nibble at. . . . And what does he read? or rather what doesn't he read? . . . [H]e nibbles everywhere. (Rubin 730)

These fears about the foraging reader recall the late eighteenth-century German ideologues' anxiety about promiscuous reading caused by the publication of an alarming number of secular texts on every conceivable topic. Also, concern about the "maverick" reader's straying from the stable to sample exotic fare serves as an inversion of nineteenth-century reservations about young women's unbridled reading, especially the reading of novels.

This chapter argues that the constructions of both the highbrow and the middlebrow reader occur in response to this anxiety about promiscuity, with the promiscuous understood to mean indiscreet, indiscriminate, and unrestrained. These negative qualities show up explicitly or implicitly in descriptions of the masses by early twentieth-century intellectuals. So the maverick reader is both inf(l)ected by characteristics of a mass ethos and at the same time denounced for being un-branded and unallied—*too* individualistic. Highbrow and middlebrow readers defined themselves in opposition to each other, yet they actually shared the same concerns about massification, standardization, and hyperindividualism.

One of the hallmarks of literary modernism was its preoccupation with teaching readers. Richard Poirier suggests that modernism can best be defined "as a kind of reading habit or reading necessity" (98). But the reading prescribed for modernist works was conflicted. On the one hand, it called for solitary and tex-tually contained reading that required sustained, almost heroic efforts from a reader who was expected to defer to the primacy of the work. On the other hand, the difficulty of experimental works and the ascendance of academic criticism, which made solitary reading impossible, resulted in reading that was mediated at every turn—truly a textual effort in Barthes's sense of text as open, polyvalent, always intertextual.

The standard view of modernism is that its intentions and effects were con-servative, even reactionary. Poirier claims that high modern texts sought through their difficulty and inaccessibility to preserve the power of literature as a privi-leged and exclusive discourse, and paradoxically to reestablish the bond/bind be-tween the reader and the writer-seer-cultural hero that the incursion of a tech-nologized mass culture had begun to undo (98). Our current interpretation of literary modernism owes much to Andreas Huyssen's term "warding off," which describes a vigilant modernism's attempts to avert the danger of an insipid and devouring mass culture (53–54) consistently gendered as female (49). In this sense, "the elegy of modernism" was an elegy for a lost patronymic and a masculine cul-ture, the feeling by the young men of Europe that they were witnessing the end of a history (Schleifer 20). British modernism under the influence of Wyndham Lewis and T. E. Hulme prized the "square bluntness" of "virile art" and excoriated all forms of aesthetic effeminacy.[1] An advertisement for the *Egoist* that appeared in the *Little Review*—journals that were both considerably influenced by Ezra

Pound's editorial suggestions—proclaimed the *Egoist* "a journal of interest to virile readers only."[2]

This conception of modernism as exclusively reactionary and elitist is a static picture that ignores the dialectical swings of the movement(s). Marianne DeKoven aptly describes the historical period of modernism as "a moment not of 'paradigm shift' but of the simultaneous coexistence of two mutually exclusive paradigms . . . [;] modernist writing simultaneously uses and undoes bourgeois Enlightenment modes of narrative and poesis" (21). This coexistence of mutually exclusive paradigms accounts for the "irresolvable ambivalence (fear and desire in equal portion)" that DeKoven sees as characterizing modernist writers' projects to wholly revise the culture (20). Modernisms differed from one cultural site to another; two examples are the marked difference between the Berlin and New York varieties and the gap between the New York movement and the Harlem Renaissance. Also, each movement was engaged in a ceaseless process of reformulation, with manifestos and position statements rapidly displaced. Michael Levenson reminds us that British modernism was individualist before it was anti-individualist, iconoclastic before it embraced tradition, and inclined to anarchism before authoritarianism (79). World War I radically changed the face of the European movement. Before the war, modern artists saw their role as provocateurs whose aim was to violently upset and disturb a moribund culture. But by 1915, artists had fixed on the problem of how best to respond to social chaos, with Pound claiming vorticism as a "sober" and "quiet sanity" compared with the insanity of war. The arrested image of a conservative and univocal modernism also overlooks the energy and excitement that artists derived from this poised, pivotal moment in history. As Perry Anderson observes, modernism occurred at a point characterized by the use of a still-powerful classical past against the capitalist degradation of culture; the appropriation of the energy and dynamism of the machine age for art's sake, an abstraction that kept art at a distance from an indeterminate technological present; and the co-optation of the "apocalyptic light" of potential social revolutions to violently reject the social order in general (105).

But the reconceptualization of literary modernism as conflicted, heterogeneous, and dynamic does not go far enough toward accounting for differences in the cultural field of the early twentieth century. James Naremore and Patrick Brantlinger have described six artistic cultures that existed simultaneously at this time. Modernist art constitutes only one of the six, occupying a place in the cultural hierarchy between high/canonical art and avant-garde art, these three followed by folk art, popular art, and mass art—the last three categories considered low and the first three high cultural forms (1–13). Because of an increasing massification in distribution and a gradual mixing of all of these categories in the course of the century, the other five cultures have anxiously defined themselves against mass art's hypostatizing and homogenizing effects (15–20).

In the United States, a sustained attempt to demarcate classes of culture began to occur in the last third of the nineteenth century, with cultural mandarins engaged in a mission to purify art by cordoning it and themselves off from noisome crowds and by instructing audiences in the etiquette of refined taste and appropriate response. As Lawrence Levine has convincingly shown, all expressive arts in the first half of the nineteenth century were joined in a general culture that was characterized by a mixing of genres and styles performed/displayed for socially and ethnically heterogeneous audiences who enthusiastically and actively registered their approval and disapproval (149). Musical concerts mixed Beethoven and Mozart with crowd pleasers such as "Home Sweet Home," and eclectic museums displayed sculpture and painting alongside mummies and taxidermic animals. But by 1870 the process of "sacralizing" culture had begun, a process given impetus in the 1880s and 1890s by Matthew Arnold's definition of culture as "the best that has been known and thought in the world . . . the study and pursuit of perfection" (qtd. in Levine 223). Levine points out that American arbiters of culture took their cues from Arnold's belief that culture was "an inward operation," such that "theaters, museums, symphonic halls, and parks were public places . . . meant to create an environment in which a person could contemplate and appreciate the society's store of great culture *individually*. Anything that produced a group atmosphere, a mass ethos, was culturally suspect" (164). Increasingly, audiences were taught to disappear into the woodwork while remaining closely attentive—docile and thus teachable.[3]

A "cult of etiquette" was imposed whereby audiences were instructed in keeping the public self separate from the private in a performance of the public self that effaced the emotional and physical aspects of individuals (Levine 199). Peter Stallybrass and Allon White's description of the construction of a rational bourgeois identity highlights characteristics of this public self, with the bourgeois community defining itself in opposition to those who "infected" public spaces "with sexuality, rhythm, noise and the obtrusive presence of their bodies" (88). As anxiety escalated about unstable ethnic and class boundaries, audiences became less mixed (Levine 177, 208).

Though pervasive, the sacralization of culture in the late nineteenth and early twentieth centuries was not monolithic. Resistance to this tendency was evident

in the continued success of the great bandleader John Philip Sousa, whose programs mixed Wagner with such ditties as "Molly and I and the Baby" (Levine
166), and in the successful parodies of Sachdeva impulses in both Chaplin's and
the Marx Brothers' films, which enlisted audiences in a conspiracy against cultural
pretensions (235). The cultural campaign to uplift the benighted masses backfired;
much of the American population responded scornfully to such concepts as the
cultivated or the highbrow (235).

The mission to make art into a religion was radically undercut also by the
emergence of the middlebrow as a transitional culture halfway between the nineteenth-century genteel tradition and the mass market of the twentieth century.
The genteel tradition, heavily influenced by Emersonian notions of self-reliance
and self-mastery, included two overlapping movements to enhance the individual
and engender self-creation: the search for culture and the search for useful knowledge. Joan Shelley Rubin has shown that this "quest for 'useful knowledge' pro-
pelled nineteenth-century Americans into lyceums and chautauquas. Those audiences . . . considered virtually any subject fair game and welcomed with equal
enthusiasm lectures about volcanoes and those about Eskimos" (785). The desire
for both culture and knowledge derived from the same impulse: self-enrichment.
The emergence of the twentieth-century middlebrow book club signaled a transition from production to consumption in America. Culture and practical knowledge were conflated so that culture became *news*. A reader of the reports written
by the Book-of-the-Month Club's selecting committee gained advance knowledge
of the books before publication, securing this reader's place at the front of the
culture pack (Rubin 792). The genteel focus on discipline and effort in acquiring
culture was fast being replaced by the ascendance of personality/style over character (788). Supplied with a steady stream of informative book reports—rather
than critical reviews—book club members found that they did not actually need
to read a book to be familiar with it. The mass-market approach reconceived the
Arnoldian notion of the best of culture to be the "best of the latest" (793).

"Americans," Bennett Cerf observed, "are notorious seekers of short cuts to
culture" (qtd. in Thomas 389). Editor at Random House when the 1934 edition of
Ulysses was published, Cerf faced the formidable challenge of marketing for wide
distribution one of the most perplexing novels ever written. He wrote to Joyce,
entreating him to consider including a reading guide for the general public. Joyce
was not moved by complaints that his work was too difficult to understand. As a
young man, he had been so eager to immerse himself in Ibsen that he had learned
Norwegian so as to be able to read him in the original (M. Anderson, *My Thirty*

Years' War 248). Joyce felt that readers should make a similar effort to read *Ulysses* and the even more demanding "Work in Progress" (*Finnegans Wake*). He insisted that no reading aids be published with the text of *Ulysses*. To circumvent Joyce's objections, Cerf included a reading guide in the Random House advertisements for the novel that appeared in the *Saturday Review of Literature*, with a map of Dublin, a chart of the principal characters, an overview of the novel's design, and annotated chapter descriptions—all packed into two oversized pages. (See appendix.) The debate between Joyce and Cerf marks the site of middlebrow culture.

ULYSSES AND THE INSTRUCTION OF THE HIGHBROW READER

I want now to analyze the cultural effort invested in rendering Joyce's *Ulysses* readable. In this discussion, *Ulysses* functions as a paradigmatic text of high modernism, Stuart Gilbert as the text's exegetical angel, and Margaret Anderson's *Little Review* as its creative vehicle. I begin by showing the gap between the reader implied by the text of *Ulysses* and the actual/historical reader of 1920 trained in the conventions of nineteenth-century realism. Then I discuss the problem of reading in serial installments a novel profoundly unsuited to that format.

Gertrude Stein boasted that "[b]etween birth and fourteen," she "was there to begin to kill what was not dead, the nineteenth century which was so sure of evolution and prayers and esperanto and their ideas" (qtd. in Berry 37). In literary terms, the nineteenth century signifies classic realism, an ideology that was both informed by and worked to bolster Enlightenment humanism and positivism. A classic realist text, such as George Eliot's *Middlemarch*, assumes a metalanguage that transcends other discourses in the novel and that is excluded from the interpretation to which the other discourses are subject (MacCabe 15). In claiming access to a truth and reality outside of language that can be conveyed in language, the classic realist text must establish a hierarchy of discourses that allows the reader to assume a transcendent discourse and subject position. In *Middlemarch*, the reader is privileged to share the narrator's metalanguage. But the readers of *Ulysses* do not occupy the subject position implied by a narrative metalanguage; rather, they are confronted by the interrogation of narrative illusions and by the deconstruction of patriarchal, imperialist, and logocentric discourses.[4]

When I say that Eliot assumes a metalanguage in *Middlemarch*, I mean to stress the unresolved tension between two definitions of the term *assume*: to take for granted and also to put on or feign. As an ideology, representational realism implies that which goes without saying, the obscured and unproblematized system of facts, beliefs, and values that underpins Eliot's narrative project in *Middle-march*. But the strenuousness of Eliot's effort to achieve representational totality and to maintain control over the narrative discourses is especially apparent in her attempt to force closure by the addition of an afterword in which she wraps up the lives of all the principal characters. This strenuous effort points to the impending crisis of classic realism and indicates that the privileges of narrative metalanguage would soon no longer be taken for granted but instead would have to be feigned. As realism evolved, it increasingly focused on the complexities of consciousness, changed to a point-of-view narrative perspective, and steadily reduced the perceptual focus—indications of what Judith Ryan calls "groping towards empiricism" (17). Perhaps what I have called the impending crisis is better described as a latent crisis, for though realist narrative attempts to be univocal, unified, and centered, it does not succeed. M. M. Bakhtin, in *The Dialogic Imagination*, points to the heteroglossia characteristic of discourse in the novel, focusing on examples such as Dickens's *Bleak House*; and Roland Barthes makes clear in his poststructuralist (re)reading of Balzac's "Sarrasine" (*S/Z*) that though a classic realist narrative would appear to be unitary and centered, an active reading uncovers a text of diverse codes and multiple layers of discursive structuration.

The experimental texts of modernism, to different degrees and using various techniques, disclose the gap between signifier and signified that represents the impossibility of the reader's (and writer's) full access to meaning, an impossibility inscribed in language that reveals a divided and conflicted subjectivity.[5] Modernist critics and readers who read defensively and conservatively took their cues from other intellectuals and artists of the time who were deeply disturbed by the conceptual shift away from the unified self—a shift reflected in the new physics, in the radical empiricism that undermined positivism, and in those aspects of Freudian theory inhospitable to ego psychology.[6] Patricia Waugh traces the impulse behind autonomy theory to this anxiety over subjectivity. The qualities that had characterized the Cartesian subject—separateness, unity, and autonomy—were displaced onto the art/literary object, with "the emphasis on *aesthetic* distance and formal unity, as strategies which substitute for a *subject*" (Waugh 84).

In Stuart Gilbert, Joyce had a guardian angel, an exegete and apologist who was as tireless in his efforts to translate and disseminate the novel as Margaret Anderson, Harriet Weaver, and Sylvia Beach had been in their sustained and costly ventures to publish it. Gilbert substituted for what Richard Ellmann in his preface to *Ulysses* describes as "the narrator figure who often in earlier novels chaperones the reader round the action" (ix). Years later, when he rationalized his much-maligned approach, Gilbert explained:

> . . . Joyce approved of [the pedantic tone]; and we who admired *Ulysses* for its structural, enduring qualities and not for the occasional presence in it of words and descriptive passages which shocked our elders, were on the defensive. . . . [I]n those early days most readers and many eminent critics regarded *Ulysses* as a violently romantic work, an uncontrolled outpouring of the subconscious mind, powerful but formless. Thus it was necessary to emphasize the "classical" and formal elements, the carefully planned lay-out of the book, and the minute attention given by the author to detail, each phrase, indeed each word, being assigned its place with *pointilliste* precision. (ix)

Gilbert's 1930 analysis concluded that the true meaning of Joyce's novel lay not in the acts or thoughts of the characters but in the text's formal design: "Thus *Ulysses* is neither pessimist nor optimist in outlook, neither moral nor immoral in the ordinary sense of these words; its affinity is, rather, with an Einstein formula, a Greek temple" (8–9). Of course, the combination of new physics with Greek classicism was shrewdly chosen to reflect the dual nature of the modernist movement defined in the Hulme, Lewis, Pound, and Eliot years. But Gilbert's interpretation swings to the conservative pole, sounding very New Critical as it repeatedly claims that all of the disparate elements form a coherent whole of beauty in repose.[7] Patrick McCarthy points out that Gilbert was in the unusual position of analyzing a novel that few in his audience had had the chance to read because of the British and American bans on distribution. So he "produced, in effect, a substitute *Ulysses*, a critical volume with such extensive passages from the original that, if necessary, it could be read without reference to *Ulysses* itself" (26). Gilbert circulated a truncated version of the infamous schema that Joyce had first shown to Carlo Linati, encouraging the notion that it had predated the novel's composition, though Pound and others were to claim that Joyce actually superimposed the schema in later phases of revision. Gilbert rightly perceived that such devices as the Homeric parallels would help the reader make his or her way through the vast narrative, but his overreliance on the schema demonstrated his desire to obscure the ironic and the incongruous (McCarthy 30). As Joyce's pedantic emissary, arguing the rationality, respectability, and conventionality of *Ulysses*, Gilbert provided helpful quotes for Morris L. Ernst, the attorney for Random House in the 1933 trial to lift the U.S. ban on *Ulysses* (McCarthy 25)—exactly the right kind of "packaging" in the Depression Era, when, as Edmund Wilson describes it, "the whole structure of American society seemed to be going to pieces" (xv–xvi).[8]

Both Gilbert and Lewis took their cues from Eliot's influential essay "*Ulysses,* Order, and Myth" (1923), which in turn was Eliot's reply to Richard Aldington's charges that "from the manner of Mr. Joyce to Dadaisme is but a step, and from Dadaisme to imbecility is hardly that" (Aldington qtd. in Deming 2: 186–87). Lewis, who had distanced himself from the conservative power base established by Eliot, undoubtedly resented Eliot's lionizing of Joyce, while Gilbert found in Eliot an allied reader. Eliot declared that *Ulysses* had given him "all the surprise, delight, and terror that [he could] require" (*Selected Prose* 177). He described Joyce's method of using myth as "simply a way of controlling, of ordering, of giving a shape and significance to the immense panorama of futility and anarchy which is contemporary history" (177) and "a step toward making the world possible for art" (178). Eliot's use of the terms *controlling* and *ordering* reflects his attempt to tame the anarchy of the novel.[9]

Eliot's struggle to achieve transcendence characterizes the attempts of modernist critics to ignore Joyce's dispersal and dissolution of the centered rational subject. Conventional literary criticism mandates that a piece of literature be complex enough to require an exegete as a mediary between the text and common reader but not so heterogeneous, conflicted, or opaque that the critic is unable to claim mastery of the literary object. Because this critic is a prominent example of the rational subject that desires transcendence, she must, at some level, protect the position of the reading subject—a conservative impulse that the seemingly diverse responses of Aldington, Eliot, Lewis, and Gilbert all share.

In a March 1922 issue of the *Daily Express*, the reviewer S.P.B. Mais sent out an alarm about *Ulysses*: "Reading Mr. Joyce is like making an excursion into Bolshevist Russia: all standards go by the board. . . . [One becomes] aware of the necessity of putting up a fight to preserve the noble qualities of balance, rhythm, harmony, and reverence for simple majesty that have been for three centuries the glory of our written tongue" (qtd. in Deming 1: 191). Compared with Eliot's and Gilbert's responses, Mais's seems reactionary, but on closer inspection, his is not so different from theirs. Mais's reader fights to maintain the "simple majesty" and "harmony" of the mother tongue, while Eliot's and Gilbert's reader works to order, control, and tame the polyvalent and heterogeneous *Ulysses*.

In the attempt to master an untotalizable text, a literary critic necessarily produces a skewed or an incomplete reading. One of the recurring concepts in *Ulysses* is the parallax effect, an effect that can be applied to critical interpretations. Simply put, parallax is the difference in views of a fixed object when that object is perceived from different reference points. In terms of literary readings, we have the parallax of different interpretations of a text from various critical positions. But what happens when the object, instead of being fixed, is perpetually moving and changing? To maintain the original or a single angle of vision, the observer/ critic must move constantly to different points of reference.[10] In this inversion of the parallax effect, the observer rather than the object gets displaced. Their displacement as reading subjects is a matter that few critics have chosen to incorporate into their interpretations of *Ulysses*. The disruption of the subject's stasis is the key to the revolutionary potential of Joyce's late works, and it is this disruption that threatens the authoritative position of literary critics as reading subjects.

A good place to begin analyzing the disruptive effects of *Ulysses* is the "Sirens" chapter, in which Joyce materializes language. When it is materialized, language reveals the gap between writing or speech and consciousness. One need only read the first lines to encounter language as sound separated from sense: "Bronze by gold heard the hoofirons, steelyringing. Imperthnthn thnthnthn." These lines are followed by two pages of fragmented impressions, lines typed one after another in list fashion, with each disconnected in meaning from the others around it. All these lines recur in contexts throughout the chapter, but until then, the meaning is deferred by interpolation, the lines originating as floating, musical signifiers. In this way rhythm takes precedence over syntax. Joyce unbinds syntactical constructions: rearranging words, omitting words, creating words. Once unbound, words float loose from meaning, for words mean in relation to other words that surround them. By requiring the reader to reread in order to construct syntactic and semantic order, "Sirens" draws attention to the task of reading, an activity fraught with division and difference.

The rhetorical effect of this chapter is often phatic rather than ideationally communicative, making connections with the reader through the body, such as in the passage that describes Lydia "leave-it-to-my-hands" Douce at the beerpull: "On the smooth jutting beerpull laid Lydia hand, lightly, plumply, leave it to my hands. All lost in pity for croppy. Fro, to: to, fro: over the polished knob (she knows his eyes, my eyes, her eyes) her thumb and finger passed in pity: passed, reposed and, gently touching, then slid so smoothly, slowly down, a cool firm white enamel baton protruding through their sliding ring" (235). This passage— full of narcissism, voyeurism, and male fantasies of being masturbated by a plump and gentle hand—anticipates Bloom's voyeurism and masturbation in "Nausicaa," conveying his feelings and desires and establishing contact with the reader not through statement as much as through phonetic combinations and rhythm.[11] Though such extralinguistic, musical effects were common to poetry, they were extremely rare in fiction when Joyce was writing. The language of realist fiction was presumed to be a window onto the world or into the individual mind, with language functioning as a transparent medium. In addition, the narrative economy of classic realism fought against the nonlinear saturation of space and the lyric stasis characteristic of poetic language.

Perhaps the most jarring effect of the musicality of "Sirens" is that the score changes so abruptly and radically. The narrator, or what David Hayman more accurately calls "the arranger," moves constantly through changes of tone and mood, from a baroque "bronze from anear, by gold from afar, heard steel from anear, hoofs ring from afar, and heard steelhoofs ringhoof ringsteel" (212) to a spare jazz riff: "Bloom ate liv as said before" (223). The music of the language changes to reflect differences among characters. Referring to Lydia Douce, the arranger says, "She smile smirked supercilious (wept! aren't men?) but lightward gliding, mild she smiled on Boylan" (219). The preponderance of the consonants *s* and *l* and the assonance of long *i*'s reflect a snakelike hissing and gliding, qualities that establish the garter-snapping Miss Douce as a fetish-temptress.

Fritz Senn claims that Joyce lost a trusted reader or a good friend with the publication of each serial chapter of *Ulysses* (66). After the publication of "Sirens," Pound began to drift from the fold. In June of 1919, he sent Joyce a letter protesting the linguistic experimentation and Bloom's fart at the end of the chapter: "[I have a] gallic preference for Phallus . . . know mittel europa humor runs to other orifice—But don't think you will strengthen your impact by that particular" (qtd. in MacCabe 170 n.1). Pound links the authority of the phallus to the dominant discourse, and he disapproves of Joyce's relinquishing the impact of phallic authority. In "Sirens," Joyce rejects the grammatical and rhetorical economy of the dominant discourse in favor of a musical excess of signifiers. This excess is what Pound could not abide.

The "Cyclops" chapter presents the reader with yet another kind of heterogeneity. Its language could serve as a caricature of the heteroglossia that Bakhtin discerns in the discourse of novels. Parodic interpolations interrupt the would-be secure patriarchal discourse of the nameless first-person narrator. These disruptive and conflicting discourses, though related metonymically to the narrator's text, undermine his narrative and distract the reader. The interruptions—which include biblical, mystical, parliamentary, scientific, and other languages—vary rhetorically and stylistically. There is, however, one characteristic they all share: self-parody. The juxtaposition of the hyperbole of the intrusions, many of them long lists overflowing with abundance, and the meanness of the narrator's and the characters' observations creates much of the antagonism that exists in this chapter. The following paired descriptions demonstrate the conflict that characterizes "Cyclops." The first passage is Alf Bergan's description of a boxing match and the second is the same event as described by the mischievous arranger:

—Myler dusted the floor with him, says Alf. Heenan and Sayers was only a bloody fool to it. Handed him the father and mother of a beating. See the little kipper not up to his navel and the big fellow swiping. God, he gave him one last puck in the wind. Queensberry rules and all, made him puke what he never ate.

It was a historic and hefty battle when Myler and Percy were scheduled to don the glove for the purse of fifty sovereigns. Handicapped as he was by lack of poundage, Dublin's pet lamb made up for it by superlative skill in ringcraft. The final bout of fireworks was a gruelling for both champions. . . . The Englishman . . . came on gamey and brimful of pluck, confident of knocking out the fistic Eblanite in jigtime. It was a fight to a finish and the best man for it. (261)

The antagonism of conflicting discourses undermines the authority of a language that would claim itself to be univocal and unilogical, that is, one-eyed like the Cyclops.

Closely related to the heterogeneity of the discourses in "Cyclops" is the instability of the irony. The interpolated texts level irony not only at the first-person narrator and character called "the citizen" but at Bloom as well. In fact, the chapter ends with Bloom objectified as the other—the Jew—of the Irish pubcrawlers' definition. And because the various texts are so diverse, they reflect ironically on each other. Describing Joyce's irony, Stephen Heath says that it "knows no fixity, and its critique is not moral"; rather, it operates according to "a perpetual displacement of sense in a play of forms without resolution" (Heath 36). This self-reflexive, unfixed irony differs significantly from traditional stable irony, which critiques positions that diverge from its own fixed, unitary position. The unstable irony coupled with the mixture of clashing discourses results in numerous centers of consciousness within the chapter so that no hierarchy of discourses exists. Rejecting this hierarchy, Joyce refuses to provide the reader with the secure subject position implied by realism.

Classic realism often features a narrator who deals in aphorisms and other kinds of familiar generalizations that encourage the reader's assent and corroboration in the narrative, allowing the reader not only to share the narrator's metalanguage but to take up the position of narratee as well. In "Eumaeus," Joyce takes this convention to absurd lengths by using a narrator who speaks only in empty, trite language, often stringing together several clichés in one sentence:

> This was a quandary but, bringing common sense to bear on it, evidently there was nothing for it but put a good face on the matter and foot it which they accordingly did. So, bevelling around by Mullett's and the Signal House which they shortly reached, they proceeded perforce in the direction of Amiens street railway terminus, Mr Bloom being handicapped by the circumstance that one of the back buttons of his trousers had, to vary the timehonoured adage, gone the way of all buttons. . . . (501–2)

Caught up in compulsive digressions, the narrator often seems to be performing for himself. Once again, the reader encounters a chapter that offers no real guidance from the narrator. "Eumaeus" is an example of omniscient narration run amok. A plethora of unimportant details and the ponderous presence of a narrative voice fabricated from dead commonplaces prevent the reader from focusing on the characters and the action. Searching through the verbal detritus for the narrative strands, the reader perceives language as matter filling up space and taking up time. At one point in the chapter, Stephen says to Bloom, "Sounds are impostures" (509), and the narrator proves this observation by stuffing his story with empty words.

In "Ithaca," Joyce levels irony not only at neoscholasticism and Jesuit catechism but at the desire for omniscience in nineteenth-century fiction. The chapter contains an enormous amount of detail, much of it scientific or philosophical minutiae. One is reminded here of Virginia Woolf's complaint in "Modern Fiction" about the material realists who labor to describe everything in a scene but fail to convey the essence of life. Despite—or, more acurately, because of—all the quantitative, analytical, "scientific" information in this chapter, Joyce offers no cognitive security for the reader. The abundance of facts in this chapter serves only to suggest the endless other facts that have been displaced. Desire for certitude leads to the discovery of the impossibility of ever achieving it. And, thus, in an endless circle, desire breeds desire.

Although Joyce considered "Ithaca" to be the end of the narrative, it exhibits no conventional closure. Fritz Senn characterizes the black sphere that marks the end of the chapter as a "grotesquely hyperbolized" period (103). Without a resolution to provide a point of departure from the narrative, the reader faces an endless play of signifiers, a characteristic of the text of bliss. Readers accustomed to texts of pleasure expect and want not only cognitive closure but some sense of emotional completeness as well. If the reader is to attain emotional stasis at the end of "Ithaca," she must work to provide it on her own.

Kenneth Burke describes form in literature as "an arousing and fulfilling of [the reader's] desires," with form being " 'correct' insofar as it gratifies the needs which it creates" (124, 138). Burke locates desire both in the reader's expectations that the textual form excites and in the anticipations that the reader has built from the conventions of a particular literary form (126). As a whole, *Ulysses* avoids satisfying those narrative needs that it begins by creating. The novel keeps alive the conventional novel as a genre, while negating its possibility with each successive chapter. Joyce begins by seducing the reader who would apply generic conventions of the realist novel to *Ulysses* and ends by betraying this reader, denying him the "innocence" and the pleasure of classic realism.

In his essay "Spatial Form in Modern Literature," Joseph Frank was one of the first critics to observe that modernist writers, through their use of spatial forms, had effectively challenged G. E. Lessing's dichotomy between the successive arts of literature and music and the simultaneous arts of painting and sculpture. Joyce went to great lengths to create the effect of simultaneity in *Ulysses*, achieving cubist results. Because of these techniques and because of the length, density, and complexity of the novel, Frank argues, *Ulysses* cannot be read, only reread, with an apprehension of the whole necessary to understand any of the parts (18–21). The only satisfactory solution to this problem, short of a reader's possessing an absolutely unwavering concentration and an encyclopedic memory, is not to begin the novel until one has read a holistic interpretation provided by a totalizing critical text such as Gilbert's.[12] Gilbert's method of relating the smallest of details to what he perceived as stable large patterns of theme and narrative strategy made him the ideal authorial reader of Joyce, who is both the encyclopedic writer fond of closed systems and the mocking puzzlemaster who encourages the reader's empirical obsession by promoting incertitude.

But Gilbert's work did not appear until the 1930s. What about all of the early readers, and especially the readers of the *Little Review*, whose reading was strung out for over two years, with some serial installments as brief as eight pages and with the publication banned in December of 1920 by U.S. censors before the journal could print the final chapters? A reader writing to the *Little Review* in 1924 asked, "Where did all these people . . . read most of *Ulysses* in the *Little Review*? From whom did they borrow their copies or where see them? The public libraries don't got them" (*LR* 10.2, 61). The U.S. postal authorities in New York seized five hundred copies of the 1922 Egoist Press edition, and the ban was not lifted in the United States until 1933. So, unless these early readers in the United States had copies of the *Little Review* issues, there was not much chance for rereading, and even then, they did not have the whole text unless they had managed to acquire a black-market European edition.

The fragmented reading experience explains in large part why Joyce lost trusted readers during the course of his writing the eighteen chapters and why reviewers like Aldington who published their opinions before finishing the novel were likely to sound so defensive or baffled. This is a point that Jane Heap overlooks when she complains about the lateness of *Ulysses* mania in her 1923 statement in the *Little Review*:

> We are Ulysses mad. It is impossible to go anywhere or read anything without getting into some jibberish about Ulysses. Ulysses ran serially in the *Little Review* for three years . . . [with] scarcely a peep from the now swooning critics except to mock it. Issues were held up by the post office and destroyed, we were tried and fined for sections of the book, but no art-sharks attended. Burton Rascoe, who runs the Bookman's Day Book in the New York Tribune, perhaps speaks for them all: when challenged for a past valuation of the book he explained that he didn't know it was a masterpiece when it was running in the *Little Review* because some of the words were misspelled, etc. . . .
>
> If there had been some of this camp-meeting ecstasy about Ulysses when it was appearing in the *Little Review* the book might have been saved for American publication, the audience that was reading it in the *Little Review* might have been able to own the book, Joyce might have

had enough in royalties to ensure him treatments for threatened blind-ness—and the disgusting profiteering on the part of dealers might have been less fat. (A single copy has already brought more than $500.) (*LR* 9.3, 34–35)[13]

The reason why Heap fails to make the connection between the lack of favorable reviews and the serialization of *Ulysses* is because the practice of serializing novels had long been common as a result of market practices and the financial exigencies of both the little magazines and the writers. As an institutionalized practice, seri-alization would not have prompted questions about its suitability as a format for publication.[14]

By the 1920s, however, the practice of serial publication had changed. The production of serialized novels had begun at a time in literary history when linear, realist narratives with episodic divisions could be written, parceled, and packaged for monthly or quarterly consumption by readers accustomed to *lectus interruptus*. Many of the major literary texts of the nineteenth century were published in in-stallments, including Dickens's phenomenally popular novels, Eliot's *Middle-march* and *Daniel Deronda*, Flaubert's *Madame Bovary*, Dostoevsky's *The Brothers Karamazov*, and Henry James's *Portrait of a Lady*. Though in the twentieth cen-tury the serial form continued to be the primary medium for texts of popular cul-ture (detective stories, serial films, comic books, radio and television programs), serial form eventually became unsuitable for "serious" literature, with *Ulysses* and Pound's *Cantos* two of the last high modern works to be serialized. The literary techniques of experimental modernism subordinated linearity to simultaneity, re-fusing to offer the linear movement that serialization required. In addition, mod-ernist criticism privileged the aesthetic artifact as well-wrought urn and required a holistic perception of the totality of the work grasped all at once, a conception of the literary object that serialization undermined.

When the complex of modernist cultural production is contextualized in the general field theory that N. Katherine Hayles calls "the cosmic web" (15), mod-ernist aesthetics reflect the paradigm shift from a developmental notion of order to a field view of order that proposes emergent interrelationality rather than pre-dictable sequence. Einstein's work on relativity and the subsequent work on quan-tum mechanics by Heisenberg and others established scientific field models that called into question linearity and simple causality. Linda K. Hughes and Michael Lund claim that "the displacing of biology by physics as dominant science, and of serialization by whole-volume publishing as premier publication format, are related events underwritten by shifting notions of order" (168). The design of individual serial installments as well as the linear development of the sequences mirrored notions of historical progress and personal growth (172), staples of the nineteenth-century cultural imaginary. Thus, the structure of *Ulysses* troubled not only the habit of linear and cumulative reading, but also the symbolic pleasure that underpinned this habit of reading.

Having said all of this about the disruptive potential of *Ulysses*, I must add that the single most threatening chapter of the entire novel for early readers—the source of most of the complaints to the *Little Review*, and the catalyst behind the charges of obscenity—was "Nausicaa." The combination of Gerty's bloomers and Bloom's masturbating to the accompaniment of church chimes set off a storm of protest.

THE *LITTLE REVIEW*, THE TRIALS OF *ULYSSES*, AND THE CONSTRUCTION OF THE "NORMAL" READER

Margaret Anderson created the *Little Review* to satisfy her hunger for intellectual conversation. Through sheer pluck (helped along, one suspects, by her extraordinary beauty), she managed to solicit $450 from Boston and New York investors for the *Little Review*'s first issue. Persuaded by Anderson's passion and energy—she had boldly declared that this would be "the best art magazine in the world"—two old publishing houses, Houghton Mifflin and Scribners, each bought two advertising pages of the first number (Flanner, "Life" 44–45).

Anderson had no such luck with the local Chicago firms. Marshall Field and Company obdurately refused to support an art magazine whose small band of readers would not constitute an appreciable number of customers for its retail business. The mischievous Anderson decided to get "gracious revenge" by devoting a full page to every local business she felt should have advertised but had not; in the center of each page was a box that stated why a particular firm should have contributed (Anderson, *My Thirty Years' War* 79–80). The message in one of these boxes seems to answer Marshall Field's excuse:

> Mandel Brothers might have taken this page to feature their library furnishings, desk sets, and accessories—of which they are supposed to have the most interesting assortment in town. I learned that on the authority of someone who referred to Mandel's as "the most original and artistic store in Chicago." If they should advertise those things here I have no

doubt the 1,000 Chicago subscribers to the *Little Review* would overflow their store. (*LR* 2, 57)

Another of the boxes is more overtly confrontational:

> Carson, Pirie, Scott and Company ought to advertise something, though I don't know just what. The man I interviewed made such a face when I told him we were "radical" that I haven't had the courage to go back and pester him for the desired full-page. The Carson-Pirie attitude toward change of any sort is well-known—I think they resent even having to keep pace with the change in fashions. (59)

A Chicago publicity "expert," James Howard Keelher, congratulated Anderson on her ingenious ploy and convinced her that she should follow it up with another visit to the firms to collect money for this free advertising. But none of the firms was convinced or amused (Anderson, *My Thirty Years' War* 80).

In the fifteen years of the *Little Review*'s existence, the financial situation was always dire. When the third number appeared, one of the magazine's most generous backers apologetically withdrew his support because Anderson had published an editorial supporting Emma Goldman's "anarchist religion" against ownership of private property and endorsing Goldman's campaign for free love and the use of violence to ensure universal equality (Flanner, "Life" 45). In response to a news report that the governor of Utah had refused to pardon an anarchist on death row, Anderson ended her editorial with the ringing question: "Why doesn't someone shoot the governor of Utah?" (*My Thirty Years' War* 75).[15] Although years later Anderson remarked that this public embracing of anarchism had not been "propitious for [her] personal destiny" (55), at the time she had not recognized that such a position would scare off advertisers. The key to making anarchism a commodity, Anderson had tried (futilely) to convince Goldman, was that "society would willingly pay to be insulted" if the anarchist were "super" enough (83). But the Chicago business establishment failed to see an investment future in anarchy.[16] Thus, after the first year Anderson relied on the donations of kind strangers and on an increase in subscriptions.

If Anderson's endorsement of Emma Goldman proved costly, her support of Joyce's *Ulysses* was costlier yet. Immediately evident in letters to the editor and later in the regular column "The Reader Critic" was the bafflement expressed by readers of Joyce's early chapters. Gradually the nonplussed responses changed to angry complaints. The following reaction to "Nausicaa" is a representative example of these complaints:

> I think this is the most damnable slush and filth that ever polluted paper in print. . . . There are no words I know to describe, even vaguely, how disgusted I am; not with the mire of his effusion but with all those whose minds are so putrid that they dare allow such muck and sewage of the human mind to besmirch the world by repeating it—and in print, through which medium it may reach young minds. Oh my God, the horror of it.
>
> With all the force of my being I reject thinking of you as part of this hellish business. . . . I hate, I loathe, I detest the whole thing and everything connected with it. It has done something tragic to my illusions about America. How could you? (*My Thirty Years' War* 212–13)

In fact, it was a concerned father whose daughter had been offended at reading an excerpt of *Ulysses* who contacted the Society for the Suppression of Vice.

In the 1921 trial of *Sumner v. Joyce*, John Quinn used three witnesses to establish the *Little Review*'s reputation and to justify its right to publish *Ulysses*. John Cowper Powys, the third witness, defended Joyce's work as a beautiful piece of art incapable of "corrupting the minds of young girls" (qtd. in Anderson, *My Thirty Years' War* 220). Quinn argued that because so few people would (or could) read *Ulysses*, it did not pose a threat to the public's morals, and so the magazine serialization should be allowed to continue. He called it "futurist literature . . . neither written for nor read by school girls." He ended his defense by claiming that he himself did not understand *Ulysses* and felt Joyce had taken his experiment too far (Anderson, " 'Ulysses' in Court" 24). Quinn's argument reflects Jane Heap's opinion that Joyce had intended *Ulysses* only for those readers "rabid for literature" and that a U.S. publisher of the novel must "have sense enough to avoid the public" (*LR* 7.1, 72). Furthermore, Heap's perception of Joyce's intentions reflects the original claim of the *Little Review* as a magazine "making no compromise with the public taste."[17]

At the point in the trial when the prosecutor announced that the obscene passages were to be read aloud, one of the three judges objected because of the presence of an attractive young woman in the courtroom—who happened to be Margaret Anderson. (His solicitous concern did not extend to Jane Heap, whom he presumably did not find attractive enough—or feminine enough—to worry over.) When this judge was told that the young woman was one of the editors, he replied that she could not have understood the significance of what she was publishing (Anderson, *My Thirty Year's War* 221). Brook Thomas points out that the legal precedent for this particular kind of paternalism was the 1868 English case *Regina v. Hicklin*, "which determined obscenity according to a work's capacity 'to deprave and corrupt those whose minds are open to such immoral influences and into whose hands a publication of this sort may fall' " (381). And those individuals whose minds were deemed most susceptible were women and adolescents.

As defense attorney in the 1933 trial, Morris Ernst challenged the decision in the 1921 case as "patently unfair, unreasonable and unsound, because it sought to gauge the mental and moral capacity of the community by that of its dullest-witted and most fallible members" (qtd. in Thomas 381). Ernst argued that experts should represent the public's opinion on obscenity, not the community's "lowest and most impressionable element" (381–82). Deriving his claims from the philosophy of legal realism, which exerted significant influence in U.S. courts during the 1930s, Ernst concluded that laws should emerge from the contemporary mores of the specific culture in which they operate. In the same way that the U.S. body politic elects officials to represent the majority opinion, so the community should select responsible and knowledgeable men to voice its views on morality (382). Justice Woolsey accepted the defense's argument that law should concern itself with the effects of obscenity on a "normal person" and that such normalcy could be represented by experts (382).

In his analysis of the difference between the subject and the object of pornography in respect to "Nausicaa," Jules David Law observes that forensically, the "normal" response to pornography is the masculine response: "[F]eminine ignorance of the obscene is both a presupposition and an intended effect of the law. The law, in patriarchal culture, assumes that in the course of 'normal' sexuality women are only the objects of, and not the consumers or producers—in other words, not the subjects—of sexual fantasy" (quoted in Thomas 383). In Woolsey's definition, the normal reader is male. Thomas adds that Woolsey's assumptions also imply a class bias, as shown in his comments that one may not want to associate with the lower-middle-class folk that Joyce describes in *Ulysses* (383). The normal reader is not only male but upper-class male at that.

Woolsey chose two of his friends, Charles Merrill and Henry Seidel Canby, to serve as "literary assessors" and speak for the normal reader. Of course, these two men agreed with their friend that Joyce's work was not obscene. Although the "acquittal" of *Ulysses* came four years after the last number of the *Little Review* was published, it took the financier Merrill and the middlebrow publisher Canby to guarantee Anderson's and Heap's assessment of the novel's literary merit. Anarchist and financier, highbrow and middlebrow—cheek by jowl.

By 1933 the heady days of early modernism had given way to a period of institutionalization and commodification that had begun years before. Lawrence Rainey's discussion of Eliot's search for a suitable vehicle for *The Waste Land* reveals that Eliot considered a simultaneous U.S. publication in the *Little Review*, the *Dial*, and *Vanity Fair*, each journal representing a phase in the evolution and success of modernism. When Pound suggested to Eliot in 1922 that he publish the poem in *Vanity Fair*, "his proposal looked forward to modernism's future, to the ease and speed with which a market economy could purchase, assimilate, commodify, and revindicate the works of a literature whose ideological premises were inimical towards its ethos and cultural operations" (Rainey 34). In this respect, Margaret Anderson's efforts to make anarchy into a marketable commodity failed not because they were based on ludicrous assumptions, but because they were premature.

The figure of Henry Seidel Canby can serve as a link between literature and the market in the 1920s and 1930s, blurring the boundary between the cultures of high and middle. In addition to acting as the mouthpiece for the normal reader in the trial of *Ulysses*, he was the editor of the *Saturday Review of Literature* and the most influential member of the Book-of-the-Month Club's first selection board.

THE BOOK-OF-THE-MONTH CLUB, CULTURAL PRODUCTION, AND THE CONSTRUCTION OF THE MIDDLEBROW READER

Virginia Woolf was one of the first to use the term *middlebrow*. The occasion was an angry letter (never sent) to the editor of the *New Statesman* in which she protested the middlebrow perspective of a reviewer who had accused her of being "invalidish," "deeply feminine," and "elitist" (in other words, a Bloomsburian). The middlebrow, Woolf wrote, "is the man, or woman, of middlebred intelligence who ambles and saunters now on this side of the hedge, now on that, in pursuit of . . . neither art itself nor life itself, but both mixed indistinguishably, and rather nastily, with money, fame, power, or prestige" ("Middlebrow" 180). Woolf criticized the Arnoldian mission of the middlebrow to instill cultural values in the lowbrow and urged "common readers" to read independently. Furthermore, she claimed to respect the judgment of lowbrow reviewers (*Letters* IV: 389). She connected the highbrow and lowbrow through a shared "vigour of language," while seeing the middlebrow as "bloodless" and etiolated ("Middlebrow" 180).

One might, as John Carey has done, describe Woolf's attitude toward the lowbrow as a variation on the pervasive "intellectual cult of the peasant" in the modernist period (36)—"[t]he demand among intellectuals for a cosmetic version of the mass, which prompted the quest for peasants and primitives in pastoral settings" (38). With no peasants available at that time in history, English and American intellectuals had to invent them, rewriting the masses to underwrite their properly leftist sentiments (38). But it was not as easy to create a cosmetic version of the middlebrow, for the middlebrow existed in profusion and in close proximity to the highbrow. Woolf wrote, "I ramble round my garden in the suburbs, middlebrow seems to me to be everywhere. 'What's that?' I cry. 'Middlebrow on the cabbages? Middlebrow infecting that poor old sheep? And what about the moon?' I look up and, behold, the moon is under eclipse. 'Middlebrow at it again!' " ("Middlebrow" 184–85). Thus, the middlebrow consumes, infects, and proliferates in a sublunary world. Woolf's exceedingly negative picture manages to project onto the middlebrow the recurring fears of artists and intellectuals about the commodification, standardization, and massification of art in the early decades of the twentieth century.

By the late 1930s, Virginia Woolf had begun to speculate about how one might recover the mutually sustaining, collaborative relationship anonymous poets had enjoyed with their audiences before the invention of the printed text and authorship, a relationship that had required the audience to listen intently to the spoken word and to watch closely the body language of actors, a relationship that had derived from the "song making instinct" and the desire both to sing and to listen (Silver, "Virginia Woolf" 626–27). But Woolf feared that the public's eyes had been claimed by cinema and its ears by radio broadcast (Silver, " 'Anon' " 358). Her nostalgia and despair are reflected in *Between the Acts* in Miss La Trobe's fears of losing a wandering and dispersing audience tenuously held together by the tick of a gramophone. This is an audience for whom literary tradition is no longer meaningful, as evidenced in the characters' inability to recall anything more than brief and misquoted snatches from Shakespeare and Keats (Zwerdling 231) and in their preference for newspapers over literature. Woolf worried about the docile public and the herd instinct (she had been reading Freud on group psychology) and in her most fearful moments imagined the populace as an amorphous, jelly-like mass that was the perfect medium for totalitarianism of all kinds. Anticipating the concerns of later thinkers such as Hannah Arendt, Woolf clung to the belief in a public sphere of liberal discourse, a Kantian public sphere marking the site of critical judgment that was threatened by totalitarianism, by an all-consuming marketplace, and by the homogenizing effects of mass media. Along with the juridical "normal" reader and the advertising industry's "average" reader, we must add Woolf's "common" reader to a collection of reader constructs in the modernist period. This common reader—independent, possessed of cultural memory and a sense of history, and exercising a well-honed critical judgment—was for Woolf the last line of defense against fascisms both foreign and domestic.

Henry Seidel Canby was also in the business of idealizing the masses. In an October 1926 issue of the *Saturday Review*, he complained, much like the *New Republic* essayist worrying over the maverick reader, about the effects of literacy in a world in which too much trash was being published: "[T]he literate modern can connect his mind, like a telephone, to anything, anywhere. . . . Excessive reading of the flat and the flatulent has developed length at the expense of depth. The print-fed modern is shallow and curiously inexpressive of his emotions; by comparison with peasants and primitive types generally he seems to have no emotions that are not echoes of something he as read" (2).[18] The etiolated middlebrow and the vibrant peasant.[19] In Canby's view, the "news reading man" and the "magazine reading woman" were reading (consuming) too much of the wrong thing (2). Of course, the overwhelming irony of this position is that the learned Canby was looking back nostalgically to the good old days of illiteracy from the vantage point of editor of a publication that was a combination of newspaper and magazine.

Janice Radway argues that Canby was one of the few intellectuals involved in the heated debates about book clubs and the loss of the individual's cultural autonomy who did not attempt to deny the presence of the masses ("Scandal" 720). By the 1930s Canby was beginning to speak of an actual working class. In one of his editorial essays in the *Saturday Review*, titled "Proletariat Literature," he insisted that the time had come for a literature written not *about* the proletariat, but *for* the proletariat. The depiction of hardship and capitalist exploitation in the fiction of such writers as Dos Passos and Dreiser was not what steelworkers would cuddle up to in their leisure time (161). As an antidote to the standardization and mindless escapism that he saw as leading most directly to cultural barbarism, Canby urged that the masses be weaned away from tabloid newspapers and pulp magazines, just as business executives and lawyers should be discouraged from reading "the detective story and the pre-digested hash of the labor saving magazine" (160). He claimed that the history of workers' reading habits in the United

States, Britain, and the Soviet Union indicated that the new classes would choose good literature as readily as they would the mediocre: "only the defeatist and the intellectual snob will believe that the masses with new reading time are incapable of better reading than the slush now offered them" (160). "Slush," "hash," and proletarian "trash"—these were the negative terms that inspired his campaign.

Canby's editorial essays in the *Saturday Review* reflect his genteel Quaker ancestry and his years at Yale. He was concerned about the materialism outside the university and the tendency toward specialization within, as Plato lost ground to John Rockefeller and the study of philology replaced the humanist study of literature (Rubin 797). He perceived three main threats to American culture: (1) literary modernism, which he saw as disruptive, anti-intellectual, and barbaric; (2) technology and the resultant standardization; and (3) the commercialization of art (797). Despite his fears about the effects of commodification and technology, Canby's Arnoldian beliefs about the necessity of disseminating culture among lower classes led him to seek a middle ground between the genteel conservation of cultural values and the mass-market distribution of culture. But this struggle to resolve the tension between the positions did not succeed. Radway points to Canby's

> often tortured efforts to rationalize his work for the Book-of-the-Month Club in his editorial columns in the *Saturday Review of Literature*. . . . His repeated return to the question of taste and aesthetic excellence demonstrates how difficult it was in the early twentieth century to cope with the implications of mass education and literacy. . . . No matter that Canby could eloquently defend the political justice of cultural inclusion . . . [,] [h]e returned always . . . to the issue of cultural authority. ("Scandal" 719)

Canby's position on democratization differed from that of most of the other intellectuals involved in the argument about book clubs (Radway, "Scandal" 720). His communitarian notion of democracy stressed collectivity and equal rights, while the standard conception of democracy was a plebiscitary one, focusing on the autonomy of atomized individuals. Thus, critics of the clubs charged them with preventing the self-regulating individual from freely exercising his own critical judgment; they saw the clubs as actively destroying the public sphere. This Kantian objection derived from the belief that the categories of the aesthetic and the commercial must be kept separate. In response to these detractors, Henry

Scherman, the advertising executive who initiated the Book-of-the-Month Club, coyly answered that the book club member still was required to make her own decisions, for the selecting committee merely presented a range of possible choices (Radway, "Scandal" 718). But Scherman's rhetoric glosses over the fact that book clubs were in the business of selling a particular collection of books selected by a small panel of cultural authorities.[20]

If Canby conceived of the lowbrow reader as a steelworker with time on his hands, Margaret Widdemer, in another *Saturday Review* essay, depicted the middlebrow as "a garden club-reader"—the clubwoman and occasionally her husband (94–95). Widdemer wrote that "[s]ometimes [the middlebrows'] wives managed to force a Book-of-the-Month on their notice but . . . by and large they read biographies and detective stories" (93). The clubwomen thus constituted the vast majority of middlebrow readers, and they had "such books on the living-room table as their literary station in life demanded" (99). In her lectures to these clubwomen, Widdemer recommended that they think for themselves and not read books simply because someone told them to (100). But, of course, that is exactly what Widdemer was appointed by Canby to do: review and recommend books to the magazine's readers.

One of the regular features of the *Saturday Review* was a column called "The Reader's Guide," written by May Lamberton Becker. Just below the column head was a box labeled "A Balanced Ration," with reading described explicitly in this phrase as consumption, in the metaphors of food for thought and nourishment for the soul. But more significant for a discussion of the middlebrow reader is the implicit meaning of consumption here. The reviewer doled out the reader's share, her allotment of culture, in balanced proportions—a form of infantilization that bespoke (yet again) an anxiety about the ravenous and indiscriminate reader, roaming and feeding. In the prescription of balance, we discern the ascetic's fear of impulse, digression, and excess.[21]

Just as the lowbrow and middlebrow readers were herded and corralled, so were consumers in general. The principal challenge for advertisers, as Roland Marchand has shown, was to quicken the flow of an ever-increasing number of goods through the marketplace by preventing "any friction from consumer resistance" (Radway, "Scandal" 728). Because it required docile buyers, advertising needed to quell the consumer's independence and idiosyncratic tendencies. In this way, the publishing industry was no different from others. The "magic" of advertising results from its ability to endow commodities with meanings unrelated to their use values and to persuade subjects sold on the notion of agency and free choice that they should adhere to the value system of a defined group. Early advertising brochures for the Book-of-the-Month Club exhorted potential members to join "the intellectual elite of the country" (Rubin 793). Another advertising technique involved promoting anxiety about the self, instilling guilt in readers. The first advertising copy for the club read: "How often have outstanding books appeared, widely discussed and widely recommended, books you were really anxious to read and fully intended to read when you 'got around to it,' but which nevertheless you *missed*! Why is it you disappoint yourself so frequently in this way?" (qtd. in Rubin 790). In this scheme, Henry Seidel Canby and other stewards of culture became therapists of culture.

The success of a magazine like the *Reader's Digest* stemmed from its selection, condensation, and repackaging of material from a flood of textual information too enormous for readers to grasp. As Earl Rovit points out, the journalistic identity of such publications as *Reader's Digest* and *Time* derived from their being purely redactive, with each editor suppressing the idiosyncratic to attain "a collective voice of political centrality" that appealed to a public weary of nineteenth-century reform and early twentieth-century muckraking (545–46). Although this identity would seem to establish *Reader's Digest* in diametric opposition to the modernist literary creations with which it was synchronous, Rovit argues that its style significantly resembles that of experimental modernist texts: paratactic, improvisational, parodic, stylistically heterogeneous, fragmentary, and featuring a tone of "intimate *im*personality" (548). Such a style derives from a modernist kinetics marked by a radical shift in space/time perceptions (552).

The most modern of the modernists, the ad man and the experimental artist, together rewrote self, culture, and public sphere according to the rhythms of the twentieth century. Their aspirations come together in the advertising canvasser Leopold Bloom's habitual bedtime meditation: "Of some one sole unique advertisement to cause passers to stop in wonder, a poster novelty, with all extraneous accretions excluded, reduced to its simplest and most efficient terms not exceeding the span of casual vision and congruous with the velocity of modern life" (*Ulysses* 705). In Bloom's vision, the ad is a canvas and advertising is an art keyed to the speed of the modern world, a power to be reckoned with. His dream is of a perfect semiosis in which the challenge is to arrest the gaze of the passerby, the modern flaneur with a short attention span. The flaneur is another version of our maverick reader, idly wandering and g(r)azing.

CHAPTER TWO

Sexing the Text: Postmodern Reading, Feminist Theory, and Ironic Agency

■ The archetype of all fiction is the sexual act. . . . [W]hat connects fiction . . . with sex is the fundamental orgastic rhythm of tumescence and detumescence, of tension and resolution, of intensification to the point of climax and consummation.

—Robert Scholes, *Fabulation and Metafiction*

■ Text of bliss: the text that imposes a state of loss, the text that discomforts . . . , unsettles the reader's historical, cultural, psychological assumptions, the consistency of his tastes, values, memories, brings to a crisis his relation with language.

. . . [I]t grates, it cuts, it comes: that is bliss.

—Roland Barthes, *The Pleasure of the Text*

With the advent of French poststructuralism in the early 1970s, numerous new critical methods reconstructed the literary reader in a reaction against the construction of the reader by Anglo-American formalism. Along with statements about the reader and the reception of literature came models for an unprecedented mode of reading in the poststructuralist performances of Roland Barthes, Jacques Derrida, Paul de Man, Shoshana Felman, J. Hillis Miller, and others. Such performances embraced the affective fallacy, undoing Wimsatt's and Beardsley's work from the 1950s. Poststructuralist theory implies the response of an active, constitutive reader (such as Barthes's writerly reader), with the agency described in conventionally masculinist terms: the deconstructive reader as conquistador seek points of entry and "violates" the text. But the problem with this conception of reading is that it disregards reading as immersion in or fusion with a text, and more accurately describes a process of criticism that requires the reader to distance him- or herself from the text and act upon it from the outside. Literary reading, as I argue throughout this study, is almost always a dynamic process of in and out—immersion and critical distancing, fusion and differentiation. The relationship between the text and the reader is a dyadic one of mutual influence in which the particularities of each determine the transaction.

Although Barthes showed us how to be masterful but playful reading subjects, we should remember that his most celebrated demonstration of poststructural reading occurs in his (man)handling of Balzac's realist text *Sarrasine*, which is a classic text of pleasure in Barthes's lexicon, a *readerly* text that is "linked to a *comfortable* practice of reading" (emphasis in original, *Pleasure of the Text* 14). However, the modern text of bliss, the *writerly* text, discombobulates the reader. Barthes celebrates both the reader as the producer of the text and the blissful text as the deconstructor of the reader—not a contradiction but a recognition of the dual nature of reading in which the reader both takes pleasure in the persistency and coherence of his or her selfhood and attempts to lose it in a state of bliss (14).

At this point, I want to stress my intention to avoid conflating poststructuralism and postmodernism, which are of different categorical orders. Poststructuralism refers to a specific group of continental (mostly French) philosophical discourses that took shape in the 1960s and, as the name implies, attempted to bring various modern structuralist theories to a crisis. Poststructuralist theories engaged in a methodological shift away from (1) a closed system of signification, (2) order and hierarchy through oppositional or binary operations, (3) explanation by origin, and (4) the person as a unified subject. Postmodernism is a broad term that includes sociohistorical, theoretical, and aesthetic phenomena. Postmodern theory draws many of its conclusions from the poststructuralist theories of Lacan, Barthes, Foucault, and Derrida; but in the forms of cultural studies and theories of gender, ethnicity, and postcoloniality, postmodern theory also exceeds, departs from, and critiques poststructuralism. Though the two most common forms of postmodern reading, the ludic and the resistant, can both be traced back to poststructuralism, resistant reading turns a critical eye on the refusal of poststructuralist theory to allow for (or its inability to account for) agency. Postmodern theories interrogate conventional constructions of subjectivity and reconceptualize alternative notions of the subject. Whereas poststructuralist theories concentrate on deconstruction, postmodern theories engage in deconstruction and *re*construction (Michael 27).

It is true that the modernist fiction of writers such as Joyce and Woolf began to displace readers from the privileged position they had enjoyed in respect to works of classic realism, a position deriving from their admittance to the imaginary space of a metanarrative from which autonomous rational subjects determine truth and reality. But in representing the experiences of a bourgeois subject, modernist texts were still committed to the Enlightenment project of rendering "subjective experience in all its uniqueness and irreplaceability" (Bürger 96). Postmodern fiction, on the other hand, works against the recuperation of the autonomous subject; instead, it demonstrates the subject as a discursive construct engaged in a performance of subjectivity that involves the reiteration of cultural norms. In postmodern fiction, the writer as subject is subsumed by the author function; narrative perspective is fragmented or constantly in flux; fictional characters often dissolve or fuse with other characters and sometimes are the other(s) who refuse to fulfill the conventional role of the appropriated other. By pushing the reader to take up a different relationship to otherness, postmodern texts frustrate the reader's identification with the subjectivity implied by the cogito of Enlightenment thinking, but offer alternative possibilities for agency. Through opacity, heterogeneity, heteroglossia, and the lack of a master narrative, postmodern texts open themselves to a plurality of readings and admit that all readings are misreadings, in the sense that a reader's interpretation is not constitutive of *the* meaning of the text. Though achieving interpretive agency—the ability to resist being fixed in the subject position of the textually implied reader—this reader is not a self-regulating subject.[1]

The most significant difference between modern and postmodern texts is the relationship established between the subject and the other/object. Whereas modernist texts are absorbed in the project of exploring challenges to subjectivity, these challenges are ultimately resolved through the author's autonomy as well as through thematic and narrative resolutions. However, postmodern texts undermine and deconstruct this conception of subjectivity and offer up other subjects with whom the reader is not meant to identify. An experience that allows readers to more fully perceive and acknowledge otherness, including their own otherness, strikes me as being a positive effect of postmodern fiction. By not only identifying hegemonic cultural perspectives but moving beyond them in our teaching, we might achieve a political effect from this kind of reading that extends well beyond the isolated experiences of discrete readers.

Literary reading generally involves performance, with the actual reader playing the role of the ideal textual reader. Postmodern reading often consists of a sustained, complex performance composed of several roles—such as reader as co-

conspirator, detective, confidante, priest, voyeur, student, dupe—the most challenging of which may be the learned responses required by the political imperatives of feminist and multiculturalist postmodernism.[2] To think of the postmodern reader as always playfully but aggressively having his or her way with a text
that invites such treatment is to overlook the range of the various writer-text-
reader relationships that characterize actual postmodern transactions. The stria-
tions of different codes and layers of meanings that Barthes's promiscuous reading
uncovers below the smooth surface of a classic realist text are on open display in a
postmodern text, which exhibits the fact that it is not natural, finished, and seam-
less but rather is constructed, open, fragmented, and plural. This exhibition can
be playful and promiscuous in tone, or it can be harsh and honest. Often the tone
is mixed. In any event, the postmodern reader oscillates between immersion and
interactive distance.

I want to begin by analyzing the overt reading lessons offered in the early
postmodern fiction of Vladimir Nabokov and the later postmodernism of Italo
Calvino, lessons unsuited to postmodern reading because they avoid coming to
terms with questions of gender difference. I agree with Craig Owens's claim in
"The Discourse of Others" that the postmodern critique of modernity and modernism was largely made possible by the feminist interrogation of the metanarratives of modernity, and I further concur with Diane Elam's argument that "the
persistence of gender boundaries as a site of either impasse or perfect resolution
marks a failure on our behalf to make one last effort, if we were to become postmodern" (18). Unfortunately, gender boundaries have persisted. As Meaghan
Morris observes, "in spite of its heavy (if lightly acknowledged) borrowings from
feminist theory, its frequent celebrations of 'difference' and 'specificity', and its
critique of 'Enlightenment' paternalism, postmodernism as a publishing phenomenon has pulled off the peculiar feat of reconstituting an overwhelmingly
male pantheon of proper names to function as ritual objects of academic exegesis
and commentary" (378).

Because all constructions are strategic (McHale, *Postmodern Fiction* 1–3), it is
important to consider the motivations behind the theoretical construction of the
postmodern reader. In particular, I am concerned with why this construct is disconnected from feminist, ethnic, and postcolonial literatures. To challenge academic theory's predominantly masculinist model of postmodernism and the postmodern reader, I turn to the feminist writers Kathy Acker and Angela Carter,
whose fiction dispels the notion that postmodernism and feminism are incompat-

ible perspectives. The discussion focuses on Acker and Carter as disrespectful readers, undutiful daughters of their literary fathers, laughing Electras who give their own lessons in postmodern reading.

I have chosen Carter and Acker over mainstream postmodern feminist writers such as Marge Piercy or Margaret Atwood because the former take more risks in terms of their formal experimentation and in their relation to feminist ideology, and as a result they have troubled many feminist readers. In pointing to the discord among feminist responses, my aim is to emphasize differences among allied readers and to argue against a static, monolithic notion of what it means to read as a feminist. I make bedfellows of postmodernism and feminism so that they might keep each other honest, with postmodernism checking the essentialist tendencies of feminist theory and feminism grounding postmodernism.

Although my discussion of the novels in this chapter does not allude to Barthes in much detail, he is everywhere present, cruising in the shadows, loitering. Barthes's efforts to make the textual sexual, to tease out the text's and the reader's desires, uncovered what reader theory did not know about itself. As a self-described *draguer* (someone who endlessly changes bearings, affections, interests), he constructed a complex and polymorphous textual pleasure. When one unscrambles Barthes's gendered roles in his description of the jouissance of reading, one finds him endorsing a man's becoming "feminized" in the process of reading. So, in Barthes's scheme, if a woman reads a blissful text, she is a woman reading as a man reading as a woman (Suleiman, *Subversive Intent* 39).

Barthes's model of reading is based on the erotic economy of homosexual anal intercourse and thus might seem an odd choice in an argument calling for a feminist reconception of textual pleasure. But the switching of sexual roles, the trading off between in and out, adds another dimension to my conception of reading as performing the self by getting outside the self. Certainly, Barthes's model is infinitely preferable to the conventionally masculinist model of a critic such as the Freudian formalist Peter Brooks. In her groundbreaking essay "Coming Unstrung: Women, Men, Narrative, and Principles of Pleasure," Susan Winnett criticizes Brooks (and Robert Scholes) for taking the Freudian pleasure principle as a universal principle and applying it to narrative structure as the master plot explaining textual pleasure strictly in terms of male sexuality. Freud claims that when an organism has been aroused out of an original quiescence, it seeks to regain equilibrium by returning to the quiescent state, which requires discharging the energy invested in it. Desire is thus desire for the end. In Brooks's application of this trajectory to narrative structure (*Reading for the Plot*), the terms

become "tumescence and detumescence," "arousal and significant discharge"—
without any self-consciousness on his part about how androcentric his Freudian
model is. Winnett argues for the recognition of alternative models, and suggests
that tumescence and detumescence be reconstrued in terms of female morphol-
ogy and experience as birth and/or breast-feeding. Such a model based on female
experience produces a much different narrative logic: for example, the end in
terms of the birth cycle does not mean closure but the beginning of a new life;
and in breast-feeding, the pleasure occurs throughout the process without culminating in a climax at the end (505–9). Unlike Brooks, Winnett recognizes the danger of essentializing and universalizing pleasure in her birth and breast-feeding
model, which is why she insists that it be read as merely another model and not
as a replacement of the one proposed by Brooks. I offer Barthes's model of polymorphous pleasure as another alternative.

READING LESSONS FROM NABOKOV AND CALVINO

Nabokov's *Lolita* was published in France three years before any U.S. publisher would take the risk. When the novel appeared in the United States in 1958,
it caused a scandal, with many readers complaining of its obscenity. Though con-
demned as obscene, the novel was widely read and reviewed, an indication that
the American public found it compelling. Part of the attraction derived from its
entangling the reader in the narrative as a kind of accomplice in the statutory rape
and murder. The reader convinced by Humbert's blandishments is more than a
mere voyeur. It is for this reason that David Richter considers *Lolita* to be among
a small group of "genuinely subversive" texts (including Melville's *The Confidence
Man*, Gide's *The Counterfeiters*, Camus's *The Fall*, and Hawkes's *The Cannibal*)
that attempt "to undermine our native confidence that we can remain guiltless in
our fallen world, that we can display our clean hands and ignore the misery, the
crime, the brutality our society produces" (151). Nomi Tamir-Ghez discusses the
considerable skill with which Nabokov constructs Humbert's rhetorical performance, a performance in which Humbert the smarmy lecher changes in the end
into the anguished, penitent lover of Lolita the human being rather than the nym-
phet (82). Though Humbert addresses his narrative to different audiences of the
jury—"[f]rigid gentlewomen" (134) and their open-minded and lusty male counterparts—Nabokov indicates no awareness of gender differences among actual
readers. (In the 1950s there was no such theorized thing as gender; unmarked by
gender, audiences were always already male.) The reader who ends by sympathiz-

ing with Humbert is a reader who is dazzled by Nabokov's mind and language games. Nabokov is the master tease who baits and tricks the reader, the master baiter turned on by his own tongue placed deep in cheek, as in the following passage: "Push the magazine into the butt. Press home until you hear or feel the magazine catch engage. Delightfully snug. Capacity: eight cartridges. Full Blued. Aching to be discharged" (294).

In *The Rhetoric of Fiction*, first published in 1961, Wayne Booth expressed his reservations about the moral ambivalence of narratives such as *Lolita*, seductively written to make the reader sympathize with depraved characters such as Humbert. Influenced by feminist criticism in the intervening thirty-five years since the publication of Nabokov's novel, resistant readers now respond much differently to the narrative tricks and feel no complicity in the kind of brutal crimes and scopophilic guilt to which Richter refers; resisting Nabokov's imposition of the masculinist subject position on all readers, feminist readers (female and male) will not fail to notice the nearly hidden clues to Lolita's misery. The traditional scopophilic position of the reader-as-voyeur simply will not work for feminist readers.[3] In his afterword to the American edition of *Lolita*, Nabokov entreated readers to understand the novel as an experiment in "aesthetic bliss," belonging to the amoral and rarefied world of art, as opposed to other kinds of literature that he scornfully described as "topical trash" or "Literature of Ideas" (316–17). Spoken like a true modernist.

In *Pale Fire* (1962), Nabokov moved to a postmodern form, with the narrative an exaggerated whodunit constructed from a tapestry of interwoven perspectives in the form of a foreword by the literary scholar Charles Kinbote, John Shade's long narrative poem in four cantos (called "Pale Fire"), and Kinbote's lengthy commentary to the poem that makes up the bulk of Nabokov's novel. There is much slippage between the identities of the poet and the commentator as well as between Kinbote and Shade's assassin, Jakob Gradus, and between Kinbote and the Zemblan king, Charles II. Because Kinbote is a narrator who may in fact be a madman, readers cannot be sure what elements of his story are actual and what are imagined. We are in his power—and he is a coercive narrator. He concludes his foreword with the following directions for the reader:

> My Foreword has been, I trust, not too skimpy. Other notes, arranged in
> a running commentary, will certainly satisfy the most voracious reader.
> Although these notes, in conformity with custom, come after the poem,
> the reader is advised to consult them first and then study the poem with

their help, rereading them of course as he goes through its text, and perhaps, after having done with the poem, consulting them a third time so as to complete the picture. I find it wise in such cases as this to eliminate the bother of back-and-forth leafings by either cutting out and clipping together the pages with the text of the thing, or, even more simply, purchasing two copies of the same work which can then be placed in adjacent positions on a comfortable table. . . . Let me state that without my notes Shade's text simply has no human reality at all since the human reality of such a poem as his (being too skittish and reticent for an autobiographical work), with the omission of many pithy lines carelessly rejected by him, has to depend entirely on the reality of its author and his surroundings, attachments and so forth, a reality that only my notes can provide. (28)

Not only does Kinbote prescribe three readings of his Commentary to one reading of Shade's poem, but he suggests that the reader buy two copies (doubling the profit) of the text. Typical of Nabokov's mischievous sense of humor, this passage takes some swipes—in this case, at literary critics, who at the time he was writing *Pale Fire* in the early 1960s occupied secure academic positions and wielded what must have seemed to writers an inordinate amount of power and influence in an institutionalized production of criticism. Also at this time, the hegemony of New Criticism was being threatened by other kinds of criticism that moved outside the textual artifact to the context beyond, reestablishing the importance of the author and the author's world. Kinbote represents the coercive critic as mediary between elliptical text and reader.

The following directions in the Commentary notes are typical of the demands Kinbote makes of the reader:

Line 71—"(see eventually my ultimate note)" (101).
Line 80—"as described in notes to lines 275 and 433–434, which the student of Shade's poem will reach in due time; there is no hurry" (112).
Line 171—"I have staggered the notes referring to [Gradus] in such a fashion that the first (see note to line 17 where some of his other activities are adumbrated) is the vaguest while those that follow become gradually clearer as gradual Gradus approaches in space and time" (152).

Line 270—"(see, see now, my notes to lines 993–995)" (172).
Line 802—"(see Foreword, see Foreword, at once) . . . " (260).

The desired effect of these and other directions is titillation, anticipation, deferral (prolonged foreplay), repetition (with the reader moving back and forth, back and forth), and sudden urgency—until Kinbote is finished, his "notes and self . . . petering out" (300).

In *Pale Fire* Nabokov engages in what Beth Boehm calls performance literature. Boehm applies the term to John Barth's fiction, referring to Barth's preference for virtuoso performance over a discussion of ideas (102). In "The Literature of Exhaustion," Barth explains that because it is so easy to discuss ideas, he is impressed only by the kind of literature that few writers can do. Barth's critics complain that his metafictional performances are solipsistic and profoundly unsatisfying to readers seeking fictional/narrative satisfaction (Boehm 102–3). Although Barth's fiction provides little satisfaction for those readers hoping for mimesis and plot, it offers much in the way of verbal play, which is reward enough for some readers. And it is Boehm's claim that, in *Lost in the Funhouse*, Barth educates his readers along the way, transforming actual readers into his authorial audience (116). Over the course of the stories, Boehm points out, Barth becomes increasingly more metafictional and playful; he ends by refusing to provide readers with the illusion of transcendence through art, relinquishing all moral responsibility to readers and setting them free to create order from the chaos in his pages (114–15). In *Chimera*, Barth describes his reader as a lover, not a romantic mate but a sexual partner, and their relationship as a mutually satisfying one-night stand, with reader and writer reveling in each other's virtuoso performances (Boehm 114).

Such equal-opportunity loving does not characterize the relationship between Italo Calvino and his readers in *If on a Winter's Night a Traveler*. Though this metafictional novel, crafted from the beginnings of ten different novels and woven together through the intertwined textual quests of two readers, is structurally inventive, its postmodernism is of the conservative sort. Indeed, Teresa de Lauretis accuses Calvino of being part of a "neoconservative reaction" to the feminist movement that has led "so many writers, artists, and theorists to employ their labor and their talent in order to re-contain women in male-centered systems" and, thus, silence the other's discourse that has threatened the status quo (82). Not only does Calvino's narrative prevent the reader from becoming the writer of Calvino's text, but Calvino (or a thinly disguised narrator-surrogate) insists on assuming the position of the reader, often thrusting himself between the Reader (his male reader, addressed in the second person through most of the novel) and the Other Reader/Woman Reader. At the conclusion of chapter 8, the narrator admits to devising a ruse to separate the readers:

> But I wouldn't want the young lady Reader, in escaping the Counter-feiter, to end up in the arms of the Reader. I will see to it that the Reader sets out on the trail of the Counterfeiter, hiding in some very distant country, so the Writer can remain alone with the young lady, the Other Reader.
>
> To be sure, without a female character, the Reader's journey would lose liveliness: he must encounter some other woman on his way. Perhaps the Other Reader could have a sister. . . . (198)

In this configuration the prized object is the young lady Reader, Ludmilla, while her sister, Lotaria, is rendered in negative terms. Ludmilla is the masterful writer's wet dream: she is a hungry but passive reader, bowing to the mastery of the text's desires and avoiding analysis at all costs—exemplifying "a condition of natural reading, innocent, primitive" (92).

This image of the natural and innocent woman reader opening herself to the text recalls the anxiety expressed in the nineteenth century about the woman reader. Kate Flint in *The Woman Reader 1837–1914* has drawn attention to the plethora of Victorian and Edwardian Age paintings and photographs of women reading. The woman reader who is the object of the spectatorial gaze in these works is engrossed in a text (almost always a novel), variously lounging, kneeling, or seated and staring dreamily into space as she listens to another young woman read—in all cases, (en)rapt(ured). There is another common nineteenth-century depiction of the woman reading; in this portrayal, the woman does not read alone but in the company of other animated young women, reading aloud, excited by the feeling of transgressing boundaries and engaging in forbidden pleasures.[4]

Calvino's sweet, docile reader bears no resemblance to the paper knife–wielding reader-as-conquistador to whom most of the narrative is addressed:

> Progress in reading is preceded by an act that traverses the material so-lidity of the book to allow you access to its incorporeal substance. Pene-trating among the pages from below, the blade vehemently moves up-

ward. . . . Opening a path for yourself, with a sword's blade, in the barrier of the pages becomes linked with the thought of how much the word contains and conceals: you cut your way through your reading as if through a dense forest. (42)

Except for the paper cutting, Calvino's male reader is not much interested in foreplay ("reading around [the book] before reading inside it"); he considers such foreplay important only insofar as it "serve[s] as a thrust toward the more substantial pleasure of the consummation of the act" (9). Because this is "a novel composed only of the beginnings of novels," with the actual reader and the reader-protagonist "continually interrupted" (197), Calvino's reader will not experience a conventional consummation—unless the reader's economy of desire is very Catholic, in which case *lectus interruptus* would be not only tolerable but preferable.

Ludmilla has no desire to write, explaining that "[t]here's a boundary line: on one side are those who make books, on the other those who read them. I want to remain one of those who read them, so I take care always to remain on my side of the line. Otherwise, the unsullied pleasure of reading ends" (93). Lotaria, however, has crossed over the line to inhabit the other side. As such, she represents the Critical Woman Reader. Her thesis on Silas Flannery involves content analysis achieved through computer reading of his novels, much to Flannery's disgust. She is a militant feminist whom Calvino portrays as a castrating Amazon (de Lauretis 77). I concur with de Lauretis's observation that Lotaria can represent a reader of postmodern resistance (80)—the sort of reader who discovers that Calvino's text, despite its experimental "play," reinscribes the same old (always already) gender determination found in realist and most modernist fiction.

KATHY ACKER AND THE PAIN OF READING

The central project of Kathy Acker's writing has been the attempt to convey new relations to the body and to represent woman as a desiring agent. In this respect her work resembles that of other contemporary feminist writers and artists. But for Acker, writing (about) the body has proved difficult. During sex, she perceives a head full of images that she feels would lend themselves to rich description of the body's experience, but once the act concludes, these images, like dream pictures, quickly dissolve, and words fail to take their place, refuse to "give head" (Rickels 62). In considering Acker's comments about the difficulty of writing the body, we should recognize that she works under a self-imposed constraint in using only spent language; such a constraint characterizes the asceticism of the punk movement.

Acker's method relies to a large extent on literary appropriation, sometimes called metaplagiarism, and in her work we encounter postmodern and postapocalyptic renderings/readings of texts from various literary periods. Acker is promiscuous, having had relations with Cervantes, Hawthorne, Rimbaud, Dickens, Twain, and numerous other literary fathers. In her fiction we experience such corporeal effects as Richard Crashaw's array of liquids gushing from bodily orifices and John Donne's desire for battering and ravishing as expressed in "Batter My Heart, Three-Personed God," but in a language evacuated of the rapture and bliss of the early modern spiritualist and metaphysical poets.[5] Her "bad writing" is an ugly language composed of the detrital and the cloacal, an abusive appropriation, a rape of master texts. For Acker, writing is an act of jouissance, in the sense of usufruct, enjoying someone else's (literary) property without owning it. But Acker abuses the privilege of usufruct in that she vandalizes the property she uses. She is a pirate (one of the recurring figures in her novels), having her way with canonical texts—with impunity.

All of the students in my recent graduate course on postmodernism and feminism responded negatively to Acker's *Empire of the Senseless* (which includes numerous passages "sampled" from William Gibson's *Neuromancer*, published just four years before). They felt themselves abused and unrewarded. Acker refuses to court the reader in any manner, which is why her subversion is much more radical than Nabokov's in *Lolita*, for in her abuse she risks losing readers. To illustrate my point, I will quote a passage from Acker's *Empire of the Senseless* that rewrites perhaps the most infamous scene in *Lolita*, the scene when Humbert first has Lolita in his lap and manages to rub his "gagged, bursting beast" (61) against the schoolgirl thighs to the point of a muffled but frenzied climax.

> At the moment my mother was whining, daddy was smelling my cunt. "I've reached my best moment!" he explained. . . . "This is the moment of truth!!! . . . I'm going off off off jacking it off!!! . . . I know you're mine!!! . . . I made you!!! . . . I'm making you!!! . . . I swore I'd live for pleasure!!! . . . My tongue is fucking enormous!!! . . . feel it!!! . . . it's reaching down to my waist!!! . . . nothing matters!!! . . . you're my God!!! . . . my daughter: I worship you!!! . . . I beg you to do it, show I can please you!!! . . . now look at it, it's big. . . . kiss it!!!"

. . . "God is in heaven I'm in heaven I've died the whole world in
heaven!!! . . . I'm coming all over your face!!!"
    I licked up his sperm. (15)

I would argue that the scene in Acker's novel and the scene in Nabokov's have
much in common, though of course Acker's "dirty old man" is not the honey-
tongued Humbert (delighting in the multilayered linguistic connection between
uvula and vulva [242]), but a Humbert so full of himself and his own voice that
his tongue reaches down to his waist—a wonderfully ironic conflation of talking and fucking, a cunning lingus. In Acker's scene Lolita becomes daughter and
Humbert father, which merely removes the thin veneer from the relationship in
Nabokov's narrative.

Brooks Landon aptly describes Acker's narrative and language as "blurring
our notions of textual and bodily identification, both presented by her only as
mutability—one thing always slipping into something else" (7)—word made
blood and cum, transgressing boundaries in ways that exceed George Bataille's.
The character Abhor in *Empire of the Senseless* describes this process as "feel[ing]
like I'm taking layers of my own epidermis, which are layers of freshly bloody scar
tissue, black brown and red, and tearing each one of them off so more and more
of my blood shoots in your face. This is what writing is to me a woman" (210). In
a series of projects to reread and rewrite the body, Acker has tapped into her experiences with tattooing, bodybuilding, and dream writing in which she awak-
ened herself five times a night to record images and sensations. Currently experi-
menting with writing while masturbating with rectal, vaginal, and clitoral
vibrators, Acker hopes to record the sexual body in process. She points out that
the techniques of masturbation and dream writing result in very different kinds
of writing. The writings she "get[s] from masturbation aren't fantasy narratives
but are descriptions of architectures, of space shifts, shifting architectures, opening spaces, closing spaces . . . [and] the language accessed during sex has some relationship to Kant's categories" (Rickels 63). Acker's masturbatory writing sounds
a lot like Calvino's and Eco's fiction.

We know that Acker is having a good time, but what about her readers? Judging from the blissful responses of a number of (male) critics, I have decided that
my graduate students must prefer pleasure to bliss. They do not find pain erotic,
at least not the variety that Acker deals out. But Brooks Landon is enthralled,
forever in Acker's debt for "throwing her body against language, throwing language at the bodies of her readers, desperately and bravely trying to narrow the

gap . . . between blood and word" (7). Larry McCaffery is similarly impressed. So is Laurence Rickels, who marvels at Acker's ability to open up the space of adolescence in her fiction, with the "adolescent metabolism" being a "perpetual ambivalence machine" not limited to preteens but a channel that is always there for us, especially in our group experiences (61). Her techniques make her a punk queen, with punk denoting a nihilism beyond existentialism. And for those readers who enjoy theory-driven fiction, fiction as ideological critique, Acker provides the goods—anti-aesthetic, brutal, bracing as a hair shirt. Acker's method, translated into psychiatric terms, resembles the response of someone experiencing borderline fragmentation syndrome who sticks pins in her body, searching frantically for just one live nerve.[6]

As a transgressive feminist, Acker does unspeakable nasties to those old masters, the Humbert Humberts of literature. Both a thief and a vandal, she refuses to recognize the force of property. And that is her most threatening achievement for those readers who think she should grow up, straighten up, respect the property of others, and own property. Her fans, postmodern readers equally excited by transgressions against the laws of literary property and modern myths of origin(ality), are probably among those who attend the "plagiarism festivals" announced in the electronic journal *Postmodern Culture* (see, for example, vol. 3 no. 2). More significantly for feminism, Acker's transgressions take her beyond the pale. Although she has often mentioned Hélène Cixous's theory of a feminine writing "through the body" as having influenced her own efforts, Acker has sampled from Cixous and made something very different in the process. Cixous's work has been enormously influential because it is playful and poetic, deliberately overthrowing the prevailing mode of literary criticism. In addition, she has sought to empower her female readers; in the manifesto for a libidinal feminist writing, "The Laugh of the Medusa," Cixous insists that "Woman must write her self" (309) in a form that would be recursive, polyphonic, dialogic, expansive, digressive, rhythmic, open-ended. But about herself Acker says, "I'm so queer I'm not even gay" (Rickels 103). Taking Cixous's advice, she has written her self, in a way-beyond queerness that disallows the reader's identification with any emancipatory feminist perspective. Despite Rickels's insistence that Acker appeals to the "deferred adolescents among us" and "the adolescent turbulence inside us" midlifers, there is little chance of readers fusing with her texts. Eschewing the essentialism of Cixous's description of *l'écriture féminine* by taking it to extremes, Acker writes in a style that, although occasionally beautiful, is fragmented, brutally graphic, paratactic, even psychotic. Acker's texts are texts of bliss; they grate, they cut, they come. Cixous's texts can also be construed as texts of bliss, but not in the Barthesian sense of the term. The difference between the two stems from their disparate relations with readers.

The demonumentalization and aesthetic appropriation that characterize Acker's writing typify postmodern art and reiterate the historical avant-garde movement's effort to erase the boundary between art and life. Though we might expect anti-aestheticism to undermine the authority of an art elite and to deconstruct the binary relation of high culture and low culture, thus making art accessible to a mass audience, this was not the effect of the historical avant-garde movement, nor is it the effect of Acker's work. There is a limit to Kathy's promiscuity. There are, however, feminist writers and visual artists who do seek to connect with a mass audience, sometimes through public display on television and even electronic message boards. Barbara Kruger's work is exemplary in this respect. By contrasting the markedly different relationships that Kruger and Acker establish with their respective spectators/readers, we can begin to perceive the range of effects possible in postmodern feminist art. Kruger's work is more accessible than Acker's, yet it can hardly be called accommodating. And although she works with cultural clichés and stereotypes—for example, inserting the line of text "We don't need another hero" (from a 1980s Tina Turner top-40 song) into the Norman Rockwell print of a pigtailed girl in awe as she feels the barely discernible bicep of a boy her age—Kruger's use of the impoverished language of the tribe manages to infuse the site of the stereotype with agitation and life. Evacuated of reference, a stereotype takes on phatic importance by keeping communication alive through the circulation of familiar but empty signifiers and embracing the user as part of a collective that traffics in such currency. By drawing attention to the ideological function of the stereotype, Kruger's work distances the spectator from his position as replicant, clone, interpellated subject of a homogeneous collective. The reader is both inside and outside, offered the lie of the collective imaginary only to have it immediately exploded. In making manifest the ideological construction of desire, Kruger highlights what ideology obscures.

ANGELA CARTER'S POSTMODERN NARRATIVES OF RESISTANCE

Although Barbara Kruger's work differs from Angela Carter's in terms of media, their works achieve similar effects. Wreaking havoc on the "consolatory nonsense" that sustains the master narratives of Western culture, Angela Carter engaged in a project she described as demythologizing. For Carter, gender constitutes subjectivity through "a relation of power, whereby the weak become 'feminine' and the strong become 'masculine' " (Robinson 77). As a relation of power, with such relations subject to change, the normative construction of gender can be deconstructed and reconstructed according to different economies of desire—a form of agency inscribed in Carter's writing and invoked in the reader's participation. Carter claimed to feel a common bond with Third World writers who, through the transformation of fictional forms, manage both to reflect and to effect changes in the way people perceive themselves and others ("Notes" 77). Her narratives incorporate postmodern parody and feminine masquerade, techniques that resemble the subversive strategies of colonized subjects in a system of colonial mimicry whereby, as Homi Bhabha has pointed out, the colonized uses the colonial discourse to undermine the power of the colonizer ("Of Mimicry" 126).

To examine Carter's privileging of the ex-centric and her use of parody and carnivalesque abjection to undermine the culture's master narratives, I will first look at the story "Black Venus" (1980) before focusing on the novel *Nights at the Circus* (1986). When I use the term *master narrative* in the context of this discussion of literature, I refer to narratives that (1) police the boundaries between and maintain the ordering of the terms in binary dyads such as subject and object, high and low, masculine and feminine, (2) shape themselves according to the teleology of the Oedipal plot, in which there is a struggle over woman's body but an ultimate reconciliation of the son with the law of the father, and (3) render female characters as fetish-objects. In "Black Venus" Carter gives voice to one of the others of Western patriarchal culture, granting an enunciative space to Jeanne Duval, Baudelaire's mulatto mistress and the object of his sublimated desire. As the narrative subject, Jeanne is a walking, talking fetish. It is in *Nights at the Circus*, however, that Carter makes her grandest and most garish spectacle of the politics of desire and representation, exposing the ways the fetish and the gaze function in the complicity between masculine desire and domination. The narrative intermingles the high and the low, conflates the excremental with the intellectual, and celebrates the abject that social, political, and philosophical systems attempt to deny. Mary Russo in "Female Grotesques" summarizes the political effects of such transgressions: "The masks and voices of carnival resist, exaggerate, and destabilize the distinctions and boundaries that mark and maintain high culture and organized society"; furthermore, the masquerading of carnival is not "merely oppositional and reactive," but active and transformational—"a site of insurgency" (218).

Brian McHale calls postmodernism "the heir of Menippean Satire" and argues that literary carnivalization serves as a fictional surrogate for the real carnival absent in the modern world (*Postmodernist Fiction* 172–74). Bakhtin felt that to realize the subversive aims of carnival, such literature must establish a fantastically defamiliarized situation and a free space "for the provoking and testing of a philosophical idea" (*Problems* 114). The more extraordinary and fantastic the carnivalized situation, the better the chance of destabilizing norms, deconstructing binary logic, and, thus, challenging the dominant order. Carter's carnival stages an interrogation of Western patriarchal standards of value and concepts of truth and provides readers with an aesthetic space for imagining possibilities for emancipatory change (Michael 183). Of course, the subversive potential of carnival is realized only if the carnival-goer brings the transgressions back into everyday life. Otherwise, the carnival has served to bolster and sustain the dominant hierarchy by allowing the subjects to blow off potentially dangerous steam in a cordoned-off space and return placidly—or, better yet, guiltily—to the "real world." Likewise, the ideological critique enacted through the feminine carnivalesque must permanently alter the reader's perspective.

As insurgent acts, Carter's stories deny readers the male gaze of arrested images of femininity that literature abounds in, thus making visible the gap between woman-as-object and women-as-subjects. But in subverting the patriarchal conception of Woman, Carter does not substitute a utopian fiction of female subjectivity; she rejects the essentialized "notion of a universality of female experience . . . [as] a clever confidence trick" (*Sadeian Woman* 12). The reader is not offered a representative of the eternal feminine or any version of the affirmative woman with which to engage in sympathetic identification. The female protagonists of "Black Venus" and *Nights at the Circus* are not characters with whom readers can identify. Magali Michael suggests that this identification is what distinguishes a "woman's novel" from a subversive feminist novel. Although the more realistic novels of writers such as Doris Lessing, Margaret Atwood, and Marge Piercy have claimed a larger readership, that does not mean that they are necessarily more politically effective. In fact, readers and critics find their more subtle feminist arguments easier to overlook (Michael 216–17). In preventing readers from immersing themselves snugly in the narrative and fusing with the characters, Carter's carnivalesque fiction mounts a more overt feminist argument and disallows passive reading. Carter wants her readers to engage interactively in the postmodern ideological critique.

Typical of postmodern narrative form, "Black Venus" interweaves several texts: Jeanne Duval as the dark seductress of Baudelaire's "Black Venus" poems and of his diary entries, and Duval as a signifier for the nude model for Manet's *Dejeuner sur l'herbe,* who sits naked in the company of men in dress suits and stares provocatively at the spectator of Manet's painting (Hutcheon 144, 149). In turn, these nineteenth-century texts recall for the reader the significance of the prostitute in the texts of male modernists such as Picasso and Joyce, who not only continued to use the prostitute's nude body as the quintessential object of the male gaze and as object of exchange between men, but who felt themselves to be prostituted in the commodity culture that had engendered modernism—and therefore appropriated the experience of female prostitutes to describe their own conflicts.

Much of the ironic insight in "Black Venus" comes from the marked difference between Jeanne Duval's perspective and Baudelaire's. Her materialist realism constantly undercuts the discourse of Baudelaire's romantic and decadent fantasies, subverting both the language of male eroticism and the conventional representation of woman as aesthetic object and muse. As Linda Hutcheon points out, this story is a complex example of intertextuality on multiple levels: "the discourses of desire and politics, of the erotic and the analytic, of the male and the female" (146). Baudelaire sees Jeanne as "a vase of darkness; if he tips her up, black light will spill out. She is not Eve but, herself, the forbidden fruit, and he has eaten her!" ("Black Venus" 117). But Jeanne's perception of the relationship paints a much different picture: "she will sometimes lob the butt of her cheroot in the fire and be persuaded to take off her clothes and dance for Daddy who, she will grudgingly admit when pressed, is a good daddy, buys her pretties, allocates her the occasional lump of hashhish, keeps her off the street" (113). The narrative irony undercuts Baudelaire's—indeed, the male artist's—erotic rhetoric with Duval's realism, her abject corporality, and the materialism that constitutes her desire. She is a dusky, musky, dreadlocked goddess on an expense account. Jeanne displays her deconstructive power every time she uses one of "Daddy's" manuscript pages to light her cheroot. In "Black Venus" as in Carter's other texts, the "consolatory fictions" that obscure the actual power relations between men and women are exposed and deflated. The agonized romantic—that is, impotent—poet begs the muse, "Jeanne, get it up for me" (123). The muse—a "beautiful giantess" with big feet, rotted molars, "a persistent vaginal odor that smelled of mice" (117)—"had been deprived of history, she was the pure child of the colony. The colony—white, imperious—had fathered her" (119). Characteristic of Carter's irony, when the colonized object finally has the chance to become a speaking subject, she hasn't much to say and is certainly no poet.

Nights at the Circus features the adventures of another businesswoman: Sophia Fevvers, a six-foot-two, bleached-blonde aerialist with swan's wings—the literalized progeny of the Zeus-swan's rape of Leda, and the "other" sister to mythological Helen, the legitimated offspring of the Zeus and Leda coupling. Fevvers's wings—a fetish par excellence ("throbbing bulges at the base of her shoulders" [185])—have launched a fair number of ships themselves. The novel revels in the idea that gender is constructed through performance, with Fevvers as the consummate performer. In a relationship of power, spectacle is gendered female and the spectator is male (Robinson 118). But in this novel, the spectacles gaze upon themselves, thus becoming both spectating subjects and objects of spectacle. Through feminine excess, Fevvers as narrative subject and object works to deconstruct the logic of masculine desire.

The novel begins with what seems to be the typical narrative trajectory of the Oedipal scheme: the American journalist Walser pursues Fevvers, who has been the "object of learned discussion and profane surmise" (8), in order to uncover and expose the truth, penetrate the veil of enigma that masks her identity. Walser's desire represents the Oedipal pleasure of narrative, which Barthes describes as the desire "to denude, to know, to learn the origin and the end" (10). Sally Robinson points out that the novel starts out by parodying "the 'seek and destroy' narrative that is so popular in classic Hollywood cinema: the feminine enigma must be 'solved,' or the troubling female presence must be eradicated" (122). But this solution or eradication can occur only if the female character can be exploited as a vulnerable object of the penetrating and consuming gaze. From her childhood experience posing as Cupid in the tableau vivant in Ma Nelson's brothel, Fevvers began to see the connection between performance/spectacle and sexual desire. And as the Angel of Death who guards the naked body of Sleeping Beauty in Madame Schreck's "museum of woman monsters," she understood that the male visitors did not pay for the use of the women's bodies but for "the use of the idea of [them]" (70). Fevvers, who becomes a shrewd entrepreneur, learns to control the gaze. She is the one who promotes the slogan "Is she fact or is she fiction?" to capitalize on the enigma of her difference. She understands that to capture the public's attention, to maintain the titillation, she must sustain the unresolved movement between woman masquerading as bird-woman and actual bird-woman. She is the master of ambiguity and plays her freakishness for all it is worth. The anxiety in the narrative is Walser's; the undecidability of Fevvers's identity threatens his controlling vision of the world. "She owes it to herself to remain a woman [masquerading as a bird-woman], he thought. It is her human duty. As a symbolic woman, she has meaning, as an anomaly [an actual bird-woman], none" (161). By "human duty" Walser means that Fevvers must not reveal herself as the abject other who would undermine the phallogocentric conception of the knowable, ordered, closed universe.

As an anomaly, Fevvers signifies what Bakhtin, in his discussion of carnival in Rabelais, theorizes as the grotesque body. Bakhtin observes that the "unfinished and open body . . . is not separated from the world by clearly defined boundaries; it is blended with the world, with animals, with objects" (*Rabelais* 26–27). Bakhtin also points to the importance of the grotesque body's manifesting "the lower body strata" that philosophical and political systems attempt to deny by viewing the body as a classical whole cut off from the physicality that connects the body to the world and to the effects of time. As a grotesque hybrid, Fevvers subverts any attempt to conceptualize her as a classical whole (Booker 227). Visible "under the splitting rancid silk" of her dressing gown were "her humps, her lumps, big as if she bore a bosom fore and aft, her conspicuous deformity" (19). The narrator describes Fevvers's dressing room as a place of "feminine squalor," with soiled undergarments spilling out everywhere and "a powerful note of stale feet" (9). Fevvers's excessively physicality extends to her eating habits: "She gorged, she stuffed herself, she spilled gravy on herself, she sucked up peas from the knife" (22). She devours a bacon sandwich "with relish, a vigorous mastication of large teeth, a smacking of plump lips smeared with grease" (53). And when she yawns, she "open[s] up a crimson maw the size of a basking shark" (52). Offstage and on the circus train through Siberia, we see "Fevvers, in her petticoat, stockingless, corsetless . . . present[ing] a squalid spectacle" (200).

Carter's connection of feminine physicality with abjection is one of the staples of misogynist representations of women. Her transgressive effect lies in the carnivalesque excess that applies to Fevvers and all the other "freaks" of the circus. One of the most common criticisms of Carter's method involves her risky use of sexist and racist stereotypes, which always carry the danger of being misread and appropriated in an oppressive manner. Of course, this concern of feminist critics is valid. We learn to become postmodern readers, and a text cannot guarantee a transgressive or an emancipatory effect, cannot force the actual reader to coincide with the subject position(s) it offers. Although Carter makes identification with characters and immersion in the narrative nearly impossible—denying the comfort of realism—she cannot secure a postmodern feminist reading that fully perceives her extensive irony.[7]

The carnivalized space of Carter's fiction also describes the site that Teresa de

Lauretis theorizes as the space of the subject of feminism, a discursive subject characterized by "the movement in and out of gender as ideological representation," a "movement back and forth between the [male-centered] representation of gender and what that representation leaves out or, more pointedly, makes unrepresentable" (26). (This movement from inside to outside at the level of ideology mirrors the in-and-out, in-and-out that is the source of pleasure in postmodern reading—the oscillation between immersion in the text and critical distance from it.) The subject in process does not settle at the site of the Woman of normative gender construction or outside this patriarchal place in a feminist utopia; rather, the subject moves back and forth between them. Angela Carter's fiction invites readers to occupy this space—which is no longer a gap—and thus provides them with the opportunity to become postmodern agents of reading.

Having considered the kinds of reading that postmodern feminism makes possible, I am reminded of the disparity between my conclusions and those of Patrocinio Schweickart in her influential essay, "Reading Ourselves: Toward a Feminist Theory of Reading," which won the 1984 Florence Howe Award for outstanding feminist scholarship. Schweickart's essay is significant in feminist theory and criticism because it moves beyond Judith Fetterly's defensive uncovering of an all-pervasive, monolithic pattern of misogyny in American literature written by men. Though Fetterly's work, published in 1978, now appears defensive and reductive (in part because it ignored the poststructural theories of French feminists that claimed the power inherent in the practice of deconstructive reading), it also played an important part in an evolving feminism in that it took up and deepened the project of cultural analysis and critique that Kate Millet had initiated in *Sexual Politics* (1970). Schweickart, embracing essentialism, constructs a notion of author and reader as two women engaged in intimate conversation. Her feminist mode of reading is "defined by the drive 'to connect' . . . the desire for relationship . . . and the desire for intimacy, up to and including a symbiotic merger with the other," rather than the mode that is "implicit in the mainstream preoccupation with partition and control—namely, the drive to get it right" (55). For Schweickart, there is *either* dialectical/dialogic reading *or* deconstructive reading; furthermore, she sees deconstruction as offering only the prospect of "impossibility" (56). From this perspective, deconstructive reading is divisive and hostile, antifeminist and unfeminine. Thus, to go along with the juridical construct of the "normal" (male) reader and the marketing construct of the "average" (female) reader prevalent earlier in this century, we have the reader prescribed by feminism.

The reification of an "authentic" feminine or feminist reading overlooks a range of pleasures and of resistances possible in acts of reading. In her provocative article, "Feminism and Trash," Imelda Whelehan claims that academic feminism is failing to reach many of today's students, not because of political apathy, but because feminism has become too punitive, puritanical, and prescriptive. Like other cultural police, academic feminists, who have created their own canon, frown on promiscuous reading: "Many women (not necessarily 'unenlightened' ones) read romance, fantasy or bestsellers for 'pleasure' or 'escape.' . . . To deny the role of pleasure that one can take in seemingly repetitious and hackneyed formulae is to . . . impl[y] that there are proper books to read, as well as proper reading practices" (233). A highbrow feminist theory's implied reader is one who can readily discern the boundary between literature and trash, and dismisses trash as ideologically regressive (Mills, introduction 17). Because of the mixture of high and low culture and the anti-art impulses in postmodern literature as well as the symbiotic relationship between mass culture and canonical literature in the contemporary film-novel nexus (including the recent *The Scarlet Letter*, with the embroidered *A* advertising the augmented breasts of Demi Moore—"Hester Prynne as she was always meant to be," said one film reviewer), the dichotomy between high and low does not hold anymore. In leaving the lowbrow to cultural theorists, feminism compromises its political influence.

To engage in postmodernist reading, which entails the deconstruction of the subject of modern metanarratives, does not mean that agency becomes impossible; rather, we read as postmodern subjects-in-process who can never respond again from a position of theoretical innocence. Earlier feminist scenarios of the joys of intersubjectivity and communal harmony have been complicated in recent years by testimonials and theories of cultural differences among women. Along with lesbian and queer theories, theories of race, ethnicity, and postcoloniality have asked tough questions of feminist theory and have provided for other kinds of resistant postmodernism.

As I mentioned in the beginning of this chapter, the culmination of the postmodern performance of reading might in fact lie in the actualization of multiculturalism. If we could learn to put ourselves in the position of other, become other to ourselves, this would enact a resistant reading taken to another level and perhaps be a concrete example of what is implied by the still shadowy but often repeated term "radical democracy." But as my discussion in the next chapter will claim, becoming the other to oneself is not a simple matter of cultural cross-dressing. Cary Nelson aptly observes that "happy family multiculturalism"—already apparent in the cultural samplers that the textbook industry is pumping out in large numbers—is merely the most recent version of the same old U.S. political imaginary, whereby *antagonistic* differences between marginalized cultures and the dominant hegemony are whitewashed to achieve a monoculture. A more contestatory multicultural reading experience—the reading of differences—would result in "moments of self-interrogation and historical anguish" in addition to moments of "epiphanic identification across cultural differences" (54).

In her recent book, *Risking Who One Is*, Susan Rubin Suleiman, long a believer in the political potential of a postmodern aesthetics, now expresses concern about the political status of postmodern subjectivity after the dismantling of the Berlin Wall and in the time of the Bosnian war:

> What has changed for me . . . is that I have lost my innocence about the "happy cosmopolitan." Things are not so simple; the idea of a postmodernist paradise in which one can try on identities like costumes in a shopping mall ("I'm a happy cosmopolitan; you can be a happy essentialist; they can be happy ironists or defenders of the one and only Faith") appears to me now as not only naive, but intolerably thoughtless in a world where—once again—whole populations are murdered in the name of (ethnic) identity. (230)

I share Suleiman's concern about the urgent necessity of constructing an ethics of postmodernism and find her suggestions compelling. Taking as a starting point Richard Rorty's emblematic figure of the ironist as the postmodern subject, she argues that Rorty stops short of envisioning the political potential of irony in his delimiting irony to the domain of the private. She wonders why this ironist with her (the gender of Rorty's allegorical figure is female) awareness of the contingency of belief systems and her sense of the self as unfinished/in process cannot "act as an agent of ethical choice." Furthermore, she asks, "[w]hy can't a community aim for a similar combination of self-doubt and responsible action? Since public rhetorics of certainty, whether of the historicist or the universalist variety, don't seem to have worked all that well in preventing war, genocide, and other forms of political murder in the past two thousand years, why not try a public rhetoric of doubt?" (237). It is precisely this irony, the recognition that values and beliefs are contingent and that the self is, as Julia Kristeva has shown us, always on trial and in process, that has informed my construction of the agency of postmodern feminism. To read as a postmodern feminist is to read as an ironist. Donna Haraway describes the political imperative of such a project in her "Manifesto for Cyborgs": "an ironic political myth . . . [characterized by] the tension of holding incompatible things together because both or all are necessary and true" (65).[8]

CHAPTER **THREE**

Beloved and *Middle Passage*: Race, Narrative, and the Critic's Essentialism

■ Given today's race industry, we are talking about millions of individuals—politicians, preachers, professors and poets among them—who can no more budge from the belief in racial (and gender) differences than the Inquisition could give a fair hearing to Galileo.

—Charles Johnson, "Inventing Africa"

■ Statements to the contrary, insisting on the meaninglessness of race to the American identity, are themselves full of meaning. The world does not become raceless or will not become unracialized by assertion. The act of enforcing racelessness in literary discourse is itself a racial act

—Toni Morrison, *Playing in the Dark*

T his chapter stages a dialectical encounter between the narrative techniques of Toni Morrison's *Beloved* and Charles Johnson's *Middle Passage* to focus on the different positions required of readers of the two novels. By readers, I mean both the reader(s) implied by the text and actual/historical readers. I argue that it is necessary to answer questions about identity politics and competing models of multiculturalism in order to construct an adequate social model of reading response. Robert Stepto rightly concludes that because the reigning social models of reading response ignore race, they do not tell us much about "an American act of reading" (315). Also significant is Joe Weixlmann's observation that African American literary critics have shown little interest in reader-response approaches to African American texts (55).[1] There are several probable reasons for the lack of exchange between African American criticism and reader theories. First, African American literary criticism has tended to focus on the text and the writer. Second, the European ethnocentrism of most reader-response and reader-reception theories (to which Stepto alludes) results in incomplete or skewed generalizations that ignore differences among readers. And third, when reader theory does manage to look closely at audiences and individual readers, it problematizes the emblematic function of race. What *essentially* does it mean, can it mean, to read as an African American? As a Latina? Such questions entangle us in the thorny issues of identity politics. Thus, the relationship between a theory of racial essentialism and reader-response theory can be characterized as a dialectic without resolution, and it is in the context of this larger dialectic that I analyze the differences between Morrison's and Johnson's narrative methods. In the final section of this chapter, I focus on the essentialism of critical responses that derive from an institutional need to read race in literature, causing critics to fetishize difference instead of grappling with the complexities of the social construction of race.

A CONTEXT FOR READING *BELOVED* AND *MIDDLE PASSAGE*

Ralph Ellison's "The World and the Jug" is a rare early example of a text that draws attention to race and reading response. This essay, composed of two pieces directed to Irving Howe, is a powerful critique of the oppressive tendencies of white intellectuals who attempt to prescribe, according to their own socialist political agenda, the aesthetics of black writers. Ellison observes that "Howe makes of 'Negroness' a metaphysical condition, one that is a state of irremediable agony," and that this condition as Howe conceives of it arises "from a collective experience which leaves no room for the individual writer's unique existence" (130). Ellison says that Howe faults him for choosing art over " 'black' anger and 'clenched militancy' " (120) and for failing to follow the path laid down by Richard Wright.[2] Claiming Ernest Hemingway as his literary father, Ellison speaks of "an American Negro tradition which teaches one to deflect racial provocation and to master and contain pain," and adds that "[i]t takes fortitude to be a man and no less to be an artist" (111–12). His response to Howe reveals a faith in modernist humanism's emancipatory project: the individual's ability to transcend the material conditions of history through an autonomous art.[3] Thus, Ellison is loath to speak of victimage, powerlessness, and racial determinacy.

More than twenty years later, Stanley Crouch's critical essays and reviews recall Ellison's comments. Yet in significant ways the dynamics of the scene have changed: the debate is no longer between black writer and white reader/critic, but between black critic and black writer. Crouch accuses Toni Morrison of pandering to an audience of white liberals and of ruining her writing through heavy-handed ideology and sentimentality, while he warmly praises Charles Johnson's talent and his independence. In his *New Republic* review of *Beloved* (reprinted in *Notes of a Hanging Judge*), Crouch criticizes Morrison for focusing on gender oppression, a focus that he claims derives from a white feminist agenda and simply reinscribes the age-old stereotypes of black male (mis)behavior. He argues that *Beloved* "is designed to placate sentimental feminist ideology, and to make sure that the vision of black woman as the most scorned and rebuked of the victims doesn't weaken" (205). Crouch calls Morrison's book "a black face holocaust novel [which] seems to have been written in order to enter American slavery into the big-time martyr ratings contest, a contest usually won by references to, and works about, the experiences of the Jews" (205). He ends by indicting Morrison as "a literary conjure woman" who has profited mightily from her position (209). Notes of a hanging judge, indeed.

At the end of his review of *Beloved*, Crouch turns to Charles Johnson's *Oxherding Tale* as a shining example of a cliché-free novel about the complexities of slavery. Unlike Morrison's novel, which Crouch calls "trite," "counterfeit," and "crass[ly] obvious," Johnson's is one of those rare books that "exhibits not only talent but the courage to face the ambiguities of the human soul, which transcend race" (208). Johnson has chosen "human nature over platitudes, opportunism, or trends" (143). Crouch also responded favorably to Johnson's *Middle Passage*; in fact, his was one of two blurbs chosen to grace the dust jacket of the book. Crouch observes that "*Middle Passage* is further proof of Charles Johnson's unwillingness to be overwhelmed by the complexity of the American story. . . . [and] it places him within the universal minority whose will to mastery is made manifest by the quality of their creations."

Beloved did not win the National Book Award, much to the outrage of the African American writers and critics—Crouch excluded—who signed a petition to register their protest. *Middle Passage* did win the 1990 National Book Award. What can we make of the connection between the two situations? Was Johnson's a compensatory award, bestowed, in the better-late-than-never tradition, on a black writer by the overwhelmingly white jury?[4] And can we attribute Johnson's success with the jury to the fact that his narrative is much more accommodating to the educated white male reader than Morrison's is?[5] My affirmative answer to the second question makes me wary of Crouch's responses to *Beloved* and *Middle Passage*. In engaging Johnson's narrative method in an encounter with Morrison's method, I find that Johnson's novel seeks to transcend race and to suppress the feminine, and indeed, these are the very qualities that Crouch valorizes. Although this chapter focuses primarily on race in reading response and critical reception, my analysis of race is necessarily inflected by questions of gender and class. Still, there remains more to be said about Johnson's narrative in terms of gender and reading than space allows me here.

Before elaborating on the differences in readers' positions in *Beloved* and *Middle Passage*, I want to consider the conventional relationship between the narrator and the reader of the nineteenth-century slave narrative, the ancestral literary genre to which Morrison's and Johnson's novels respond. These postmodern middle passage narratives speak from the silence of their literary forebears. The gaps and silences in the slave narratives resulted from rhetorical constraints and generic conventions, textual restrictions that applied to the postbellum novel as well. John Sekora has observed that "[o]utside the narrative, slavery was a wordless, nameless, timeless time. It was a time without history and without imminence. Slaveholders sought to reduce existence to the psychological present and to mandate their records as the only reliable texts" (163). By mastering language and providing an oppositional text, slaves and ex-slaves wrote themselves into existence. But by no means was this creative agency unfettered, for the narrators were bound by the political exigencies of their white sponsors and by the literary taste of a white audience. Most sponsors co-opted the narratives for their own purpose, believing that the fugitive slaves had no stories to tell until the abolitionists provided one for them; the abolitionists were not interested in the narratives as texts of identity but as eyewitness accounts of victimage (Sekora 162, 154). Even the most well-meaning of sponsors, editors, or guarantors encouraged narrators to uphold generic conventions to satisfy the desires and expectations of readers.

The slave narrator's rhetorical burden involved enlightening an audience with gruesome and life-shattering facts. Narratives of the 1830s and 1840s, during the high point of the abolitionist movement, adopted a forensic/judicial kind of rhetoric. They attempted to persuade readers to take political action, with the primary form of persuasion being verifiable evidence of the horrors of slavery; the evidence often included legal documents and the endorsements of white authorities. Narratives written after the Civil War, such as the 1893 version of Frederick Douglass's autobiography and Booker T. Washington's *Up from Slavery* (1901), no longer conveyed an exhortatory voice. Instead, these narratives expressed the slave's gratitude at having been emancipated in the course of a progressive social movement.[6]

Although narrative perspectives and rhetorical strategies changed in the evolution of the genre, the stories contained common components that readers came to expect. Covering a prescribed sequence of experiences that ranged from violent whippings by cruel masters to narrow escapes from the jaws of bloodthirsty hounds (Olney 153), the slave narrative by turns horrified and titillated its white middle- and upper-class readers. Narrators such as Frederick Douglass and Harriet Jacobs were uncomfortably aware of the distance between their experiences and those of their readers. One reason why the slave remained the other/object was because the genre of the slave narrative diverted the reader's attention from the individual slave's experiences and shifted the focus to slavery as an institution.[7]

To establish the agency of the slave, contemporary African American writers have defamiliarized the predictable institutional story and granted the authority of the story to the individual narrator (McDowell 160). Readers of slave stories written in the postmodern period are denied the position of detached spectators and involved in a discursive relationship very different from that experienced by nineteenth-century readers. Yet the methods used to bridge the gap between reader and text vary widely, as an analysis of *Beloved* and *Middle Passage* reveals.

BELOVED AND THE NARRATIVE EXPERIENCE OF OTHERNESS

Toni Morrison has claimed that she writes with a black audience in mind.[8] By audience she means narrative audience, and in the case of *Beloved* this narrative audience would include those African American readers who find no overwhelming dissonance in the fact that Beloved seems to be alternately a haint and an actual person, who have no trouble "listening" to a story that accumulates in layers as narratives do in oral tradition, and who understand a mother's decision to kill her child rather than relinquish that child to the brutality of slavery. But Morrison also writes to an audience that she tests and tries, an audience I will describe as rhetorical-authorial.[9] Speaking of her intentions in *Beloved*, she says she wanted the reader to be in a situation similar to the slave's, denied information needed to make connections, without preparation or defense ("Unspeakable" 32–33). Does Morrison want to make it hard on her black readers? Or just some of her black readers, those so distant from their African heritage and from the horrors of the middle passage that they cannot be part of the ideal narrative audience? This black audience, confronted by intraracial difference, can become the narrative audience only by engaging in cultural "cross-dressing." And interracial difference constitutes the cross-dressing for other readers. Although an understanding of this cultural cross-dressing or border-crossing is important to any theory of reader response, thus far, the reader's identification—or failed identification—with fictional characters or fictional worlds has been explained almost exclusively in aesthetic or psychological terms that largely ignore the implications of racial and cultural difference.[10]

Beloved charts the conflicts of Sethe's mother love. In the conflicted urge to tell her children about the past but to keep silent about the enslavement and racism so as not to stifle the hope and potential of the children, the African American mother's plight becomes clear. Like other mothers who have suffered through the unbearableness of being, Sethe feels the desire to recover history but also the need to deny history. For her, history acts as Platonic *pharmakon*, both poison and cure. Though Sethe's conflict was shared by many female slaves and ex-slaves, Morrison tells a story that other African American writers have avoided: the story of a woman who sacrifices her children in order to constitute herself as an agent. Sethe kills her child in an act of love, murders her child to save her from the effects of slavery, and thus "outhurt[s] the hurter" (234).[11]

Expected to be powerful matriarchs who shoulder the burdens of an oppressed race,[12] black women in this culture have also been forced to recognize the passive, receptive white woman as an iconograph of the feminine ideal. Hortense Spillers observes that in contrast to those African American writers who submerge their characters in a "tide of virtue and pathos," Morrison dramatizes the fact that "virtue is not the sole alternative to powerlessness" (181, 183). According to Barbara Christian, *Beloved* originated in Morrison's impulse to fill gaps—both unconscious and deliberate—left in the narratives of former slaves (326). Christian points out that Sethe represents what the ex-slave Harriet Jacobs could not speak in her narrative. Writing under the pseudonym Linda Brent, Jacobs used a code to avoid seeming immodest and to avoid offending the sensibilities of her readers (329). The domestic novel—primer of ideal womanhood, modeling chastity along with marital and maternal success—served as Jacobs's literary model; her ethical appeal depended on her ability to convince readers that she was a chaste, victimized woman. Sethe's particular form of agency would have relegated her to the status of crazy slave in the record of white history.[13] Likewise, Sethe troubles those readers schooled in the prescribed forms of African American female literary characters: characters whose anger and agency are diffused/defused in servitude to a white employer, in mysticism, in hysteria, or in suicide.

As the narrative progresses, readers are encouraged to admire Sethe and meant to agree with Paul D when he says, "You your best thing, Sethe. You are"

(273). Yet readers are also likely to share Paul D's conclusion that "[t]here are too many things to feel about this woman" (272). It is one thing to deal with Beloved's otherness, understanding her as a haint or the palpable spirit of both a repressed racial memory and the child that Sethe killed, but it is quite another thing to come to terms with Sethe's otherness. Very few contemporary readers—of any culture—can know the kind of love that "it took to drag the teeth of that saw under the little chin: to feel the baby blood pump like oil in her hands; to hold her face so her head could stay on; to squeeze her so she could absorb, still, the death spasms that shot through that adored body, plump and sweet with life . . . " (251).

Paul D, who loves Sethe, also fears her, for her "love is too thick" (164). Sethe's daughter Denver, unable to trust her mother, has kept a twelve-year vigil, never leaving the house and yard for fear that "the thing that happened" (205) might happen again if she is not there to stop it. Denver says she needs to understand that which made it all right for Sethe to kill her own child, but she does not really want to understand. She, too, is caught up in the tension between recall and repression. Sethe recognizes that she can never fully explain the murder, "never close it in, pin it down for anybody who had to ask" (163). Her daughter cannot fathom the "dirtiness" of the white racist consciousness that worked to rob Sethe of both an identity and the ability to reconstitute an identity.

If Sethe's daughter cannot fully understand her mother's experiences as a slave, what about readers today, and especially white readers? It is customary for white academics and New Age liberals outside of academe to take up a position that allows us to condemn the brutality of a white consciousness that diminished (and diminishes) the African American to the status of commodity-beast. In this position, when the white reader identifies with Sethe and the other characters, the reader identifies in opposition to her or his own culture, assuming a position comparable to that of the abolitionist readers of the nineteenth-century slave narratives. But when Sethe kills her baby to "outhurt the hurter" (234) and thus to become a subject rather than an object in her fight against the schoolteacher, for many readers the identification ends. Though Morrison has succeeded in drawing readers close enough to Sethe to enable them to sympathize with her, Morrison's narrative effect ultimately depends on the reader's inability to infuse Sethe's character with his or her own subjectivity. Sethe occupies the gap between the terms of the colonizer's necessary contradiction: the other as both completely knowable and wholly mysterious. The design of Morrison's narrative works to prevent readers from responding to Sethe and her story through either introjection or rejection, which Gabriele Schwab describes "as the earliest modes [in the development of the self and in the genesis of cultural relations] of relating to otherness" (114).

Morrison offers readers the opportunity of relating to otherness in a way that does not involve abjection. Subject formation requires that a person differentiate him- or herself from others, and there are numerous ways of differentiating the "I," with the worst being those that abject and degrade others from whom the "I" must be distinct. I join in Judith Butler's call for forms of differentiation that do not require the systematic repudiation and disavowal of others and that result in "fundamentally more capacious, generous, and 'unthreatened' bearings of the self in the midst of community. That an 'I' is differentiated from another does not mean that the other [must become] unthinkable in its difference, nor that the other must become structurally homologous to the 'I' in order to enter into community with that 'I' " ("For a Careful Reading" 140). In the reader's relationship with Sethe lies the possibility of acknowledging difference without introjecting or assimilating Sethe to the reader's own identity or rejecting her as unthinkable in her absolute difference.

Morrison was committed to an *in medias res* opening designed to be abrupt, meant to throw the reader into "an environment completely foreign," and as such to construct a shared experience for readers and characters. The reader would be "[s]natched just as the slaves were from one place to another, from any place to another . . . " ("Unspeakable" 32). Morrison wanted to achieve "the compelling confusion of being there as they (the characters) are: suddenly, without comfort or succor from the 'author,' with only imagination, intelligence, and necessity available for the journey. . . . No compound of houses, no neighborhood, no sculpture, no paint, no time, especially no time because memory, pre-historic memory has no time" ("Unspeakable" 33). Unlike the slave narrative, which provided a multitude of facts to demonstrate the inhumanity of slavery, *Beloved* withholds ordered facts and resists the insulated, detached reading position offered by the slave narrative. Like the characters in the novel, readers must construct a narrative from randomly remembered incidents and from seemingly incomprehensible occurrences. The appearance of Beloved confounds the reader's ability to distinguish the real from the supernatural, for Morrison's intertextuality combines the epistemology of fictional realism with that of the African folktale.[14] Morrison describes her use of the haunting as both "a major incumbent of the narrative and sleight of hand . . . to keep the reader preoccupied with the nature of the incredible spirit world while being supplied a controlled diet of the incredible political world" (32).

At one point in the second section of the novel, Morrison temporarily removes the narrator as mediator, and the narrator—along with the reader—becomes a listener. In this part of the narrative, Beloved, Sethe, and Denver tell their stories to themselves and to each other, their voices finally intertwining in counterpoint. These are the voices silenced in the slave narratives, speaking in a language, a semiotic, that not even Morrison's narrator could translate. The strangeness of this fugue results from the voices having been silenced for so long. The fugal quality, with contrapuntal voices simultaneously expressing variations on the same theme, reflects not only the narrative structure of the novel but the collective effort of the African American slave narratives as well.

The teleology of the slave narrative involved the progression from slavery to freedom. Implicit in the slave owner's cruelty and in the slave's ability to survive, as described in the opening chapters of the narrative, was the design of eventual emancipation and the triumph of justice, providing readers with emotional and aesthetic closure. By ending on this positive note, the slave narrative suppressed troubling questions about the experiences of the ex-slave. But the narrative structure of *Beloved* is not teleological. Perhaps the most unsettling aspect of the novel is Morrison's problematizing of the emancipation narrative, in respect to both political history and individual life experience.

In addition to its fugal structure, *Beloved* evokes another meaning of fugue: the psychiatric term for a form of amnesia. The narrator's refrain, woven through the two-page coda of the novel, warns that "it was not a story to pass on," and we are told that all of those persons connected with Beloved have disremembered her, for "[r]emembering seemed unwise" (274). But Toni Morrison warns us that we risk fragmentation unless we embrace the wholeness of our cultural and racial histories; we must remember even—perhaps especially—those parts we would most like to forget (Christian 340–41).

After talking about *Beloved* with my students and with readers outside of academe, I have decided that it is one of those novels one can both admire profoundly and not finish, for in its otherness it is painful. Those readers for whom the *pharmakon* seems more poison than cure engage in their own kinds of disremembering. The narrative forces African American readers to recall experiences so horrible that they were not only omitted from the narrative of American history but were repressed in personal memory as well. By requiring European Americans to occupy the position of the other in all of its abjection, *Beloved* both calls for identification with Sethe and makes it ultimately impossible. These readers confront the limits of cross-cultural identification.

MIDDLE PASSAGE: TRANSCENDING RACE THROUGH NARRATIVE

Charles Johnson might seem to have transcended race by creating *Middle Passage* from an amalgamation of cultural and literary sources, drawing from the *Brihad-aranyaka Upanishad*, Plato, Homer, Aquinas, Swift, Defoe, Melville, and African folklore in a story narrated by a freed bondsman who sounds at moments much like a university professor of the 1990s. When interrogated by the method of *Beloved*, the transcendence of *Middle Passage* appears suspect. The tension between the narrative methods results from the fact that Morrison's rhetorical-authorial audience is composed of nonblacks and those black readers who have separated themselves from the painful history of African Americanism, while Johnson's rhetorical audience is composed of those African American writers and critics who make racial resentment the primary determinant of their aesthetic endeavors. This resentment Johnson sees as a residual aesthetic response from the period of Black Nationalism and separatism that characterized the African American political and cultural movement of the 1960s and 1970s. Johnson feels that such a response is retrograde in the 1990s and should be replaced by an aesthetics and a politics of cultural synthesis.

The middle passage Charles Johnson offers to his readers is much more accommodating than Morrison's *foreign environment*. The narrator, Rutherford Calhoun, occupies an intertextual space-time—a middle passage—into which he invites the reader, and it is through the intersubjectivity made possible by this narrative interstice that readers understand Calhoun's experiences on the slave ship *Republic*, perceiving him not as a static historical other but as a historical agent with whom they are implicated in an ongoing construction of the African American experience. Considered from the perspective of intertextuality, Calhoun's numerous anachronisms are performative; they are interfaces that mediate the textual relationship between the world of contemporary readers and the world of nineteenth-century Africans and African Americans. Furthermore, Johnson's narrative intersubjectivity advocates a political position beyond the Scylla and Charybdis of cultural assimilation or cultural separatism, a postmodern position that acknowledges the coexistence of unity and difference.

Calhoun is a warm, palpable presence, ever attentive to the reader's needs. Though he frequently speaks directly to the reader, using rhetorical gestures such as "as you know" (10), "[y]ou have seen" (11), and "[s]urely you can understand why" (100), Calhoun is not obsequious, is not slavish.[15] He manifests none of the anxiety that the traditional slave narrator expressed in writing for a white audience. From the first sentences of his ship log, Calhoun sounds not only comfortable but droll.

By the second page of the novel, Calhoun admits to being a petty thief, defying the literary stereotype of the honest, steadfast bondsman who not only survives slavery but, in a perverse turn on the work ethic, attains true nobility of character through the test of slavery. Although possessed of a wily, mischievous nature, Calhoun is not the stereotypical African American male trickster of literature. Like Odysseus, with whom he compares himself (207), Calhoun is wily with words. But, more than merely a skilled rhetorician, he is nimble with ideas, erudite as a result of the efforts of his former master, the Reverend Peleg Chandler, "a fair, sympathetic, and well-meaning man" (111), who hoped Calhoun would become a preacher. Having explained his classical education, Calhoun is free to make liberal use of strikingly unslavelike metaphors and allusions. The following examples occur within the brief span of eight pages: "Never in my life had anyone loved me so selflessly, as the hag in the Wife of Bath's Tale had loved her fickle knight" (17); "like the monocular witches outwitted by Perseus" (22); "[H]e'd be the kind who could do Leibnizian logic or Ptolemaic astronomy" (25). Although some narrators, such as Frederick Douglass, were extremely eloquent, a slave narrative would not have made repeated allusions to medieval literature and Renaissance philosophy. The rhetorical purpose of the antebellum genre required an ethos quite different from the one projected by Rutherford Calhoun.

Johnson created an atypical ex-slave narrator and placed him in a completely unfamiliar situation to jolt readers from their preconditioned responses. In his critical and theoretical study *Being and Race: Black Writing Since 1970* (1988), which can be read as a blueprint for the design of *Middle Passage*, Johnson claims that the best fiction "fling[s] the reader . . . toward revelation and unsealed vision" (32–33). He adapted the narrative method of *Middle Passage* from Husserlian phenomenology. Husserl's method involves bracketing the data of consciousness by suspending all preconceptions, especially those derived from the naturalistic perspective. Husserl believed that such bracketing made it possible for the observer to experience the object in all of its complexity and to grasp the object's essence intuitively. Objects of pure imagination are especially important in this theory because they prompt responses free from the naturalized preconceptions that adhere to data taken from the objective world.

On the slave ship *Republic*, existence is bracketed off from the world. The crew and captives inhabit a strange middle passage between worlds and between levels of being. In an ironic reversal of Plato's Republic, the slave ship contains absolutely no immutable forms; rather, what we encounter is a brilliant but mad captain with a motley collection of misfits and degenerates for a crew, transporting the last survivors of a tribe of magicians from their devastated African homeland, on a voyage financed by a wealthy African American slave trader, aboard a ship so ravaged by storms that the crew must ceaselessly repair it to keep it afloat. Calhoun describes the ship as "from stem to stern, a process" (36). Heterogeneity and flux characterize the situation of the *Republic*, with the unfamiliarness constantly evolving.

But when we consider particular instances of humor and intellectual musing, it becomes clear that Johnson intended more than defamiliarization. In passages such as "his face looked, so help me, like five miles of bad Louisiana road" (54) and "the high-flown inscrutable way whites made the Cherokees talk in dime novels, or the Chinese in bad stage plays" (83), Calhoun's humorous anachronisms establish a bridge between his historical and cultural situation and the situation(s) of his readers. In another example of a performative anachronism, Squibb, as part of "the competition [among the crew] to prove the purity of one's gender," recites a sexist barroom riddle new to his companions but (too) familiar to the readers of the novel: "Q: What's the difference between a dog and a fox? A: About four drinks" (41). Calhoun's comment about gender purity indicates an awareness of sexism that makes his favorable reaction to the riddle a politically incorrect response. But more to the point, his calling Squibb's riddle "memorable" indicates that he is an observer straddling a fence between two worlds, able to see into the future but unable to completely read the data. It remains for the reader to complete the interpretive transit.

The conversations between Calhoun and Captain Falcon contain numerous allusions to contemporary theoretical and political issues. Calhoun says Falcon has "a thinker's brow . . . , the kind fantasy writers put on spacemen far ahead of us in science and philosophy" (29). Proving the truth of Calhoun's description of him as a visionary, Falcon launches into a discussion of excellence that sounds much like the current conservative political position on affirmative action:

> "I believe in *excellence*—an unfashionable thing these days . . . what with headmasters giving illiterate Negroes degrees because they feel too guilty to fail them, then employers giving that same boy a place in the firm since he's got his degree in hand and saying no will bring a gang of Abolitionists down on their necks. . . . [T]he problem, Mr. Calhoun, is . . . that most of these minorities aren't ready for the title of quartermaster or

first mate precisely because discrimination denied them that training that makes for true excellence." (31–32)

Falcon's argument about excellence—the argument of a megalomanic, sadistic, cannibalistic intellectual—obliges the reader to re-see this familiar position posed by those who claim to be infinitely reasonable. The reader's re-seeing and enlightenment is one of the aims of Johnson's phenomenological method.

Falcon's speech quoted above, and numerous other passages like it woven through the narrative, result in a postmodern intertextual form, with the texts of the readers' world connected dialogically to the texts of the world of the narrator and other characters. This kind of narrative structure makes manifest the constructedness of history, throwing light on the historian's hermeneutics and showing the impossibility of a historical narrative purified of interpretation.

Johnson's adoption of Merleau-Ponty's theory of engagement qualifies his use of Husserlian phenomenology. Husserl's transcendental idealism—a form of subjectivism that posits a transcendental ego as constituting everything, as fully constructing the other, and as having the ability to grasp its own essence through internal perception (Madison 60)—is challenged by Merleau-Ponty's rejection of dualism and his insistence that all knowledge derives from living in the world. Instead of the binary oppositions of dualism, Merleau-Ponty's theory describes dyadic relationships, which involve intersubjectivity. The *I* becomes *I* in its relationship to *you*, with the *I* and the *you* mutually defining each other. Our own narratives are woven tightly into a tapestry with the narratives of others. In *Adventures of the Dialectic*, Merleau-Ponty claims that each of us possesses only incomplete, interrupted meanings that are "completed over there, in the others who hold the key to them because they see sides of things that I do not see, as well as, one might say, my social back. . . . Our experiences thus have lateral relationships of truth: . . . in our combined functionings we form a totality which moves toward enlightenment and completion" (qtd. in C. Johnson, *Being and Race* 44).

Various kinds of intersubjective encounters occur in *Middle Passage*, from the wondrous melding of the cabin boy Tommy O'Toole with the Allmuseri's shape-changing monster to Peter Cringle's offering his dying body as food for the survivors on the *Republic*, who are so famished that they accept this gift that requires them to kill, butcher, and eat another human being. The shared experiences of Calhoun, the crew, and the Allmuseri transcend racial and cultural binaries. When Calhoun discovers that it is Papa Zeringue, the black Creole gangster-godfather of New Orleans and the creditor he fled, who is the slave trader financing their voyage, he recognizes that they are all slaves in the configuration of capitalist property and power: "Suddenly the ship felt insubstantial: a pawn in a larger game of property so vast it trivialized our struggles on board" (150). Also, as sons involved in tortured or nonexistent relationships with their fathers, Calhoun and the white crew members share painful memories of coming to manhood, their unity deriving from shared emotional trauma. In one of his most significant epiphanies, Calhoun understands that he is "[a] man remade by virtue of his contact with the crew" (124). The Allmuseri—and Calhoun's experience of "all misery" on the *Republic*—have "irreversibly changed [his] seeing" and made a "cultural mongrel" of him (187). Furthermore, he admits to having seen the Allmuseri's "lives and culture as timeless product, as a finished thing, pure essence of Parmenidean meaning . . . when the truth was that they were process and Heraclitean change, like any men, not fixed but evolving and . . . vulnerable to metamorphosis. . . . Ngonyama and maybe all Africans were not wholly Allmuseri anymore. We had changed them" (124).

In *Being and Race*, Johnson claims that "[o]ur lives, as blacks and whites . . . are a tissue of cross-cultural influences" (43). But failing—or refusing—to recognize our "mongrelized" construction, we try to establish a unitary identity for ourselves by making others into various versions of the static, essential, homogeneous other against whom we define ourselves. Kwame Anthony Appiah, whose theories Johnson admires, observes that despite our attempts to fix Africa as the other to Europe, "[w]e are all already contaminated by each other" (qtd. in Johnson, "Inventing Africa" 8). Postcolonial writers and visual artists complain that they are tired of being "otherness machines," for they do "not see themselves as Other" (Appiah, "Is the Post-" 356) but rather as part of the diverse and dynamic mosaic of groups that constructs an evolving sense of place, time, and situation.

Charles Johnson has advised his fellow African American writers "to move from narrow complaint to broad celebration" and to engage in what Merleau-Ponty described as "singing the world" (*Being and Race* 123). Indeed, the rhetorical-authorial audience Johnson addresses in *Middle Passage* is composed of those African American novelists and critics who have helped to produce what he considers an impoverished body of narrow and homogeneous fiction—"provincial" because it fails to transcend racial polemics (*Being and Race* 124). In political terms, Johnson's narrative method suggests a way for us to get past our local and specific situations to a more expansive perspective. Johnson's narrative middle passage is the site where narrator and reader are interlocutors who, despite the differences and distance between them, for a time become in the text "a single thing:

singer, listener, and song, light spilling into light, the boundaries of inside and outside, here and there, today and tomorrow obliterated" (69). This reader is not the unreliable listener whom Robert Stepto describes as getting "told off" (forced to submit to the truth of the teller) in African American storytelling texts (309); rather, Johnson's textual reader is involved in a close, collaborative relationship with the narrator.

The model of reading that Johnson's narrative constructs resembles the model that Gabriele Schwab has derived from D. W. Winnicott's object-relations theory. In this theory, literature constitutes a protected area, what Winnicott calls the "intermediate area," where one can temporarily and safely reexperience the early pleasures of "archaic fusion" by breaking down the boundary between the imaginary and the real. In the intermediate area, which is the site of the production and the reception of literature and other cultural texts, Schwab observes that " 'otherness' as such disappears . . . , being transformed into sameness. . . . Instead of an 'annexation' of the self by the other, Winnicott would think of a fusion that transforms self and other simultaneously" (Schwab 117, 120). Furthermore, in allowing us a safe space to discover and acknowledge otherness, the intermediate space "favor[s] a continuous process of dissolving, transforming, and retracing the boundaries of our culture and our selves" (120). Johnson's narrative middle passage enacts Winnicott's notion of intermediate space.

Having described Johnson's narrative method, I am left to consider large questions that his perspective begs, for his efforts to effect the transcendence of race succeed only to the extent that actual readers can occupy the position of the implied reader. Would not African American readers' responses differ significantly from European Americans' according to desire and ability to achieve this transcendence? I can begin to answer this question by reiterating that Stanley Crouch is Johnson's ideal reader, while I (European American) am an oppositional reader who resists the transcendent effect that Johnson seeks. To offer a more complete answer, I turn now to the politics of interpretation that informs the critical reception of African American literature.

THE ACADEMIC CRITIC'S ESSENTIAL GESTURE

I want to consider the tension between *Beloved* and *Middle Passage* at the site where aesthetics and politics converge. When interrogated by Morrison's method, Johnson's is transcendent in terms of race and seems to me politically conservative. At the 1991 conference of the National Council of Teachers of English, Johnson spoke of the dangers of multiculturalism, expressing the fear that our literature as well as our cultural lives will be "balkanized" into separate spheres. To support his position of cultural synthesis, he quoted Martin Luther King along with Allan Bloom and Dinesh D'Souza. It is at this point that I pause. Has Johnson discovered the fourth way, with cultural synthesis coming after segregation (rejection), assimilation (introjection), and cultural separatism? Or is Johnson's notion of cultural synthesis simply another form of assimilation in which the dominant culture swallows up marginalized cultures?

Searching for answers to these questions, I discovered a telling statement in Johnson's 1992 review in the *New York Times* of Appiah's *In My Father's House: Africa in the Philosophy of Culture*: "By carefully examining the concepts behind such emotional issues as Pan-Africanism and 'African identity,' and by applying precision of thought—*indeed, the entire history of Western* philosophy—throughout the interdisciplinary essays that constitute *In My Father's House*, Mr. Appiah delivers what may well be one of the handful of theoretical works on race that will preserve our humanity and guide us gracefully into the next century" (emphasis added, "Inventing Africa" 8). One of Johnson's syllogisms proceeds as follows: (1) "precision of thought" is necessary to uncover the truths obscured by the emotional issues that plague Africanist theory; (2) precision of thought is constituted by "the entire history of Western philosophy"; (3) therefore, the history of Western philosophy is the necessary analytic to productively theorize race and other issues related to African philosophy and culture. It seems that Johnson employs a version of what Appiah has dubbed the "Naipaul fallacy" to refer to a "postcolonial inferiority complex" that compels African or African American critics to assign value to African texts by using European literature and culture as the universal standard.

In speculating about the likely negative or negligible response to Appiah's *In My Father's House*,[16] Johnson speaks of "personal and professional investment in the idea of racial differences." He feels that race has become an "industry" employing "millions of individuals—politicians, preachers, professors, and poets among them." And it is exactly this acknowledgment of the political utility, ideological pervasiveness, and what Toni Morrison calls "the metaphysical necessity" of race that undermines Johnson's and Appiah's efforts to transcend the concept of race. I agree with Morrison's conclusion in *Playing in the Dark: Whiteness and the Literary Imagination* that "[t]he world does not become raceless or will not become unracialized by assertion" (46). In his critique of Appiah's work on W. E. B. Du Bois, Houston Baker expresses sentiments similar to Morrison's, arguing that Appiah's efforts to reveal race as a biological fiction refuse to account for the fact that race has always mattered—historically, politically, and materially (384–85).[17] In explaining the full import of race—Africanism or blackness—to American ideology, Morrison observes: "There is still much national solace in continuing dreams of democratic egalitarianism available by hiding class conflict, rage, and impotence in figurations of race. And there is quite a lot of juice to be extracted from plummy reminiscences of 'individualism' and 'freedom' if the tree upon which such fruit hangs is a black population forced to serve as freedom's polar opposite . . . " (*Playing* 64). Thus, the presence of the racialized other shores up a faltering belief in freedom and autonomy, the emblem of race functioning in the service of a perverse postmodern humanism.

Johnson's notion of an industry of race and Morrison's notion of race as a metaphysical and ideological necessity recall Gayatri Spivak's observation that there is an institutional need to consolidate the self by definition through the other (Spivak 162). Expressing a similar conclusion, Gates points out that "[Frantz] Fanon's fascination for us has something to do with the convergence of the problematic of colonialism with that of subject-formation" ("Critical Fanonism" 458). Appearing as both "a psychoanalyst of culture . . . [and] a champion of the wretched of the earth," Fanon, according to Gates, has proved "irresistible . . . to a criticism that sees itself as both oppositional and postmodern" (458). We critics on the left, inside and outside of academe, project these desires onto the productions of contemporary writers and, thus, engage in our own version of the manufacture of otherness. I suspect that Johnson's relatively cool reception by critics and scholars results from his effort to substitute *another* for *the other*. Despite the prestigious National Book Award bestowed on *Middle Passage*, the novel is not being written about in professional journals, taught in universities, and worked into the canon the way that *Beloved* or Alice Walker's *The Color Purple* were almost immediately after their publication. Perhaps the scholarly attention to Johnson's work will come later. To posit a reason either for the dearth of or the delay in critical attention, I would return to Spivak's comment and say that Johnson's *Middle Passage*, which elides the concept of otherness in a theory of intersubjectivity, short-circuits the institutional efforts of academic critics and theoreticians to consolidate themselves through the other. Johnson's aesthetic project, though not identical to Ellison's, is related, for both writers believe in the writer's ability to transcend the material and political conditions of history through artistic production/construction. Although *Beloved* expresses Morrison's urge to return to the past and seek out gaps in personal memory and cultural history, *Middle Passage* enacts Johnson's push to move forward in a constantly evolving reconstruction of history. Johnson's narrator is a time traveler, the one doing the cross-dressing. Morrison, on the other hand, requires the reader to cross over.

An analysis of the trials of the reader must differentiate among situations of reading. For the isolated reader—that reader, of any culture, who reads independently of an academic interpretive community—reading *Beloved* is likely to be more arduous than reading *Middle Passage*. But for this very reason, *Beloved* is more accommodating to our institutional reading desires and needs. The most cynical explanation for Morrison's success with academic readers is that it is due to her narrative method, which practices a continuous withholding of information from readers and in this way sustains our institutional obsession with ambiguity and undecidability, qualities the modernists and New Critics and later the poststructuralists taught us to expect and to want. Therefore, from this perspective the critical focus on cultural or racial otherness indicates merely the latest in a series of moves to establish the specific difference of a unique literary product. In a related explanation, Valerie Smith has argued that white feminists have begun to use black women's texts to revitalize and materialize their theories, which have become attenuated from the influence of poststructuralism. Elizabeth Abel notes that this relationship between white and black women—white theorist/critic sustained by black writer—"reproduces in the textual realm white women's historical relation to the black female bodies that have nurtured them" ("Black Writing" 479).

A more positive explanation for Morrison's success and for our institutional investment in difference appears when we consider these phenomena in an oppositional political context: we seek knowledge of cultural otherness to understand how the construction of race functions and to use this understanding to oppose racial prejudice and the resultant injustice and exploitation. In this way, we can get beyond the ugly anthropological project of objectifying otherness that involves grasping and consuming what we perceive as the essence of the other in order to return to ourselves as more complete (and temporarily sated) humans/humanists. The question "What can the exotic other tell me about myself?" can no longer determine our scholarly inquiries. Charles Johnson's *Middle Passage* establishes a middle ground, a neutral space that denies the marginal and offers readers the familiar and the unthreatening. But in forcing readers far removed from the middle passage and from African American slavery to assume the position of an other with whom they cannot coincide, Morrison's *Beloved* makes these readers aware of their own otherness. The effect of this kind of reading is akin to what Spivak describes as "the unlearning of one's own privilege" (qtd. in Giroux, "Post-Colonial Ruptures" 19).

On another level, Johnson's narrative method and targeted audience underscore the facts of the demographics of reading. When I speak of "these readers" of Johnson and Morrison, what I actually mean are readers who live a fairly privileged life: they are literate, have enough leisure time to read "serious" novels, and likely make enough money to buy the books. The notion of "black reader" or "white reader" obscures the fact that class (which includes level of education) presently determines most intraracial differences as well as interracial similarities in the United States.[18] The material lives of those who read, study, and write about Morrison and Johnson are much more similar to each other—regardless of the differences in race—than they are to the lives of those in the lower classes.

Yet one's life experience entails more than the material reality of everyday existence; we must add in personal, familial, and communal memory. It is these memories that constitute the province of *Beloved*, and the differences among readers in Morrison's audience stem from the readers' proximity to these memories.[19] Johnson's concept of an ever-continuing present leaves behind the notion of a memory to be recovered; in his novel, a historical narrative reconstructed collaboratively by the narrator and the authorial audience substitutes for memory. Effecting differences among readers is the last thing that Johnson intended to do. Indeed, one of the epigraphs to *Middle Passage* is "Who sees variety and not the Unity wanders on from death to death" (*Brihad-aranyaka Upanishad*).

Yet most women with whom I have spoken about Johnson's novel claim that they feel disconnected from the narrative circle because the novel almost totally excludes female characters. The story often feels like a classic male quest narrative, a sea saga in which men are involved in self-conflict as well as battles against each other and against nature. Isadora Bailey serves the double function of Woman in Johnson's quest adventure: she is a schoolma'am who schemes to trap Calhoun in marriage, initially causing him to flee domestication and seek adventure; and she is the warm body, the open arms to which he returns. Stressing a cultural/literary patrilineage, *Middle Passage* attempts to bridge the gap between races and cultures by constructing an ex-slave's narrative in a manner that is reminiscent at one moment of Swift and at other moments of Defoe and Melville. But the narrative ignores the gap between genders.

Belinda Edmondson stresses the fact that even though Morrison has no truck with the concept of a feminist aesthetic based on the prerogatives of white women or with the essentialist claim of an all-inclusive black aesthetic, she believes that black men write like white men but that there is an "enormous difference" between the writing of black women and white women (87–88). These claims put Morrison "in the curious position of disavowing a feminist aesthetic and a black aesthetic yet affirming a black feminist—or rather, *female*—aesthetic" (88). Edmondson observes that Morrison's reasoning derives from an essentialism that posits women as the " 'natural' bearers of culture" (88). But perhaps Morrison's belief results not so much from a deductive essentialist premise as from an inductive conclusion arrived at through her many years as an editor for a major publishing house. She likely read manuscripts by many African American male writers who, like Charles Johnson, *chose* to transcend race and suppress the feminine—which would make their writing appear very similar to that of white men. Similarly, the fact that black women and white women have *chosen* to construct culture-specific narratives that openly tackle issues of gender indicates their aesthetic agency rather than an essentialism that drives their art.

When readers fault African American writers for attempting to transcend race, as I have done in disapprovingly calling Charles Johnson's ideas politically conservative and his narrative method suspect, we display what Nadine Gordimer calls "the essential gesture" of criticism, which mandates that a writer living in a politically conflicted country write about the conflict, that a female writer represent the female experience, and that the culturally marginalized author write about the experience of marginality. In the essentialist mandate, white male writers from politically stable Western countries—thought of as being unmarked by gender or race—are the only ones free to construct ahistorical, apolitical, and unrepresentational narratives. This essential gesture (the Irving Howe reflex) reveals the white critic as a manufacturer of otherness, a curator of difference to valorize and preserve her or his own autonomous essence—a sign of the institutional necessity of race in reading and a sign that we need to read more closely this criticism that passes for cultural work.[20]

In claiming that all readers who respond in this fashion display the essential gesture, I do not mean to elide the qualitative differences among gestures. For example, though both Irving Howe's and Amiri Baraka's critical responses to Ralph Ellison's fiction reflect their disappointment in his refusal to engage in a literature of protest, their responses arise from obviously different positions. When Joyce A. Joyce in "Black Woman Scholar" laments what she sees as political disengagement in the embracing of poststructuralist theory by prominent African American scholars such as Henry Louis Gates, Jr., and Houston Baker, her response derives from her experiences of sexual and racial discrimination as an African American woman in academe. As such, the motivations for her essential gesture are very different from mine.

In 1992, Toni Morrison's *Jazz*, Alice Walker's *Possessing the Secret of Joy*, and Terry McMillan's *Waiting to Exhale* were simultaneously on the best-seller list, along with Andrew Hacker's *Two Nations: Black and White, Separate, Hostile, Unequal*. Released in the fall of 1992, the anthology *Race-ing Justice, En-gendering Power: Essays on Anita Hill, Clarence Thomas, and the Construction of Social Reality*, edited and with an introduction by Toni Morrison, received favorable reviews and sold briskly. Many American readers find compelling the narratives of African American women and the scholarly analysis of race, facts that convince me we are a long way from being able to transcend race. Rather, the time has come for us to uncover the complexities and the protean functions of race as they lie hidden behind the "whiteness" of even the most liberal gestures. And we critics dressed in Kente cloths, like members of an academic Franciscan order ministering to the needs of the marginalized, could begin by uncovering the underlayers of our own needs.

CHAPTER FOUR

Reading
(in) Cyberspace:
Cybernetic
Aesthetics,
Hypertext, and the
Virtual Public
Space

■ Cyberspace. A consensual hallucination experienced daily by billions of legitimate operators, in every nation, by children being taught mathematical concepts. . . . A graphic representation of data abstracted from the banks of every computer in the human system. Unthinkable complexity. Lines of light ranged in the nonspace of the mind, clusters and constellations of data. . . .
—William Gibson, *Neuromancer*

The development of cybernetic theory and technology marks a paradigm shift: the basis of the economy is transformed from material goods to information, space and communication are reconceptualized in terms of electronic virtuality, and text and intertextuality are extended into hypertextuality. Cybernetics includes not only information technologies but the complex of effects—epistemological, ethical, social, political—that accompanies these technological developments.[1] As is true for all paradigm shifts, the effects of cybernetics have inspired fear and loathing in those committed to an earlier paradigm characterized by visual or material presence, linearity, and monologism. Conversely, those who abandoned the old paradigm years ago and who form the advance guard of the new movement exhibit an optimism that verges on rapture.[2]

In this chapter I begin by analyzing various cultural responses to cybernetics.

Then I consider the ways that the electronic reading of hypertext transforms the task and process of reading. In this part of the discussion I focus on the fiction of Michael Joyce, Carolyn Guyer, and Stuart Moulthrop. The chapter concludes with observations on the future of literature in a cybernetic system as it vies with technologies of virtual reality. Because the responses to hypertext tend to be polarized as either Luddite aversion or rapturous acceptance, too often they have been evaluative without being adequately analytical. Furthermore, the arguments from these polarized positions frequently suffer from temporal displacement, with one camp exhibiting a nostalgic wish to return to the past and the other a utopic yearning for the future. It is from the vantage point of the present—a transitional period between the paradigms of the printed text and the digitized virtual text—that I will assess the aesthetics of the evolving genre of hypertextual fiction and discuss its future as it vies with various forms of virtual reality. My own response to cybernetic aesthetics is neither aversion nor unquestioning acceptance, but a combination of the two responses—a wary openness.

As I see it, within the next few decades cybernetic reading will gradually displace the linear, close(d), solitary reading constructed by the printed text, and it would indeed seem that the process is already under way. The ideal reader for hypertext is being constructed through sustained exposure to mass media and information technologies.[3] This is a reader whose experience includes exposure to cinematic fast cuts (MTV short attention span), information as sound bites, Nintendo and Sega game systems, computer video games, and interactive fantasy adventure games in a computer network. This is also a reader who has become immersed in informatics in diverse forms such as banking, education, medicine, telecommunications, and mass media. Ironically, this situation poses special problems for hypertext as an art form. In a cybernetics culture, I want to argue, hypertext will survive as an art form only by offering the pleasures of virtual immediacy, spontaneity, intricate movement, a rich web of texts in various media (graphic, audio, and film), and interactivity for the reader in the form of creative agency to reconstruct the text, acting either alone or as part of a performance with other readers. Hypertext will not realize its potential unless it provides for the reader both the pleasure of immersion in an imagined world (the achievement of realist fiction) and the pleasure of instrumental action in that world (the goal of virtual reality technology). Cyberspatial interactivity offers the possibility of a virtual public space in a postmodern world that allows for a measure of community without assuming an impossible commonality.

CYBERNETICS AND THE TECHNO-SUBLIME

The concept of cybernetics traces back directly to Norbert Wiener's modeling of Brownian motion in the 1920s. His success at modeling the random, exceedingly complex motion of minute particles convinced him that he could construct models for any problem resistant to mathematical description.[4] The ultimate challenge for Wiener, which derived from his inability to tolerate Heisenbergian uncertainty (and was also, one suspects, a way for him to steal thunder from Freud's psychoanalysis and Watson's behaviorism), was to derive a model of human behavior and of the functions of the mind. By 1950, Wiener had popularized cybernetic theory in his books *Cybernetics: Control and Communication in the Animal and the Machine* (1948) and the more ominous-sounding *The Human Use of Human Beings* (1950).[5] Cybernetics, the science of self-regulating systems in living organisms and in machines, has developed theories of communication and technologies of control. In cybernetic metaphor, the brain is a machine.

The conceptualizing of the brain as a machine, which is accompanied by anxieties about artificial intelligence, is the most recent phase in a centuries-old response to science and technology that I will call the techno-sublime. As is true of any form of the sublime, this response includes fascination, dread, and veneration—in successive waves or in unequal portions mixed. The core issues concerned with the cultural response to science and technology involve humanness and humanity: What makes us human? What establishes the boundary beyond which inhumanity lies, lurks?

The cultural experience of the techno-sublime begins with the fearful perception of the invasiveness of science and technology that implies a viruslike colonization of the cultural identity and a threat to humanness. One kind of defense mechanism in response to this perceived threat is the acculturation of science, which includes the aestheticizing, naturalizing construction of technology by human agents in a cultural production. In this acculturation, techno-science as other is introjected and domesticated. Rob Wilson describes a variation on this response that he specifies as an American sublime characterized by techno-euphoria, whereby individuals sublimate their subjective traumas by losing themselves in the imaginal vastness and power of U.S. technological spectacles of grandeur that revive nationalistic myths and promises of historical redemption (206–8).[6] A nationalist ideology interpellates political subjects by producing what Slavoj Zizek calls "the sublime object," which occupies the place of "the impossible-real object of desire" (194). Accepting Zizek's description of the function of the sublime object, one can extend Wilson's general observations about techno-euphoria to other nations and cultures.[7] The sublime object satisfies an imaginary need for national/cultural power and effects the sublimation of subject into nation or culture.

Poised on the brink of the twentieth century, Henry Adams described himself as "lying in the Gallery of Machines at the Great Exposition [Paris World's Fair] of 1900, his historical neck broken by the sudden irruption of forces totally new" (380); "he began to feel the forty-foot dynamos as a moral force. . . . Before the end, one began to pray to [the dynamo]; inherited instinct taught the natural expression of man before silent and infinite force" (381). The awe and veneration in Adams's account also appear in fictional renderings of the techno-sublime but are complicated by what George Slusser calls the "Frankenstein barrier," a response in which the sense of wonder that impelled Victor Frankenstein's creativity bumps up against the unresolved fears and ontological hesitations of the present, which forever block access to a radically transformed future world (71). In this way, even the most futuristic science fiction is stalled in the present.

The Frankenstein barrier is evident in a film such as *Terminator 2*, which, for all its technical brilliance in terms of robotics and cinematic morphing, relies on the old shoot-'em-up formula of two guys blasting each other with guns. Because these shootists are cyborgs and the bullets merely slow them down, the shooting can and does recur ad infinitum (a literal example of shooting a film). The technology on display is the *filmic* technology, which is unproblematized and offered without restraint to the viewer. Technology—as a dark, forbidding force—is presented at the level of narrative, a narrative that is atavistic when contrasted with the technological wizardry of the film's special effects. This mix of the atavistic and the futuristic represents the pull and push of the techno-sublime.[8]

William Gibson's *Neuromancer* is the novel most frequently connected to cybernetics and the quintessential cyberpunk text. Conventional in terms of narrative form, Gibson's novel thematically conveys the experience of cybernetic virtuality. He could not have achieved the effects of the techno-sublime through a thematic approach alone, an approach used in classic science fiction narratives such as those by Isaac Asimov, which spend an inordinate amount of time educating readers in scientific and science fiction concepts. Such education works to avoid the techno-sublime through down-scaling and demystification of science and technology. Gibson says of *Neuromancer*, "It's not really about an imagined future. It's a way of trying to come to terms with the awe and terror inspired in me by the world in which we live" (qtd. in Rosenthal 85). With regard to the intended effect on the readers of *Neuromancer*, he says, "It was really a complex undertaking to measure out the information available to readers in constant homeopathic doses. I wanted to simulate culture/shock. The book can also be read on an interesting game level. About 85% of it is coherent data, and then there's stuff thrown in that's the color of weirdness" (qtd. in Larsen D-12).

Gibson attempts to convey his own feelings of the sublime and inculcate similar feelings in his readers through his descriptions of ineffable spaces. The most saturated sections of description are devoted to the protagonist Case's orgasmic sensation of "jacking in" to cyberspace from a console:

> Disk beginning to rotate, faster, becoming asphere of paler gray. Expanding—
>
> And flowed, flowered for him, fluid neon origamitrick, the unfolding of his distanceless home, his country, transparent 3D chessboard extending to infinity. Inner eye opening to the stepped scarlet pyramid of the Eastern Seaboard Fission Authority burning beyond the green cubes of Mitsubishi Bank of America, and high and very far away he saw the spiral arms of military systems, forever beyond his reach. (52)

Gibson also floods the text with cyberjargon/technospeak to trouble the reader's ability to assimilate completely the narrative and the narrative world:

> Cowboys didn't get into simstim, he thought, because it was basically a meat toy. He knew that the trodes he used and the little plastic tiara dangling from the simstim deck were basically the same, and that the cyberspace matrix was actually a drastic simplification of the human sensorium. . . .
>
> The new switch was patched into his Sendai with a thin ribbon of fiberoptics. (55)

Gibson's narrative features decentered subjects in a world in which anyone can be a cyborgian construction of lab-grown flesh, muscle augmentation, and neurological enhancement implants, or in which a character might be a holographic simulation. Personal experience is not exclusive to an individual but can be shared through a "simstim" (simulated stimulus) link. Likewise, "personal" memory can be raided, with not even death preventing memory from being appropriated by others.

Despite all these postmodern surface features, *Neuromancer* stops at the Frankenstein barrier by falling back on the realist/romantic conventions of linear, cause-and-effect, resolved plot structure and the characterization of the protagonist as a unified and self-willed subject. Case's most intense pleasure may come from jacking into cyberspace, but he is, as Claire Sponsler observes, "resolutely 'human' " (638)—and, more to the point, humanist. Sponsler criticizes Gibson for his failed imagination, his inability to envision a reconstructed sense of human agency that avoids a return to the retrogressive realist/romantic paradigm (642). As such, she finds fault with Gibson's defense mechanism as a response to the terror of the postmodern sublime. However, Sponsler overlooks the fact that the punk aesthetic—a postmodern existentialism—does not offer progressive alternatives or transformations. Thus, cyberpunk makes use of a feedback loop, the most essential aspect of a cybernetic system, which enables the system to be autocorrective and self-regulating. Without such a feedback loop, cyberpunk would spin out of the humanist orbit.

It is in this sense that the feedback loop resembles what Gibson, in one of his early stories, calls the Gernsback continuum. The story refers to and establishes a contrast with the technolatry of gleaming futurism conveyed in the work of early science fiction writers such as Hugo Gernsback. But in using the word *continuum*, Gibson implies that the Gernsback tradition of science fiction is still present in the contemporary form of cyberpunk. For all the surface changes, Gibson's fiction includes the characteristics instituted by Gernsback: (1) a narrative text interrupted by passages of "hard" scientific information; (2) a plot constructed as a riveting adventure; (3) a protagonist who must ultimately disavow and disengage himself from a technical network that has supported him; and (4) a tone of simultaneous pessimism about the future of the human race and optimism about intelligent life in general (Westfahl 90–91). Gibson's narrative appears to be caught in the Gernsback loop.

But self-correction is not the only function of a feedback loop. Feedback also can provide the information necessary to enhance performance and to move to the next level of productivity or creativity. Because it refuses this latter effect of the feedback loop, cyberpunk seems to some critics to be merely regressive.

The Frankenstein barrier, marking the site of the differentiation of the human from the machine, constitutes the fourth stage in a sequence of ego-shattering events in history engineered by Copernicus, Darwin, and Freud. Before the impact of Darwinian theories, the barrier was erected between the human-cultural and the natural, but after Darwin, humans could not be split off from nature and became themselves objects of scientific study and technological control. Subsequently the boundary separated the human-cultural from the technological. Much of the anxiety in contemporary science fiction concerns the instability of body boundaries, with alien others fluidly morphing into human form and with humans metamorphosing into alien forms.[9] In a sense, we are forced to return through the looking glass but are then denied the imago of the mirror stage, seeing only and everywhere a reflection of the fragmented body. To mark the distance between the Freudian revolution and the cybernetics revolution, Baudrillard describes ours as "a system where there is no more soul, no more metaphor of the body—the fable of the unconscious itself has lost most of its resonance" (*Ecstasy* 50–51). In the Baudrillardian postmodern picture, technology has displaced the unconscious as technology has become ideology.

One of the few texts to get beyond the paralyzing effects of ontological anxiety in response to technology is Donna Haraway's "Manifesto for Cyborgs," which is "an argument for *pleasure* in the confusion of boundaries" (emphasis in original, 66). Beginning with the recognition that we are already living in the brave new world of texts, surfaces, and "the informatics of domination" (80), Haraway suggests that we need to make the best of the situation and speculates about how to have a feminist-socialist-materialist theory in the integrated circuit. She includes a discussion of feminist/antimasculinist science fiction by writers such as James Tiptree, Jr., Octavia Butler, and Samuel Delaney that offers an alternative to the same old scenario of the overdetermined masculine hero beseiged on all sides by forces that would penetrate, drown, or consume him. Haraway's is a utopia arrived at only by proceeding through the dystopia of technocratic instrumental rationality and its attendant ideological domination (Bukatman 323). As such, this utopia is a far cry from Marx's idealistic vision of the industrial worker as a repository of scientific and cultural knowledge who in leisure time has taken the initiative to become educated enough to transcend the potentially dehumanizing effects of mechanization. Marx's utopianism constructs a picture of advanced technology as providing "a space for a kind of rarefied humanness" (Rosenthal 92). Haraway's materialist socialism provides an antidote to such marxist idealism. In her conception the cyborg is a chimera in a postgender world, "resolutely committed to partiality, irony, intimacy, and perversity . . . wary of holism, but needy for connection" (67, 68). While precybernetic machines did not threaten the dualism between human and machine, "[l]ate twentieth-century machines have made thoroughly ambiguous the difference between natural and artificial, mind and body, self-developing and externally-designed. . . . Our machines are disturbingly lively, and we ourselves are frighteningly inert" (69).

As Gibson puts it in *Neuromancer*, we "gradually and willingly accommodate the machine" (203). It is not just that we consciously choose to accommodate the machine. It is also that technology works as hegemony in the Gramscian sense: our resistance is neutralized as we gradually—even if *un*willingly—accommodate the machine by internalizing technology. When the machine disappears, becomes transparent, the technology has achieved perfect interface with the human. Immersed in informatics of diverse kinds such as banking, education, law enforcement, medicine, telecommunications, and mass media, we live in a technoculture. The techno-sublime involves the constant reestablishing of borders between the human and the other. Technology that was awesome and terrifying thirty years ago has been accommodated. Donna Haraway's "Manifesto," written a decade ago, should be dated by now in terms of the normally rapid turnover and obsolescence rate in theory, yet references to it appear ubiquitously in the most recent literary theory and cultural studies. That Haraway's essay still appears radical is an indication of the generational gap between current academics engaged in cultural theory and our students, who were born into the information age.[10]

Mark Johnson points out that bodily orientation in time and space creates experiences that are encoded in language in the form of extensive metaphorical networks (18–35). Supplementing Johnson's claims, N. Katherine Hayles suggests that when bodily orientation and functions change through technological innovations or cultural shifts, the transformed experiences of embodiment will infiltrate the metaphorical network of language ("Materiality" 164–65). Gestalt psychologists have shown that perceptual schemae are culturally acquired. If, as I have argued, technology is inextricable from culture and ideology, then our students, who have grown up in a world of informatics, will operate in a metaphorical web influenced by cybernetic experiences and will be capable of perceptions and conceptions that differ from those of us born into an earlier metaphorical web. Which is to say that this generation of readers will not feel much threatened by cyberspace, virtual reality, or hypertext.[11] It is not that they have gotten beyond the Frankenstein barrier, it is that the site of the barrier will have changed in a world in which the human and the technological are markedly coextensive, integrated, and mutually defining. Scott Bukatman refers to the posthumanist subjectivity constructed by electronic technologies as "terminal identity" (9, 22).

Henri Lefevbre has argued convincingly that "every society . . . produces a space, its own space" (31), this production of space seeking to reconcile mental/ theoretical space with the actual physical and social spaces of everyday life. We are living in a time in which natural space is disappearing; not only will natural space "soon be lost to view," but nature will soon be "lost to thought" (30–31). Working from Lefebvre's claim, I would argue that this culture is in the process of producing cyberspace. Dissolving the boundary between mental space and social space, cyberspace functions as an analogue for the invisible space of a postmodern multinationalism. The cybernetic matrix is a complex configuration of power, a space of potential emancipation as well as oppression, and a space in which we locate ourselves and produce social relationships.

To theorize a politics of cyberspace, one might look to the work of Michel de Certeau, which begins with but exceeds Foucault's theories in that de Certeau accounts for the heterogeneity of micropolitical forms that Foucault tends to generalize and homogenize (until his late work on aesthetic self-fashioning). Foucault's conception of the panopticon in *Discipline and Punish* has come to represent for some thinkers an analogue for existence in a cybernetic society.[12] In this system, surveillance works because individuals participate in an institutional encoding process that differentiates them according to increasingly smaller microcharacteristics. Foucault observes that "individualization is 'descending,'" with the sources of power and knowledge becoming increasingly anonymous and the objects of discipline more and more individualized (*Discipline* 193). But de Certeau claims that in the system of late modern capitalism, consumers move in a system "too vast to be able to fix them in one place, but too constraining for them ever to be able to escape from it" (40). Cybernetic networks in this system do not have origin points, nor do they offer fixed sites of political identity. Effective resistance in this space must occur in the micropolitical form that de Certeau calls "tactics," which result from the condition of displacement, as opposed to "strategies," which derive from fixed (often institutionalized) power locations/ bases (35–36). De Certeau perceives limits to the totalization of postmodern cybernetic control in the very vastness of the system (Bukatman 212). He foresees the emergence of a cybernetic society characterized by "the Brownian movements of invisible and innumerable tactics. One would thus have a proliferation of aleatory and indeterminable manipulations within an immense framework of socioeconomic constraints and securities: myriads of almost invisible movements, playing on the more and more refined texture of a place that is even, continuous, and constitutes a place for all people" (40).[13] There is a wonderful irony in the idea of a vast cybernetic system providing the space for Brownian motions that will undermine the system's control—the return of what Norbert Wiener sought to repress.

Provocative as de Certeau's ideas are, his is a theory of micropolitics, politics conceptualized as the resistance of isolated individuals. Aesthetic and cultural self-expression need not translate into collective empowerment. Skeptical analyses of the cyberspatial myth decry its inherent monadological idealism (Markley 498). Though de Certeau's individual, like the individual of Deleuze and Guattari's *A Thousand Plateaus*, is more accurately described as "nomadilogical"—that is, characterized by nomadic wandering—than monadological, the nomad and the monad share the same space when it comes to the celebration of local action, self-organization, and self-actualization. Cybernetic communication has been lauded by Richard Lanham, George Landow, and Howard Rheingold—three prominent explicators of digitized information, hypertext, and virtual reality—as a democratizing process, providing agency and extending voice to individuals silenced in conventional forms and forums of communication. But as Charles Ess astutely point outs, there has been a lack of conceptual clarity in hypertext and computer literature about the definition of democracy. Ess points to three conflicting conceptions of democracy that have existed in American history: "plebiscitary, emphasizing individual autonomy and maximizing the number of persons directly involved in government; communitarian, stressing service in the common good and the importance of [public participation]; and pluralist, stressing free competition among diverse interest groups" (256, n. 16). Too many writers arguing for the democratic potential of computer-based communication seem to be implying a plebiscitary form of democracy, which has not proved to be a particularly liberatory form. I am more concerned about the future of group and communal politics and with larger structural solutions to political problems in cyberspace.

I want to consider the aesthetic, social, and political issues of cyberspace by focusing first on hypertextual reading and then on the experience of interactive virtual reality in the net.

READING HYPERTEXT

The concept of hypertext traces back to Vannevar Bush's article "As We May Think," published in 1945 in the *Atlantic Monthly*, which envisioned a mechanical system to help scholars deal with an information explosion that was already under way. Bush's "memex" apparatus was meant to enable individuals to store all their records, correspondence, and books; to construct paths between these texts; and to retrieve specific information within them (Yankelovich, Meyrowitz, and van Dam 60). Underpinning Bush's project was the assumption that memory is organized in a semantic network with concepts linked by associations; thus, the memex would structure data in a manner similar to human cognition. Influenced in part by Bush's vision, Theodore Nelson and Douglas Englebart in the 1960s developed computer systems to link texts. Nelson coined the term *hypertext* in 1965 and fully explained the concept in his 1980 *Literary Machines*, describing this new textuality as "non-sequential writing with reader-controlled links" (1).

Structuralist, poststructuralist, and postmodernist theories as well as modern and postmodern literary experimentation laid the groundwork for hypertext. Mikhail Bakhtin's theory of dialogism and heteroglossia in novelistic discourse anticipated the hypertextual proliferation of narrative strands and voices. Claude Lévi-Strauss's metaphor of bricolage, in which heterogeneous chunks of information are taken from a variety of sources and reassembled in a new combination, fits both the writing and the reading of hypertext. Distinguishing texts that require the reader to be a producer/writer from texts that require the reader to be a passive consumer, Roland Barthes pointed to the interactive relationship between hypertextual reader and writer. Jacques Derrida's decentering of logos and his deconstruction of the presence/absence binary describe an open, interactive, and electronic (virtual) text. Gilles Deleuze and Félix Guattari's concept of the rhizome book, which is characterized by principles of connection, heterogeneity, multiplicity, ruptures in signification, and cartography, closely approximates the structure of hypertext. What Michel Foucault calls the author function is the position assumed by the hypertextual reader, who makes decisions about focus, perspective, and arrangement formerly exclusive to the author, and, in the case of fully interactive hypertext, the reader actively rewrites the text. The reader provides the only center hypertext can have, with the center changing in each reading.

The challenge for writers of hypertext fiction has been to improve upon the hypertextual effects already achieved in experimental texts of modern and postmodern literature. *Ulysses* abounds in discrete discursive spaces and in words that yield and open into layers of allusion, and *Finnegans Wake* is a hypertextual(ist's) dream.[14] The prose of Woolf's *The Waves* is full of saturated, lyrical moments, and the characters of *The Waves* are monads connected in a loose web. Gertrude Stein, in *The Making of Americans*, uses chunks of prose segments arranged in an associational and antihierarchical construction. *Gravity's Rainbow* is hypertextually encyclopedic, with more than three hundred characters and as many narrative spaces, including interstitial spaces between nodes or links, and the interweaving of a myriad of texts and discourses ranging from salacious jingles to historical exposition to quantum mechanics. Nabokov's *Pale Fire* is ironically intertextual, coercing the reader into cross-referencing movements that interrupt simple linear progression through the narrative. Calvino's *If on a Winter's Night a Traveler* offers the beginnings of ten narrative paths.

The novels mentioned above come closer to representing hypertext than does Gibson's *Neuromancer*, the novel that most critics associate with cybernetics. Echoing some of Sponsler's disappointment with Gibson's work, Stuart Moulthrop describes the cyberpunk loop as a circle that runs "back to the same old future so neatly packaged for us in dystopian novels and films" ("Deuteronomy," par. 25). He finds fault with cyberpunk writers such as Gibson for not using an electronic mode of writing, which offers the radically different experience of virtual culture. As one of the rhapsodic practitioners of hypertextual writing, Moulthrop criticizes the timorousness of those creative writers bound to the codex book, with the printed text functioning as the Frankenstein barrier for those cyberpunk writers who are obsessed with representing cybernetic reality but stop short of instantiating it in cybertextual writing.

Moulthrop's rapture over hypertext is understandable if one considers that he is one of the premier (in both senses of the word) creative writers to use this form. But some of the same claims are heard from Robert Coover, who has had a long and illustrious career as an experimental printed-text writer. Coover started Brown University's hypertext fiction workshops and has spoken enthusiastically about the experience. He especially enjoyed the group-writing component, which he found wild and constantly inventive—characterized by twists, sabotages, and reversals as well as less mischievous forms of collaboration: "This space of essentially anonymous text fragments remains on-line and each new set of workshop students is invited to check in there and continue the story of the Hypertext Hotel. I would like to see it stay open for a century or two" (25).

Coover was surprised to discover that most of the writing experience occurred in the interstices and paths between text fragments, with the fragments functioning merely as stepping stones for momentary stasis, while "the real *current* of the narrative runs between them" (24). Hypertext creativity is more concerned with linking, routing, looping, and mapping than with plot and character development, which are the mainstays of the Aristotelian poetics of classical narrative. In the hypertextual writer's relationship with the reader, the emphasis is on avoiding hierarchical structure and, instead, offering discrete constituent bits of information; these bits do not become narrative until the reader arranges and joins them. Reading hypertext becomes a version of choose-your-own-adventure. The most effective hypertext is the one that provides the reader with the most complex and intriguing ways of organizing the textual lexia. The buzzwords in hypertextual poetics are "[f]luidity, contingency, indeterminancy, plurality, and discontinuity" (Coover 25).

Although Coover is convinced that hypertext is the way of the near future, he is not quite exultant over the fact. He has reservations not only about the threat it poses to the genius of the solitary writer (and other vestiges of idealist aesthetics), but also about the excesses of hypertextual decentering and multiplicity and its trading linear narrative movement for "expansion." Hypertext "runs the risk of being so distended and slackly driven as to lose its centripetal force, to give way to a kind of static low-charged lyricism—that dreamy, gravityless, lost-in-space feeling of the early sci-fi films" (25).

After reading Michael Joyce's *Afternoon, a Story*, Carolyn Guyer's *Quibbling*, and Stuart Moulthrop's *Victory Garden*, I tend to agree with Coover's cautionary statements about the tendency of hypertext to produce for the reader a kind of spaced-out drifting through scenes and characters' conversations and reveries, touching down occasionally in a saturated lyrical spot or in an excerpt from a historical, theoretical, or popular culture text, and at other moments being up-ended by a narrator who wants to talk directly to the reader. What is unexpectedly pleasurable, at least in the first few hours of reading, is making one's way through the maze of paths, which *feels* like a maze in that you bump up against the end of paths and must retrace your steps or strike off in another direction, never knowing what might pop up. But this pleasure does not provide any deep or lasting satisfaction, because what impels a trip through a maze, whether it be a physical space or the textual space of a tortuous detective-story plot, is the lure of the (re)solution—which is exactly what the reader is denied in hypertext. Another aspect of the pleasure of reading hypertext involves low-level kinetic activity, using the mouse to seek out words that yield additional textual links, to switch to an alternative menu option, and to move to another lexial string on the text map. Once again, this does not constitute a substantial pleasure. Though more active than in reading a print novel, one is not engaged in *creative* cybernetic interactivity, the kind of interactivity provided already by real-time (as opposed to e-mail lag time) electronic discussion groups and by the MUSHes (Multi-User Shared Hallucinations) and MOOs (Multi-User-Dungeon Object Oriented), which are virtual clubs of collaborative fantasy in the Internet.

Considered the *Ur*-text of hypertextual fiction, Joyce's *Afternoon* (1987) has received most of the critical attention so far. Because this text is brief and features the intertwined stories of five discernible characters, one can almost imagine it in print form, though to capture the complex interweaving and to provide the five-plus closure points would require a great deal more print space, comparatively speaking, than the small amount of electronic space it occupies. In addition, print could not adequately convey the simultaneous multidirectionality of movement in the narrative field.

Though Joyce's story is not a mystery, generically speaking, it is mysterious. Extramarital affairs occur, potentially occur (as in fantasy affairs), might have occurred, and/or do not occur (with the slash between *and* and *or* important). The same is true of a tragic car accident, which does and/or does not happen and in which a frantic and/or insouciant character's son dies and/or is severely injured and/or is not involved. The *and*s and *or*s are both operative when the reader has read all of the lexial strings, but if she chooses a single linear path, she discovers the interpretive basis of one of the *or* choices for the narrative situation. The intricacy of Joyce's narrative derives from the fact that readers can reach certain nodes (hypertext places) only after they have traveled through a required sequence of other nodes, but these determined paths crisscross each other in many places, making it necessary for the junctions or links to function differently according to each path that runs through. As J. Yellowlees Douglas points out, the node/place called "Asks," which features a question "How . . . would you feel if I slept with your ex-wife?," appears in four or more contexts in the narrative, each time with a different inflection (17).

The Storyspace software program in which *Afternoon* is written offers the reader a default option to enable her to move through the text—page by page, as it were—without making any choices. Such passive, linear, unadventurous reading would seem to defeat the purpose of electronic reading. But perhaps the Storyspace designers (who include Michael Joyce) perceive this default option as offering a transitional position for the reader still tied to print habits but attempting to make the change. After having coasted along on default all the way through a narrative path, she might then decide to cruise on her own, get a little wild, actively seek out those words that give way like revolving doors into another narrative space. Searching for and finding the words that yield is enjoyable, but the default option diminishes some of that pleasure, because in a default scheme any word the reader clicks on will take her to another screen. The reader must circle back to the previous screen and try numerous other words to discover the actually yielding words. No instant gratification here. In fact, reading an interactive hypertext short story the length of *Afternoon*, which contains 538 screens, takes longer than reading a three-hundred-page novel.

In his instructions to the reader, Joyce writes, "The lack of clear signals isn't an attempt to vex you, rather an invitation to read either inquisitively or playfully and also at depth. Click on words that interest or invite you."[15] A (coy) word that fails to yield on one path might give way on another path. He suggests that the yielding words are often those with "texture" as well as character names and pronouns, and that the real interaction between himself and the reader "is in pursuit of texture" ("in my mind"). By texture, presumably Joyce means resonance resulting from connotational energy and from strangeness. In *Afternoon*, for example, when one clicks on the strange-textured adjective *emphysematous*, the screen titled "Dublinissimus" appeared with the single question "Who's she?", this screen being one in a path containing James Joycean ludic, gnomic word games. Michael Joyce's hopes for significant interactivity are realized only if he has targeted as interesting and inviting those same words that the reader chooses. Of course, *emphysematous* jumped out at me. But many of the other words I clicked on did not yield and so were not textured in Joyce's perspective. In fact, I got hooked on this treasure hunt aspect of the reading game and clicked on many words, my hopes for Joyce's inventiveness outstripping his actual production (yield). Judging his own achievement in promoting interactivity in this pioneering text, Joyce admits it is a "partially failed attempt, a text which empowers more than it reciprocates" ("Notes," par. 28), more an "exploratory" than a "constructive" text (pars. 18, 25). When Joyce uses the term *exploratory*, he refers to hypertext that limits the reader's agency to freedom of movement among the narrative paths, while *constructive* hypertext permits the reader structurally to alter the text.

The gap between reader's expectation and writer's production is a real problem for hypertextual narrative claiming to be interactive; there must be numerous interfaces between readers and textual author(s), and in the case of yielding words, there must be enough to repay the efforts of a range of readers. If interactive narrative takes its cues in part from the choose-your-own-adventure model, then it must deliver the goods in terms of lures for the reader, which in the case of adventure would mean, at the very least, narrative surprises. The twists, turns, and loops employed by hypertextual writers, however, do not guarantee surprise and, in fact, seem to substitute for it. When I first came to the end of a lexial path in *Afternoon*, I felt disappointed. My first hypertext experience did not live up to the hype: this text was rather simple, far from the nearly endless narrative I had expected (in the manner of the Kantian quantitative/mathematical sublime), and the text was subtle and understated, not wild and unconventional.

Although the lyrical beauty of Joyce's text is one of its memorable aspects, this same lyricism stalls the narrative movement, which is exactly what Coover complained of when he described hypertextual narrative as "slackly driven." *Afternoon* includes numerous passages of arrestingly vivid descriptions (most of them scenes of nature, some of them scenes of lovemaking) in prose so beautiful that one wants to linger or to return to them: "By five the sun sets and the afternoon melt freezes again across the blacktop into crystal octopi and palms of ice . . . as we walk out to the car, the snow moaning beneath our boots and the oaks exploding in series along the fenceline on the horizon . . . " ("begin"). Lyrical concentration need not result in narrative stasis, but in a story that is delicately drawn, fragmented, elliptical, and open, such concentration might in fact contribute to a stasis that could diminish the kinetic potential of the hypertext medium.

Carolyn Guyer's *Quibbling* is much less finished and tightly constructed than Joyce's text. Many free, unlinked spaces float through the text, encouraging readers to fill in their own associations. Guyer's text contains sections of gorgeous prose, some of the most striking passages describing the medieval nun Margaret, who becomes involved in a sensual relationship with Henry, a priest. (The Margaret–Henry narrative is a story within a story within a story . . . , written by one of Guyer's contemporary characters and shared with a woman he loves/has loved, with allusions to Fowles's *The French Lieutenant's Woman* and to other love affairs among Guyer's characters.) These lyrical passages are woven into a more extensive, heterogeneous, and dialogic text than Joyce's. Guyer's is a resolutely anti-idealist aesthetics, rejecting the notions of (1) the artist as (singular) genius, (2) the work of art as an organic totality, and (3) reception as contemplation from a distance.

Guyer begins the narrative with maps and charts for the reader: a global map with linkage arrows between the lexial places, a tree map, and a chart view of the places. These locational aids characterize Guyer's careful attention to readers throughout the text. Often the narrator-writer poses questions to readers that draw attention both to the writer's narrative choices and to the reader's narrative wishes: "Well, let's see. I could simply put a link here, so you could find out [the answer to this narrative riddle]. Some of you really like the mystery part, don't you?" ("moon-view"). Her irony is leveled at reader expectations and the narrative conventions of which her own narrative is guilty: "I don't *want* you just to follow me around in here. Get the mutable one and have Heta turn raving bitch who demands Priam make still another choice in his life. . . . In fact, that's exactly what does happen. What *doesn't* happen is anything about real life for anyone who isn't an American white person" ("aliens").

While Joyce's narrative moves according to the interactions of the main characters, Guyer's text often ripples out through sensory associations. For example, she begins with the tactile-visual curve of a man's forearm, moves to the curve of a woman's back as she bends over a baby, then to the curve of a melon in one's hands, extending to the curve of a clay bowl and a host of other lunules. Largely eschewing narrative coherence for other forms of coherence, Guyer constructs a fluid web to allow the proliferation of connections among the textual elements and "to evoke WHAT IS without graceless elaboration" ("secretary days").

At one point, the writer-narrator wonders what the effect would be if she suddenly changed the narrative's organization. Answering her own question, she helps to explain her intentions to the reader: "But it strikes me that each of the men is developing as himself and in relation to his lover, while the women are developing as themselves but also kind of like sisters. . . . I believe what I was (am) doing is helping the women stay independent. Also, giving them access, through proximity, to each other" ("topographic"). In one of the numerous journal entries woven through the text, Guyer mentions that she has read a review of Mary Gordon's recent collection of essays that makes her want to rethink the Gordon paragraph she has used in *Quibbling* as well as in IZME PASS, her collaborative hypertext with Martha Petry. The screen "Aleph" contains two letters from Guyer to another hypertext writer (perhaps Moulthrop); the second letter begins, "Have not read all of Borges like a good little hypertexan, so was surprised to find the reference to 'The Aleph' in Landow's new book." Guyer engages in direct dialogue with other writers' texts, whereas Joyce includes other texts without overtly referring to them.

What Guyer's text illustrates is the way that intertextuality in hypertext fiction tends to work epigraphically or in collage fashion, the screens of text from other writers or speakers (Borges, Barthes, Baudrillard, Gregory Bateson, George Bush, David Byrne—these are merely some of the names beginning with *B*) woven into the web with no direct commentary. It is up to the reader to make the connections between and among texts. The reader also can use the "marginal notes" menu option to add other texts to the hypertext. The inclusion of other writers' texts as discrete chunks without the assimilation of these chunks into the primary text has the effect of eroding the hierarchy of the "main" text.

As such, hypertext comes closer to being what Bakhtin terms dialogic and heteroglossic than does a printed text that subordinates the perspectives and voices of other texts to the single-voiced narrative or argument of the author. There is a sense in which a univocal/monological text turns all other writers—whether quoted, paraphrased, or alluded to—into straw (wo)men, attenuated versions of the originals that enable the author to shore up his or her own position. George Landow observes that Bakhtin's own method of citing the work of other critics is more characteristic of hypertext than of the book form. Caryl Emerson, Bakhtin's translator and editor, says that when Bakhtin quotes, "he does so at length, and lets each voice sound fully. He understands that . . . there is an outrageous privilege in the power to cite others" (Emerson xxxvii).[16]

Stuart Moulthrop's *Victory Garden* is even more complex than Joyce's *Afternoon* and Guyer's *Quibbling*, and this increasing complexity characterizes the evolution of the hypertextual genre. Moulthrop includes a partial map of story nodes and the connecting paths in the form of north, mid, and south garden sections. Without such a map, the reading would be very difficult because there are a number of loops in this narrative that offer no exit to the reader who merely clicks the default button. In fact, Moulthrop uses Storyspace's "guardfield" or narrative gatekeeping feature, which forecloses access to certain paths once one has chosen a particular path. *Victory Garden* requires the reader to make a choice within the first few screens; otherwise, the narrative will not proceed. In "Reading from the Map," Moulthrop discusses his 1986 hypertextual adaptation of Borges's "The Garden of Forking Paths," detailing his construction and its reception by student readers. Clearly this experience informed his creation of the *Victory Garden* web. Moulthrop's early critical work focused on Pynchon, and while at Yale he developed a hypertext unit on *Gravity's Rainbow* to enable a group of readers to share their responses to the novel (Landow and Delaney 33). In *Victory Garden* the influence of Pynchon is everywhere apparent. The Vietnam War and the Persian Gulf war are interwoven as are World War II and the Vietnam War in *Gravity's Rainbow*. One of the main characters is a Pynchonian paranoiac named Boris Urquhart, who is involved in a research project to interface electronically with the unconscious and produce "the world's first Interactive Dream." The narrative is full of other outlandish characters, including historico-media constructs such as Norman Schwarzkopf, a.k.a. "Stormin' Norman," "Ike on Steroids," and "the Norminator." The tone of the narrative changes suddenly and markedly in the paratactic juxtaposing of humorous passages, serious political passages, critiques of postmodern media simulation, and scraps of telespeak.

Moulthrop's yoking together of vapid and contradictory Gulf War commentary from such correspondents as Bernard Shaw, Peter Jennings, Tom Brokaw, and Bob Simon as well as his pairing the speeches of Bush and Saddam Hussein effectively conveys the media circus quality of the "event" and the obscene opportunism of all parties involved in the spectacle. Following a graphics screen titled "Norman Coordinate," which depicts Schwarzkopf's face in military map coordinate points, is a screen containing the narrator's theoretical reading of the gulf war: "Catastrophes are nation-forming, they weave networks in the air, they call communities into being, a thousand points of light, compelled, electrified, we tuned in" ("war zones").

Like Joyce and Guyer, Moulthrop includes metanarrative observations on hypertextuality. Hypertext, in his account, becomes a necessary tool for actively managing and manipulating a constant influx of information, a medium for "inventing, discovering, viewing, and testing multiple, alternative, organizational structures" in order to reconstruct and map knowledge ("hyperspace"). He argues that the recombinations of the bricolage effect that hypertext facilitates will lead to breakthroughs in knowledge. This belief explains the significance of yielding words: "Though yield-words often create discontinuities, they also map connections" ("welcome"). Moulthrop uses the term *paraknowledge* (suggestive of Lyotard's *paralogy*) to suggest the relation between paranoia and knowledge, to consider the possibility that everything is connected—at a deeper or less obvious level than conventional perspective allows us to see. Not surprisingly, Moulthrop invokes chaos theory with its attendant ideas of order arising out of chaos and the importance of stochastic elements in a complex system. Hypertext requires a reader who will veer from the default path to make connections and find ways through a sea of information. Out of the seeming chaos of hypertext, the reader engages in aleatoric, improvisational combinations that construct order.

Any attempt to judge the aesthetic merit of hypertextual literature must use criteria suited to the medium; the hypertextual medium is fully realized only if the text provides a maximum level of reader interaction. Without this focus on interactivity, the fetishizing of form will likely occur—which seems to be what is happening in the production and marketing of some recent hypertext fiction, such as the technological potlatch of *Uncle Buddy's Phantom Funhouse* by John McDaid, which an Eastgate Systems sales brochure hypes as "Five disks / Two basement tapes / One chocolate box / Too many links to count / A postmodern classic." A blurb from Gavin Edwards of *The Village Voice* describes McDaid's text as "[p]rofoundly frivolous." One is reminded of Coover's observation that "the author's freedom to take a story anywhere at any time and in as many directions as he or she wishes . . . becomes the obligation to do so: in the end it can be paralyzing" (qtd. in Landow, *Hypertext* 119). As the ante is upped and upped again, randomness and expansiveness might come to feel just as oppressive to hypertextual fiction writers as linearity and closure did for modern and postmodern writers. One can imagine the reaction against the conventions of hypertext taking the form of arcane, minimalist, and closed narratives, ordered according to strict linearity, and composed in quaint media (typewritten text or even scribal manuscript).

When multiplicity and expansiveness enable multiple readers to expand text, hypertext has realized its potential and is constructive rather than merely exploratory. One work that has achieved this effect is Deena Larsen's *Marble Springs*, which readers describe as an open constructive hypertext. Larsen's text is interactive poetry that explores the lives of frontier women of the American West. The design features poems by anonymous authors found in an abandoned ghost-town church and invites readers to discover the poets' identities hidden in textual clues scattered throughout. It is a complex web of interconnections among women of diverse cultures, constructed from Larsen's exhaustive research, with nodes linked to extensive bibliographies on such topics as law, religion, quilting, and cooking. As a constructive hypertext, *Marble Springs* encourages readers to establish new connections by contributing additional characters and narratives. One can also envision Larsen's text as enabling interactive learning and creative collaboration among reader-writers in history and literature classes.

Writing six years ago in *New Literary History*, Richard Ziegfeld predicted that hypertext software soon would not only allow the reader to interact in the reconstruction of the literary text but would collect data from reader responses that would enable writers to refine the hypertext medium to achieve enhanced participation by readers in future texts—an example of a cybernetic feedback loop. Though the software does not yet have the built-in capability to collect reader responses, many of the writers most committed to the new medium are academics who have used hypertext in their courses and presumably have shared their own texts with their students. The trajectory from Joyce to Larsen, along with what seems to be reader-prompted self-reflexiveness in Guyer's text, convinces me that readers' wishes for more interactivity have been granted. This aspect of hypertextual reading, perhaps more than any other, differentiates it from the reading implied and sometimes prescribed by aesthetic theories from the eighteenth century on. Stemming from idealist aesthetics, such prescribed reading characterizes a pedagogical method of imposing culture from above, requiring readers to transcend the limitations and peculiarities of their subjective experiences in order to become competent literary readers and to ensure that aesthetic reception matches creation. Hypertextual literature, however, aims to work from the culture of the reader up, rather than from high culture down to the reader.

Yet if hypertext promises to become an extensively used teaching tool to facilitate writing, reading, researching, and critical thinking, as an art form hypertext will have to vie with the printed text, which will continue for some years to be the dominant literary medium, for numerous reasons. Not the least of these involves the entrenched institutions of publication and critical review: imagine the task of reviewing a text such as McDaid's. In addition, the literary status and popularity of neorealist writers such as Raymond Carver, Jayne Anne Phillips, Brett Easton Ellis, and Bobbie Ann Mason attest to the staying power of realist narrative in a postmodern world. As long as there are enough readers who prefer conventional narrative structure and enjoy the material sensation and portability of the bound book, there will be a literary printed text industry, which is currently considered a "sideshow for publishers," amounting to less than one fifth of the total book-publishing industry (Max 68).

Ultimately, though, the biggest challenge to hypertext will come from virtual reality technologies: the full-immersion virtual experiences (requiring visual and audial headset, gloves, and sometimes a body suit), which are becoming increasingly refined; and the more than 60,000 electronic discussion and performance groups in the United States alone (Rheingold 132). The power of the virtual reality experience, as Marie-Laure Ryan points out, derives from the reconciliation of "immersion and interactivity through the mediation of the body" (par. 39), while in literature these two effects cannot occur simultaneously (par. 28). The more immersive a literary text is (so lifelike that the reader suspends disbelief), the less interactive (metafictional, drawing attention to itself as textual construction) it is. Though postmodern fiction promotes a high degree of interactivity by making the reader aware of his or her active role in the construction of textual meaning, it often denies the reader the pleasure of being caught up in a fictional world (Ryan, par. 27). Hypertexts provide even more interactivity than postmodern printed texts, but unless this activity of the reader takes place in a role-playing experience—an immersive dialogue or shared creation in real time—with the writer or with other readers, the activity is more exploratory than constructive. Thus, the cultural survival of hypertextual literature likely will depend on its providing virtual immediacy in a CD-ROM format with enhanced graphics, video and audio capabilities, and meaningful interactivity so that the reader becomes more of a dramatic performer in the virtual reality of the fictional text.

THE VIRTUAL PUBLIC SPHERE

There's no substitute for a planned simulation.
—Don Delillo, *White Noise*

Speculating on the libraries of the future, with the new Bibliothèque de France project serving as a model, Geoffrey Nunberg attempts to counter the exaggerated claims of those invested in electronic publishing who have predicted the death of the book. He argues that it is precisely because electronic technologies "transcend the material limitations of the book that they will have trouble assuming its role" (15). Writing in the wake of poststructuralism, Nunberg is defensive in his belief that material presence constitutes public visibility. He conflates the Enlightenment concept of public sphere with a material space/place, what Stanley Aronowitz wryly calls "a mythic town square in the sky" (qtd. in Robbins viii). In addition, he credits literature and newspapers with constructing the contemporary *sensus communis* while overlooking the importance of other forms of mass media. As Greg Ulmer has observed, "Everything now, in its own way, wants to be television" (qtd. in Moulthrop, *Victory* "wannabe").

Nunberg's argument, which centers on the disembodiment of experience and the further erosion of the public sphere caused by virtual reality technologies, typifies the prevailing critiques of a thoroughly commodified and cyberneticized culture that can only simulate reality. It is around the issues of embodiment and the public sphere that I want to frame a discussion of aesthetics in a cybernetic world.

As a result of the dematerializing effects of poststructural theories, we cannot seem to get enough of the materialized body these days, with much of theory and cultural studies engaged in various projects of reembodiment. This fixation on the body cannot be explained fully as a dialectical movement of theory to compensate for an overinvestment in discourse but must also be seen as a response to the dematerializing effects of informatics and cybernetic virtuality. The philosopher and self-described Taoist Michael Heim says that when he first tried virtual reality in 1989, his "philosophical seismograph went crazy," because the shift from simple computer use to virtual reality immersion constituted an ontological rupture: the experience of a full-blown substitute reality (xiii). Heim argues that software is not simply a tool; rather, its systems of language and methods of representation will end by governing our psychology and robbing us of our identity (79). He also warns that we will lose touch with our internal body awareness (80).

Industry enthusiasts project the development of full-immersion virtual reality that will require not only visual and audial headsets but gloves and body suits that will provide precise tactile simulation. This form of virtual reality has received the most attention in mass media, as we all wait breathlessly for virtual sex. Once again we are faced with a case of the technological imagination outstripping existing technology, for virtual reality technology is still primitive. This situation supports my thesis that cybertexts do not have to construct their audiences. Primitive or not, virtual reality is being marketed to an audience with preconstructed notions of what it wants. With amusement parks and arcades charging $10 to $15 for ten minutes, this full-immersion simulated hallucination is no cheap thrill.[17]

Though her tone is much less alarmist than Heim's, Katherine Hayles, in "The Materiality of Informatics," makes some of the same points about disembodiment that he does. Interrogating the theoretical truism that discourse writes the body, she distinguishes between *the body* inscribed/constructed/normalized by culture and *embodiment,* which refers to the incorporating practices, performances, and habits of individual and specific bodies. Taking into account both meanings of the body and the constant interaction between them, Hayles claims, "The body produces culture at the same time that culture produces the body" (157), which is why theories of discourse by themselves will not tell us what we need to know about informatics. An adequate theory of changes wrought by information technologies requires that theories of discourse engage in dialogue with theories of materiality (154).[18]

To understand the knowledge that embodiment imparts, it is necessary to invert the cogito: "the body exists in space and time and through its interaction with the environment defines the parameters within which the cogitating mind can arrive at its 'certainties' " (Hayles 160). Thus, embodiment constantly redefines the significance of context to cognition (161). So, the important question to ask about the context of virtual reality is what the effect will be on the enculturated body—both inscribed body and embodied practices—of a dematerialized, virtualized space. Dematerialization in terms of embodiment relates directly to proprioception, the sense of bodily boundaries and of inhabiting one's body, which is experienced through the inner ear and internal nerve endings (167). Proprioception involves a feedback loop between the body and objects habitually encountered, but in virtual reality the feedback loop connects the body with a simulation (167–68). Thus, in virtual reality, when one's hand touches a simulated object (for example, a door), changes occur in the visual field (the door opens), but no tactile sensation/resistance occurs, so the physical touching is deactualized, the hand seeming to be amputated. One has the impression of one's dematerialized body controlling the objects in a visual field; as Hayles describes it, the body is transformed into "an informational pattern interacting with the informational patterns on screen" (169). The term *split subject* takes on a meaning not accounted for in psychological theory when applied to the sensation of the virtual reality user, the subject, controlling herself as an object in a virtual realm. If, to liberally paraphrase Virginia Woolf, the perspective of the world changed about the time of Picasso's painting of *Les Demoiselles d'Avignon*, with the women in the painting staring back at the spectator and thus refusing to behave as conventional artistic *objects*, what about the perspectival change brought about by virtual reality, whereby the user as subject is gazed on by him- or herself as simulated object?

In *The Ideology of the Aesthetic*, Terry Eagleton is engaged in a project to bring embodiment back to aesthetics. He points out that aesthetics was "born as a discourse of the body" in the work of the eighteenth-century philosopher Alexander Baumgarten, which posited a rational and sensate individual, with aesthetics as a necessary form of cognition mediating between reason and sense (13–17). But the connection to embodiment, evident in Baumgarten's concept of the aesthetic, is elided later in Kant's notion of aesthetic judgment in which taste derives from universals that oppose the subjectively sensuous, supporting instead a kind of "sensuous communis." Bourgeois aesthetic theory sprang from what Eagleton calls "a dream of reconciliation—of individuals woven into intimate unity with no detriment to their specificity, of an abstract totality suffused with all the flesh-and-blood reality of the individual being" (25).

This dream of reconciling the individual with the universal was predicated on the concept of a public sphere that would allow for the cultural production, reception, and judgment of art protected from marketplace consumption and other forms of debasement connected with vested interest and functional ends. In this conception, art would act as a critical counterforce to the hegemony of the marketplace. Kant's theory required categorical integrity so that aesthetic experience would not be mixed with other faculties of experience. Furthermore, this categorical integrity was meant to prevent the aesthetic from subsuming the political. In the forms of critical/reflective judgment, aesthetics and politics enjoy a close relation in the public sphere. Because the public sphere is both necessary to and assumed by critical judgment, the end of art signals the possible disappearance of the public sphere.

Late modern theories of the public sphere generally take one of two courses: those who nostalgically believe we have lost the public sphere and those who believe we never had one to lose. Those who mourn the loss of the public space attribute its death to contamination by the marketplace, and specifically to an unholy alliance between commodification and aestheticization. The critical judgment of the public sphere has been displaced by the unreflective consumption characteristic of what Guy Debord calls "the society of the spectacle." Mass media and a commodified popular culture transform all experience into entertainment, with such spectacles facilitated by the simulated reality of electronic technologies. For example, we encounter nature as meteorological spectacle/entertainment in *The Enemy Wind,* advertised as "the best-selling cable weather channel production"—a forty-eight-minute video of tornado footage and the heroics of the camera(wo)men who battled the elements. For historical spectacle, there are theme parks such as the one Disney wanted to build five miles down the road from the Manassas National Battlefield in Virginia: "Disney will split the American story into nine playlands which, planners declare, will let visitors participate in the nation's creation but without getting shot or even dirty." This park promises "cheek-pinching real 'audioanimatronic' Presidents—computer driven mannequins that will spout historic speeches and debate each other. It will have a genuine-looking Army airfield where computer animation will let 10-year-olds fly World War II bomb runs and parachute behind enemy lines" (Wines A8). As Eagleton observes, this is an aesthetics evacuated of art's potential to exceed and trouble a repressive rationality (368), a commodified aestheticization of culture that renders all experience in terms of entertainment, pleasure, diversion, style, surface, and intuition and that substitutes cultural consumption for democratic participation.

A string of arguments about the rise and fall of the public sphere has secured for that perspective the status of conventional wisdom, reiterated in texts such as Habermas's *Structural Transformation of the Public Sphere* (1962) and Allan Bloom's *The Closing of the American Mind* (1987). But, as Bruce Robbins points out, "the appearance of the public in these narratives is something of a conjuring trick" (Introduction viii). Those who argue that the public sphere has never been anything but a phantom take their cue from the "as if" in Kant's imperative. In fact, it is a logical extension of Kant's conception to insist that the commonality of the public sphere mandates that it be open and indeterminant in order to forestall the imposition of *particular* forms of politics and identity (Carroll 174). Thomas Keenan aptly sums up this position: "The public—in which we encounter what we are not—belongs by right to others, and to no one in particular" (133).

Agreeing that a public sphere is dynamic, diffuse, and heterogeneous rather than concrete or locatable, I would argue that the dialogue in the public computer network constructs the postmodern public space par excellence—allowing for communication and community without attempting to enforce an impossible commonality. The technology of the worldwide net enables more people to form the empirical collectivity than ever before and from a much wider range of international cultures. Also, the ability to effectively debate issues is enhanced tremendously by the ready access to a wealth of data necessary to refute or support a position.

Government and media research reveals that people are not very interested in accessing information on a computer unless they are also provided with the means to interact with other computer users (Rheingold 277). Users do not want canned information if they can have personalized information through networking that results in immediate answers to questions from persons with knowledge of and experience related to the topic of the inquiry. Information alone cannot substitute for experience. Networkers want to chat, to debate, to collaboratively create a virtual world. The most extensively used forms of virtual reality include e-mail, computer bulletin board systems and real-time chatting, and interactive game-playing and collaborative virtual creations in the MUSHs and MOOs. Unlike the expensive full-immersion amusement park and arcade fantasies, chatting and gaming on the worldwide Internet or on a local and/or specialized bulletin board are, as of yet, free or minimally priced and (with the exception of a few commercial ventures such as Prodigy and America Online) unregulated—because unowned by the corporate lords of telecommunications. Anyone with access to Internet, which presently links more than three million computers around the world, has an equal right to participate in this public sphere.

Why the overwhelming desire for interactivity? There is the obvious answer: existence in the modern world is a lonely, fragmented, depersonalized, shallow, and passive experience for many people. A less obvious answer lies in the fact that information media have created a world awash in events but largely devoid of shared experience (Morley and Robins 144). In a commodity culture, interactivity in mass media spectacles constitutes an aestheticized republican virtue, substituting for participation in a critical politics of the public realm the consumer's participation in the constructing, mobilizing, and selling of public opinion—a simulation of shared decision making and political agency. Referring to the home polling and voting staged by the Warner Qube service in the early 1980s, Jean Betheke Elshtain called the television-voting model an "interactive shell game [that] cons us into believing that we are participating when we are really simply performing as the responding 'end' of a prefabricated system of external stimuli" (Rheingold 287). In his analysis of the consumer's position in the current global economy, Arjun Appadurai observes that a fetishism of the consumer masks the sites of actual agency—the producer and the many forces constituting production: "Global advertising is the key technology for the worldwide dissemination of a plethora of creative, and culturally well-chosen, ideas of consumer agency. . . . [T]he consumer is helped to believe that he or she is an actor, where in fact he or she is at best a chooser" (286–87).

Interactivity has become the media industry buzzword. Perhaps we want (more) interactivity because we have been fed a steady diet of it—or what passes for it—in recent years. Selected viewers have served as test audiences for the preview of films before wide release, often prompting directors to make last-minute changes in plot or character, such as the much-discussed rewriting of the ending of *Thelma and Louise*.[19] There is the public's seemingly endless fascination with Phil and Oprah talk shows in which issues are presented in the form of warring personalities with whom the studio and telephone audience are invited to wrangle. The *Today Show*, which also transforms newsmakers into entertainment personalities, has a new $15 million set that has moved to the ground floor, with the back walls replaced by glass so that a smiling and gesticulating crowd of arrested flaneurs is exhibited in a window to the world. Recently, on-line computer services—Prodigy, America Online, and Compuserv—have added network bulletin boards for the four major television networks so that viewers can pass on their opinions and chat with other viewers. Television executives read the bulletin board postings with great interest, because finally they are getting some valuable feedback from a valuable audience segment that was previously difficult to reach through the conventional methods of mail and telephone, an audience described by a CBS executive vice president of marketing as "upscale, upper-income, educated, techno-friendly viewers, almost all of whom have cable TV" (Lorando E2). This interactive connection between audience and programmers is not limited to the commercial networks: PBS had America Online forums every week after its controversial independent film series *P.O.V.*

The best-case scenario is that this interactivity functions as a post-Fordist feedback loop, with mass media responding to the opinions of its consumers, who in turn respond to the modifications in media offerings. The darker picture is that those in marketing want to extract as much information as possible from individuals—with or without their consent—to further individualize their pitches and avoid wasting time on a scatter-shot method of general broadcast (Foucauldian surveillance technique). If (or when) a few corporate giants gain control of all mass media, the scenario threatens to become worst case: they will not have to force entry into our home telecommunications systems and information terminals, because we will sell data about our private behavior and buying habits in exchange for access to the databases on which these corporations will hold a monopoly.

So far, de Certeau's theory that the vastness of the system subverts the systematic attempts to monitor and control the individual participants has held true. People are using computer networks to interact in emotive and intellectual ways in a system that is unregulated and getting vaster by the week. To counteract the negative effects of vastness, undifferentiation, and transience, listserv users have developed lists to capture the best of the net exchanges, serving as archives to allow exciting net conversations to be reviewed reflectively and cited in the future. One secures a place in the net archive through provocative ideas crafted in memorable language, and the same characteristics guarantee that readers will respond to one's postings.[20] Skilled writing and reading sustain interactivity. Hypermedia and cyberspatial communication threaten the book and printed-text industry, but they do not signal the end of literacy. Far from it. And although there are too many *ifs* to consider to predict the future of the vast cybernetic public space with much confidence, I remain hopeful about the possibilities of using computer technology in the classroom to construct a space in which individuals, of whatever particularities, have equal participatory rights. Used in this way, "[t]he machine is us, our processes, an aspect of our embodiment" (Haraway 99).

CHAPTER FIVE

Cultural Production and the Teaching of Reading

■ With pluralism irreversible, a world-scale consensus on world-views and values unlikely, and all extant *Weltanschauungen* firmly grounded in their respective cultural conditions (more correctly: their respective autonomous institutionalizations of power), communication across traditions becomes the major problem of our time. . . . The problem, therefore, calls urgently for specialists in translation between cultural traditions.

—Zygmunt Bauman, *Legislators and Interpreters*

I end this study with what Gerald Graff calls "the pedagogical turn" evident in recent literary theory and criticism (65). This turn has occurred for various reasons: the influence of reader and reception theories, which analyze students as readers; the increasing importance of cultural studies, which view schools and universities as important sites of cultural transmission; and the proliferation of political-ideological arguments about canon revision and multicultural education. My construction of a reading culture in the university classroom applies observations from the previous chapters. To make a case for a new pedagogy, I want to reconsider multiculturalism and computer-mediated communication, in this case taken together in what might seem at first glance to be an incongruous coupling. But this coupling is already operative in the emerging transnational culture marked by the tension between cultural homogenization (achieved through global commodification, mass media, and informatics, for example) and cultural hetero-

genization (as exemplified in identity politics and micro-political disjunctions).[1]
Thus, the electronic multicultural classroom is a microcosm of sorts, displaying in
miniature the complex pull between the universal and the particular that characterizes postmodern culture. By combining the friction-reducing technology of informatics with the friction-producing differences of multiculturalism, I hope to
deflate some of the hype connected with computer-assisted instruction and multicultural curriculum reform and to offer a more productive conception of their
potential when they are combined in a pedagogy reconceived with the actualities
of the present as well as the hopes for the future in mind.

This attempt to reform pedagogy might seem to contradict the spirit of my
institutional critique in the section on critical essentialism, in which I imply that
we who count ourselves among the academic left have constructed an imaginary
vision of our cultural work as being more radical and progressive than it actually
is. I have not meant to suggest that the academy plays an unimportant role in what
Pierre Bourdieu calls the field of cultural production; on the contrary, my criticism derives from my feeling that because the role played by universities and
schools is significant, we need to rethink pedagogy in ways that go beyond merely
adding texts and courses to the curriculum.

In arguing for pedagogical reform in the humanities, I part company with
Bourdieu's argument in *The Field of Cultural Production.* I find the basic terms of
his analytical model persuasive: he posits an agent—excluded in structural theories of social analysis and occluded in idealist conceptions of the subject—and he
describes agency as occurring in a field of cultural production, which avoids the
mechanistic determinism of most marxian analyses. But despite the dynamism
involved in Bourdieu's field model, art remains a static category in terms of
value, with individual works expressing only the symbolic value of the field as a
whole. In Bourdieu's model, the form/content of the individual art work counts
for nothing. The category of high art is determined solely by "restricted production, in which the producers produce for other producers," while low art is mass-
marketed, often on a grand scale; the more restricted the production, the more
autonomous it is (Bourdieu 39). This notion of cultural capital overlooks the
changes in cultural production in the contemporary world.[2] Postmodern marketing of literature in close connection with mass media (for example, the film-novel
package) increasingly erases boundaries between high and low culture in terms of
production and between classes in terms of reception. Though he intends to
get beyond the limitations of aesthetic idealism and structural determinism,
Bourdieu's model of cultural production is itself modern and monocultural.

I agree with Mary Louise Pratt's description of classrooms as cultural contact zones (34), but I would add that, until recently, this contact has largely excluded students as fully participating agents. The nature of this contact has changed in the course of the twentieth century with the rise and fall of various pedagogical theories and methods, these changes being especially visible in the teaching of literature. The New Critical method made clear that the teaching of literature is the teaching of competent reading; to the New Critics, literary competence meant eradication of the emotional and impressionistic affects of the amateur reader, rejection of the intentionalism of biographical and historical scholarship, and recognition of the literariness of literature. New Criticism sought to transform the reader into a reading machine or automaton, and thus the contact zone featured the teacher as drill sergeant who worked the students into homogeneous shape. By the late 1960s, New Criticism had been officially dethroned in the academy (though its effects have been long-lived in secondary and university education) with the ascendance of a combination of critical perspectives that recuperated the contexts of literary texts, the writer, and the reader. The contact zone in literature courses then began to allow expressivist disagreement over interpretation, with such disagreements subject to the dictate, "Find your proof in the text." But the text alluded to was not Barthes's multivalent text-as-texts; it was the instructor's authoritative text. Though the discussion might have begun with the instructor's asking the students what they thought of the reading, the momentary pause for affective responses soon gave way to construction of the context and to textual exegesis. Teaching literature after the New Criticism was and still is a matter of teaching competent reading, though the parameters of competence have changed. The conventional trajectory of reading in undergraduate literature courses— reader reads on her own, comes to class to have her reading supplemented and corrected by the instructor, and attempts to replicate the instructor's authoritative reading in a paper or on an examination—does not allow for much contact among classmates. Though Graff might exhort us to teach the conflicts as Stanley Fish and Dinesh d'Sousa duke it out in heavyweight matches in public arenas, the contact zone belongs to us, not to our students.

In 1929, A. N. Whitehead stated in *The Aims of Education* that the goal of literary education was to prepare students for decision making and for leadership roles in a democratic society. Though the aims he outlined were admirable, they did not adequately reflect the fact that in democratic societies in the 1920s, there was a vast populace of disenfranchised individuals and, despite unceasing attempts to extend suffrage, diminishing faith in the notion of a democratic public sphere. Several generations after Whitehead, theories about the public sphere and about universal consensus (such as those of Richard Rorty and Jürgen Habermas), which might appear on the surface to be neopragmatic, still too often seem ideal because they do not come to terms with the realities of discursive power differentials but rather bracket the fact of social inequalities. Nancy Fraser's attempt to rethink the public sphere is instructive in this respect. She observes that public life in egalitarian, multicultural societies cannot be explained by a single, all-encompassing public sphere, for there are multiple publics unevenly developed (17). Another problem with the bourgeois conception of public deliberation, according to Fraser, is that civic republicanism requires individuals to transcend their preferences and identities in a deliberation devoted exclusively to "the common good," which means that the crucial aim of the deliberative process—to enable individuals to articulate and clarify their positions—is thwarted (21). Fraser rightly argues that this idea(l) of the public sphere will no longer do for contemporary critical theory of stratified societies:

> What is needed, rather, is a postbourgeois conception that can permit us to envision a greater role for (at least some) public spheres than mere autonomous opinion formation removed from authoritative decision making. A postbourgeois conception would enable us to think about strong *and* weak publics, as well as about various hybrid forms. In addition, it would allow us to theorize the range of possible relations among such publics, thereby expanding our capacity to envision democratic possibilities beyond the limits of actually existing democracy. (26)

I believe that we should reconsider the classroom in terms of Fraser's multiple public spheres, with our reforms envisioning expanded democratic possibilities grounded in multicultural awareness. Computer networks in the classroom and a multicultural curriculum offer the promise of extended contact and meaningful interaction among students and between instructor and students, pointing to a new paradigm in the teaching of reading and in the reading of culture. Such a pedagogy suggests a way to get beyond the models of the student reader as automaton or completely autonomous individual.

THE UNCOMPLETED PROJECTS OF COMPUTER-ASSISTED INSTRUCTION AND CURRICULAR MULTICULTURALISM

The microchip revolution in the 1980s was hailed as the long-awaited breakthrough in education, with enthusiasts predicting that computers in the classroom would resuscitate the moribund public school system in the United States. These grossly exaggerated claims sound much like the ones made for television in the 1950s. The electronic educational revolution never occurred. Instead, computers in the classroom proved a failure for the same reason that television had: computer-based instruction was structured according to the broadcast paradigm, in which knowledge is transmitted in top-down fashion from teacher to student, rather than according to a network paradigm, which allows students to engage in collaborative inquiry and learning (Rheingold 244–45). Because on-line resources were limited and expensive in the early 1980s, schools used computers to deliver canned content presentations and modules to teach skills such as grammar.

Judging strictly from teacher assessments and student evaluations, computer use today appears to be a glorious success. But when Gail Hawisher and Cynthia Selfe, editors of the journal *Computers and Composition*, visited writing classes that used computers for on-line conferencing, they discovered the actually existing pedagogical situations to differ markedly from the "visionary images of technology—what we want computers to do" as described in assessment narratives (57). Teachers report that in composition courses in which computers are used, students write more, engage more often in peer tutoring, enjoy collaborative writing more, and feel more comfortable in one-on-one conferencing with the instructor than in the conventional lecture-workshop format. Hawisher and Selfe did indeed witness a lot of writing going on—but during class time. Rather than serving as a mediating force to facilitate communication, the computer obtruded between student and instructor and between student and classmates, displacing interaction and dialogue. When instructors interacted with students, they often used a central computer with an overhead projection screen to discuss an essay or a passage from an essay that the students could also read from their own computer screens; in this case, the computer served as an expensive overhead projector. Despite the high-tech setting of the computer lab, Hawisher and Selfe generally found the age-old pedagogical dynamic to be in place: the teacher talked, students listened; the teacher asked preset questions (read-my-mind questions) that students, aiming to please, struggled to answer.[3]

In these unsuccessful forays into computerized education, computers were added to classrooms, but business proceeded as usual. Much the same can be said of multiculturalism in education: insert into the old format a few brief texts by Native Americans, African Americans, Asian Americans, and Chicanas/Chicanos. In 1988 and 1989, the National Center on Literature Teaching and Learning conducted a series of studies to determine the current state of literature instruction in U.S. secondary schools (Applebee 27). A nationally representative sample of 488 public, Catholic, and independent schools participated in the studies. One study asked the respondents to list the book-length works that were required reading in grades seven through twelve; this same survey had been given twenty-five years earlier, and the replication was meant to establish a contrast. The combination of the most frequently required texts on the public school list, the Catholic school list, and the independent school list provided the ranking of the top ten titles in the 1988 survey: (1) *Macbeth*, (2) *Huckleberry Finn*, (3) *Romeo and Juliet*, (4) *The Scarlet Letter*, (5) *To Kill a Mockingbird*, (6) *Hamlet*, (7) *The Great Gatsby*, (8) *Julius Caesar*, (9) *Of Mice and Men*, and (10) *Lord of the Flies* (Applebee 28). Although these titles show up in slightly different positions in each of the three lists, they all rank in the top ten on each (with the exception of *Of Mice and Men*, which the independent school list omitted in favor of *The Odyssey*). In his comparison of this 1988 survey with the 1963 survey, Arthur Applebee points out that the study discovered "only marginal increases in the percentage of selections written by women (from 17% in 1963 to 19% in 1988) or by writers from alternative cultural traditions (from 0.6% to 2%)" (28).

So surprised were the researchers at the National Center by the narrowness of the selections that they sought out possible reasons for distortions in the results. They suspected that the categories "required" and "book-length" in the question might have skewed the results, causing the survey to overlook prose, poetry, or short fiction by women and people of color taught by a significant number of individual teachers (28). But a second study designed to describe what individual teachers did in the course of a school year uncovered the same narrow selections. The percentage of selections devoted to women writers was lower in this study than in the one for book-length texts. And although the percentage of nonwhite writers increased from two percent to seven percent, much of the increase represented poets. In fact, Langston Hughes emerged as one of the most frequently taught poets (29). Many of us who have taught literary survey courses at the university level have discovered poetry to be the least favorite genre for most students, with fiction or short fiction the favorite. I suspect the same is true of high school students; in fact, the poetry phobes in my classes generally trace their fear and aversion back to high school teachers whose (New Critical) analytical method killed the poetry. Most literary anthologies perpetuate the least-favored status of poetry by placing the bulk of poetry in "Modern Poetry" sections at the back of the text. Add to this the fact that a good many teachers march through anthologies in linear fashion, never making it to the modern poetry section (Pace 35).

Those teachers wishing for more cultural diversity cannot be heartened by the fact that modern poetry is the only genre in textbooks that offers significant heterogeneity.

We now know that the quantity is not there, but what about the quality of the selections by women and people of color in literary anthologies? In her 1991 survey of five commonly used U.S. literature anthologies, Barbara Pace found that "the dissenting, reflective voices come from white males . . . while [t]he thin sampling of protests from men of color and the absence of women's voices suggest that acquiescence to the status quo is part of the 'natural order of things' " (37).[4] Pace's observations extend Cary Nelson's contention about the "happy family" multicultural anthologies proliferating in the textbook industry. No angry differences allowed, nothing negative—only a rainbow coalition of happy voices, the happy dysfunctional American family. Henry Giroux describes this curricular model of nonconfrontational multiculturalism as a "pedagogy of normative pluralism" (*Teachers* 95). An alternative curricular model, a mirror inversion that achieves the same results as cultural relativism, makes writers from other cultures into otherness machines, with the exoticized and marginalized other functioning to redefine and recenter the Western subject and to provide new blood for an attenuated academic theory. As I discussed at length in my treatment of race and reading, this approach places the reader in the position of colonizer. The challenge for educators is to avoid fetishizing otherness and to find ways of making the experience of cultural difference meaningful and instructive for all students. A necessary step in this process involves the student's confronting a resistant other/object that refuses to be assimilated or rejected.

VIRTUAL PLACES AND POTENTIAL SPACES OF MULTICULTURALISM

Perhaps the most vehement opposition to the use of computers in university education derives from fears about the despatializing effects of informatics. Implicit in this argument is the belief that the university campus is a real space, an unmediated, natural place. It is true that in a culture increasingly given over to interstate highway sprawl, with urban architectural design determined in large part by the perspective of the automobile driver/spectator moving at high speeds, an enclave traversed by footpaths is becoming a rarity. Then again, it is perhaps not so rare if one considers the proliferation of shopping malls and theme parks, which in terms of architectural design do share characteristics of the pedestrian, walled, malled, quadrangled space of the university, derived from Thomas Jefferson's concepts at the University of Virginia.[5] These are safe urban spaces, relatively speaking, offering a replacement for the old town square now gone, or, more accurately, simulating a substitute for the town green, which itself functioned as an ideological icon for both pastoral escape and idealized community. Such contemporary urban spaces provide a place for late-twentieth-century flaneurs, who, like their nineteenth-century counterparts described by Walter Benjamin, seek public spaces that offer themselves as interiors where the flaneur can maintain his or her privacy in the midst of a milling collectivity (Gelley 250). The university where I teach, typical of urban universities, is walled off and fortified by fraternity row on one flank and by student apartments and large homes on another. Additionally, it faces a large city park and has a very exclusive street (complete with guard gate) on the right front and another university on the left—a "ring of teeth," as it were. Those who bemoan the loss of the real, natural space of the university should reconsider what they mean by these adjectives. The university is (always already) an unreal place and an unnatural space. Yet it is also one of the few architectural spaces left that suggest a public realm and a community. The significant issue, it seems to me, is whether or not the architectural space of the university actually translates into communal interaction or public engagement. I would say that generally it does not. Though the physical space of the university campus often succeeds in bringing together numerous disparate architectural objects, the architectonics does not extend beyond the physical.

That the university is cut off from the community outside its walls and is fragmented within because of disciplinary specialization is hardly recent news. Nevertheless, these facts have attracted attention in recent years, with increasing calls from the outside world for accountability. This clamor for accountability comes from conservatives who do not really care so much about university teaching's "paying off" (after all, a big part of the university's symbolic value comes from its being a space cordoned off for "pure" learning) as they do about the university's maintaining an investment in time-honored cultural (that is, Western) values. Related to the call for accountability is the push from inside academe to connect the university more closely to the outside community. This push sometimes comes from a public relations impulse and so is not necessarily concerned with a progressive social vision as much as with the desire to improve business relations with the community. But the push from inside the academy also owes to the influence of critical theories and cultural studies. Cultural studies, in particular, seek to engage students in cultural work in the community and to help students locate themselves in culture beyond the university.

The far-reaching goal of this process of location is what Fredric Jameson calls "cognitive mapping," which enables a person to get a sense of his or her place in the global system ("Postmodernism" 79, 92). Postmodern feminist theory has engaged in a sustained discussion of the process of location that can provide helpful direction for pedagogical theory. Feminism at some historical moments and for some cultural groups requires identity-formations to represent female voices and perspectives previously silenced. Yet feminism has also been influenced by the poststructural arguments for a posthumanism and the "death" of the self-regulating, rational subject of Enlightenment (masculinist) humanism. For postmodern feminists, one way out of the bind between the essentialized self of identity politics and the decentered, conflicted, constructed self of poststructural theory has been to conceptualize a politics of location that calls for women to understand their local and specific situations, and then to consider those situations within a larger cultural, political, and historical context. A politics of location acknowledges individual differences *and* the effects of structural determinism (such as capitalist consumerism) that attempt to interpellate us as discrete but homogeneous subjects.

Locating oneself in a system, whether global or local, does not mean anchoring oneself as a monadic individual who acts as a self-contained representative of the collective subject; rather, identity formation is a dialogical, dynamic process. Writing in *Profession 93* on the question of how to move beyond the culture wars, Henry Louis Gates, Jr., quotes Isaiah Berlin, whom he credits with many of the ideas currently circulating in the debate over multiculturalism, and these words of Berlin, from *The Crooked Timber of Humanity: Chapters in the History of Ideas*, bear repeating here: "We are free to criticize the values of other cultures, to condemn them, but we cannot pretend not to understand them at all, or to regard them simply as subjective, the product of creatures in different circumstances with different tastes from our own, which do not speak to us at all" (qtd. in Gates, "Beyond the Culture Wars" 11). In a multicultural pedagogy, students should not be allowed to operate solely from the position of "that's my personal opinion"—a perspective that gets students nowhere because it closes down dialogue and undermines the potential public space of the classroom. The public space of a postmodern multiculturalism is posthumanist—and this is where I part company with Berlin—in that it is not a space in which one comes to a profound sense of interiority or monadic self-realization; rather, it is public in being that space that is not-I, that is outside the self. As David Carroll points out, this "outside" does not imply the dissolution of self or the alienation from self and other that constitutes a nostalgic illusion of lost community; instead, Carroll writes, "this 'outside' must be thought [of] as the possibility of links and relations to others and to alterity in general that are not rooted in or dependent on any sense of the interiority, immanence, or essence of the self to itself or others" (183). A reconceptualized public sphere, resulting from postmarxist and post-Freudian theories of subjectivity and from the effects of devastating myths of community and collectivity such as the Nazis', calls for a reconceptualization of self-reflexivity, which too often has meant merely gazing at one's reflection in the mirror.

In the posthumanist multicultural community, the self bumps up against resistant others who refuse to be experienced as the elided difference or alterity *within* the subject. As such, objects become subjects, and the public space constitutes the interstitial place where links occur between differentiated subjects or, more accurately, agents. Sara Suleri offers a metaphorical representation of this outside or space of the not-I in explaining the cultural antagonism and resolution that occurs in Forster's *A Passage to India*. Cultural and religious differences are heightened and brought to a rather troubled resolution in "The Caves" section of the novel, which separates the sections "Mosque" and "Temple": "The caves in which nothing happens turn out to be resonant spaces. . . . Perhaps multiculturalism can be intellectually effective only if it is prepared to locate the caves of emptiness that riddle all cultures or the hollow pockets in which the distinction between the mosque and temple can be temporarily undone" (17). Suleri's description of multicultural engagements occurring in the "hollow pockets" between entrenched cultural positions recalls Charles Johnson's efforts to construct an intercultural middle passage, but, unlike Johnson, Suleri is positing not a fusion that transcends differences but a temporary encounter that results in an ambiguous resolution. The temporariness and ambiguity indicate that the process of differentiation is ongoing.

The virtual space of the electronic multicultural classroom can be the site of the hollow pockets that allow for cultural contact and understanding.[6] The past failures of computer use in education occurred because the computers were used for word processing by individual writers and not for reading, collaborative writing, and communication. Students who participate in computer conferencing are freed from the interruptions that occur in class discussion, interruptions that make the discussion format too often resemble a succession of dramatic monologues in which not enough close *listening* occurs. Recent research on computer conferencing in the classroom concluded that if students are given the time to read the texts of others and to thoughtfully craft their own responses in the context of the discussion, they participate much more willingly and tend to offer lengthy contributions (Cooper and Selfe 853).[7]

Some educators using computer-assisted communication have conducted experiments that require students to employ pseudonyms, which enables the students to leave the body behind—and get beyond what the educators perceive as restraints caused by gender and race—to an even greater degree than in computer conferences in which the students use their names. As Lester Faigley puts it, "[C]omputers joined in a network can be a means of liberation, particularly for those students who are often marginalized in American classrooms" (qtd. in Bump 50). International students in Faigley's classes at the University of Texas claimed that the computer removed the problem of accents and that "the computer has only one [skin] color," enabling them to feel more comfortable engaging in the classroom exchange. Though I find these reports of enhanced intercultural conversation to be encouraging, there is something unsettling about this electronic "passing" of marginalized students, who are empowered through the disappearance of embodied differences. Less fraught with ambivalence is another scenario in this electronic exchange: the culturally privileged student's losing through anonymity his or her advantage, which might be a crucial step in the unlearning of privilege that I see as necessary for multicultural learning to occur.

An important question arises in regard to this electronic role-playing: What can be learned from the temporary performance of identity? The answer will depend on one's theoretical perspective on subjectivity and identity-formation. In claiming that readers are both constructed and constructing, I am arguing for a self that is performed—but in a series of performances that are not unfettered. Although a game in the classroom that allows for voluntarist performance of a cultural other could be interesting, it might also turn into a trivial exercise in crossdressing. The performance of identity in electronic communication offers the possibility of significant cultural exchange, but in order to deal with the difficult questions posed by self–other relations in multiculturalism, there needs to be more at stake in performance than voluntarism implies.[8] In this case, theories of performance, multiculturalism, and cybernetics converge and interanimate each other.

Harveen Sachdeva Mann offers a cogent description of the task of multicultural pedagogy:

To attempt to truly decolonize Western pedagogical (as well as larger ideological) structures, it is necessary to adopt a multiplicity of reading

strategies in approaching post-colonial literatures: to interpret the latter
as rooted in their specific cultural and historical contexts, to read the
West and non-West "contrapuntally" [Edward Said's term], and even to
re-read the West through the non-West. (101–102)

For a course in modern British literature, this task would not mean adding, for
example, the Nigerian-British writer Buchi Emecheta or the Indo-Anglian writer
Salman Rushdie to the reading list to make the category *British* more capacious.
Rather, the addition of texts written by exiles from former British colonies, who
are situated both inside and outside British colonialism, should point to the heterogeneity and conflict obscured by the imaginary of British nationalism. The
marked differences between the cultural traditions and between the situations of
exile of these two writers should prevent their being lumped together as the exotic
but homogeneous postcolonial other. And because Emecheta's and Rushdie's novels differ radically in form, students understand that postcolonial writers do
not necessarily share literary kinship; in this case, Emecheta is much closer to
Margaret Drabble than to Rushdie, and Rushdie is more closely related to James
Joyce. Although I do not want to claim that the understanding gained through
such critical, contrapuntal reading is sufficient to guarantee respect for and sensi-
tivity to other cultures, I do think it is a crucial first step, especially if it is accompanied by multicultural performance, as discussed above.

Edward Said describes the extent of widespread cultural ignorance and its
costs in his discussion of the ideological consensus constructed by a combination
of the rhetorics of government, military, think tanks, academia, and the media to
represent, explain, and justify the Persian Gulf war:

> Never had nouns designating the Arab world or its components been so
> bandied about . . . [with so little] regard or care . . . even though the
> United States was not at war with *all* the Arabs. . . . No major cultural
> group . . . was (and still is) as little known: if one were to ask an Ameri-
> can *au courant* with recent fiction or poetry for the name of an Arab
> writer, probably the only one to come up would still be Kahlil Gibran.
> How could there be so much interaction on one level, and so little actu-
> ality on the other? (*Culture and Imperialism* 294)

Said agrees that the Arab world's ignorance of America is just as profound.
Said is not sanguine about the possibility of communications media promot-

ing intercultural relations; in fact, he has argued that the media representations of cultural others are generally regressive, serving to keep alive negative cultural stereotypes (Morley and Robins 133). Because we largely rely on the media for our images and knowledge of other cultures and events, "media imperialism" results in a one-way flow of representations and a spectatorship that prevents intercultural understanding (133). The media screen works both to screen out the perspective of the cultural other and to construct a cultural imaginary that acts as a defense against perceived threats to a cultural or national group's unity, purity, vitality, and survival.

David Morley and Kevin Robins point to the therapeutic function that the gulf war served in American culture, suggesting that it helped expiate the feelings of guilt, depression, and uselessness that had emerged in the wake of the Vietnam War. The gulf war offered America a new lease on life, a chance to heal and reconsolidate the national psyche in the process of, as George Bush put it, "kick[ing] the Vietnam Syndrome" (qtd. in Morley and Robins 140). The text of the gulf war that CNN constructed for its viewers sprang from what indeed may be the dominant metatext of contemporary culture—paranoia. Thus, cultural unity grows out of a collective defense against shared fears.

One of the few instances of cross-cultural communication of parties involved in the gulf war that was not media determined was the largely sympathetic conversation that occurred between Kuwaiti and Israeli students via an Internet link that had been established in Kuwait before the Iraqi invasion and remained operational for a week after radio and television broadcasts ended (Rheingold 185). As an increasing number of schools become linked internationally through e-mail or Internet Chat Relay, our students will be able to read cross-culturally as part of a global audience. In this way the computer screen, unlike the television screen, can facilitate multidirectional cultural exchange.

In linking Emecheta and her novel *Second-Class Citizen* to the hypertextual web for modern British literature, students can incorporate any pertinent texts they access from the Internet and can also write papers to construct links on topics such as the following:

—The British colonial era in Nigeria

—Postcolonial Nigeria

—The economic and political situation of immigrants in London

—Race relations in postwar England

—Emecheta's connections to English and Irish feminists

—Other contemporary Nigerian writers who have emigrated to Britain and the United States, including Chinua Achebe and Wole Soyinka

These links can cross disciplinary boundaries to establish cultural studies clusters. Hypertext with CD-ROM capability will make interdisciplinary collaboration much easier to achieve and will provide a shared resource that will help eliminate costly duplication of texts and course matter among disciplines.

The collaborative construction of a hypertextual web will be an excellent way to teach research method. As students move texts from the database and add them to the web, the instructor can teach paraphrasing, summarizing, the conventions of citation, and the selection and arrangement of information. These skills of discovering, evaluating, linking, and assimilating information are the ones all students will need for reading in a cybernetic world.

CYBERNETIC LOGIC, MULTICULTURAL
DELIBERATION, AND CREATIVE-CRITICAL READING

Two decades ago, when Barthes claimed that the objective of poststructural reading and blissful texts was to transform readers into producers rather than consumers of texts, he accurately predicted the kind of reading necessary in a cybernetic world. This active and creative role of the reader offers an alternative to Baudrillard's bleak description of the postmodern subject as a "switching center" through which a myriad of diverse circuits of information flow. In a world awash in information, it seems more urgent than ever that we help our students become active and critical readers of texts, enhancing their ability to maneuver through and form meaningful patterns from vast amounts of data.

One might argue that in such a world, we should hierarchize with a vengeance. Well, yes and no. Certainly the vastness of the information lode requires prioritization and coherent arrangement. But there are different ways of achieving this end. For centuries, humankind has operated according to the narrative logic characteristic of oral text, and in printed text according to the logic of expository argument. But now, as Greg Ulmer observes, because of the digitization of informatics, we have moved into a period in which another logic is operative alongside expositional argument and narrative: the logic of pattern, whose essential form is collage (163). The logic of pattern is conductive, Ulmer points out, whereas the logic of exposition is deductive and inductive and the logic of narrative is abductive (161). In collage, the directive principles of construction include appropriation, fragmentation, and juxtaposition, and the primary principle of reading collage is association. If the task of expositional logic has been to lead the reader through a hierarchical arrangement of proofs to arrive at a single, monological conclusion or solution to a problem, the task of hypertext/hypermedia logic is to give a full array of possibilities to allow the reader to trace numerous arguments through the collage or to make it possible for the reader to reframe the information in a way in which argumentation ceases to be the point of the inquiry (160).

These three logics, taken singly, represent the ways that information has been arranged in the oral, printed text, and hypermedia phases of culture; functioning coterminously in contemporary culture, they represent another meaning of multicultural. To be culturally literate in this sense of the term means to understand the characteristics and interrelations of these three logics and the ways in which they supplement each other. Long accustomed to the collage effect in advertising, television programming, and film, we now encounter hypermedia that transform the book into a collage of words, pictures, sound, and film. Antifoundationalism translates into an enormous and ever-growing web of data, and critical reading necessitates creative intervention in the web. As Richard Lanham puts it, "The criticism/creation dichotomy becomes a dynamic oscillation . . . prompt[ing] a new kind of teaching in which intuitive skills and conceptual reasoning can reinforce one another directly" ("Extraordinary Convergence" 36). I am reminded of Gabriele Schwab's observation that experimental literature has helped us make new kinds of associations, bringing back into play the primary processes of cognition (the production of alogical connections without polarity or hierarchy, the experience of simultaneous impressions, the fusion of objects and thoughts) that have been given short shrift by a positivist regime committed to the development of elaborate systems, hierarchies, and polarities (24–28).

Currently the most exciting work in the field of artificial intelligence is occurring in neural net research, the results of which help to explain the importance of alternative methods of problem solving. This research leaves behind the traditional logical approach to problem solving to build parallel processing networks that copy the structure of the brain, enhancing the computer's capacity for making associations and enabling computers to "learn" unprogrammed behaviors. Computers will become better, more complete processors of information when they can be designed to work with fuzzy logic, which is the capability of turning previously uncoded randomness into part of an enlarged pattern, or as William Paulson describes the effect, achieving "[s]elf-organization from noise" (301).

Computers will be able to cope with vaster amounts of data and with more randomly arranged data—in effect, becoming more human. Likewise, the vastness of
the information base and the increasing use of collage necessitate an extension of
the human capability for fuzzy logic.

In the midst of this fuzziness, what about the shape and place of argument in
the contemporary world? It no longer goes without saying that expositional argument is the best vehicle for intellectual inquiry or problem solving. In fact, as
Graff and others have reminded us, the teaching of literature is a collective transaction, but the rhetoric of scholarly presentation mandates a model that valorizes
originality and agonistic individuality.

Already in the academy there are the beginnings of an effort to rethink models of inquiry and problem solving. James Sosnoski and David Downing have established Alternative Educational Environments, which administers the E-Works
database and publishes an electronic circular among university instructors and
students. E-Works has as its goal "the creation of an environment conducive to
the understanding of other human beings," with the conversation specifically focused on the future of literary studies in the humanities ("Teaching" 2). Believing
that "the confrontational classroom simply maps itself [in binary fashion] as the
media would have it . . . [resulting in] a pedagogy that resembles contemporary talk shows," Sosnoski and Downing have tried to establish a forum for more
extensive interaction ("Multivalent Pedagogy" 32). The electronic cycles conversation is not meant to arrive at a false consensus and a reductive conclusion that
closes down discussion but to continue the conversation, with the result that consensual problem solving is revealed as a messy process. Though messy, the process
is not diffuse and unfocused: the conversation, which cycles around a problem
that the group identifies, is cross-referenced by the subscribers, who also contribute to a glossary of ubiquitous but slippery theoretical terms ("Teaching" 1, 3).
The cycles interaction discourages hasty refutation and encourages people to read
closely and try to understand another person's point, and to consider potential
concurrences before they rush to disagree ("Protocol" 81). Although Downing
says that on-line communication is not essentially important to the Cycles project
("Protocol" 77), it would seem that a project of this sort, which sustains a conversation among faculty and students from a number of universities, would require
the technology of computer networking.

The pedagogical practice I have outlined, which involves the recognition and
use of multiple logics and requires an ethics of careful reading and listening, seems
to me crucial if deliberation and creative collaboration are to occur. It is this de-

liberative-collaborative process that will allay the pervasive doubts about both computer technology in the classroom and curricular multiculturalism, with the suspicion being that they provide connection but do not facilitate understanding. Returning to the epigraph to this chapter, by Zygmunt Bauman, I want to agree with his claim that we no longer have the choice to insulate ourselves from culture differences and otherness. Assimilation and repudiation, introjection and abjection—both at the individual level and at the community level—as methods of differentiating "I" and "we" from the other have resulted in objectification, oppression, colonization, and genocide. The time has come for the construction of cultural empathy and for instruction in cultural interpretation, which would involve readers in a fusion or linking with other cultures, a nonviolent relation to the other, followed by a separation and contemplation of the experience of merging—the necessary next stage in reading cultures.

APPENDIX
NOTES
WORKS CITED
INDEX

474   THE SATURDAY REVIEW OF LITERATURE   FEBRUARY 10, 19

How to enjoy
JAMES JOYCE'S
great novel

FOR THOSE who are already engrossed in the reading of *Ulysses* as well as for those who hesitate to begin it because they fear that it is obscure, the publishers offer this simple clue to what the critical fuss is all about. *Ulysses* is no harder to "understand" than any other great classic. It is essentially a story and can be enjoyed as such. Do not let the critics confuse you. *Ulysses* is not difficult to read, and it richly rewards each reader in wisdom and pleasure. So thrilling an adventure into the soul and mind and heart of man has never before been charted. This is your opportunity to begin the exploration of one of the greatest novels of our time.

JAMES JOYCE

STUART GILBERT, in his masterly essay on ULYSSES, says: "It is like a great net let down from heaven including in the infinite variety of its take the magnificent and the petty, the holy and the obscene. In this story of a Dublin day we read the epic of mankind."

This monumental novel about twenty hours in the life of an average man can be read and appreciated like any other great novel once its framework and form are visualized . . . just as we can enjoy *Hamlet* without solving all the problems which agitate the critics and scholars. The structure of Ulysses is composed of three elements: the symbolic narrative of the Odyssey, the spiritual planes of the Divine Comedy and the psychological problem of Hamlet. With a plot furnished by Homer, against a setting by Dante, and with characters motivated by Shakespeare, Ulysses is really not as difficult to comprehend as critics like to pretend.

The real clue to Ulysses is simple: the title itself. Just as the Odyssey was the story of Odysseus, Telemachus and Penelope: the father who tries to find his home; the son who seeks his father; the constant wife who puts off her suitors and waits for her husband's return . . . so Ulysses is the story of Leopold Bloom, Stephen Dedalus and Molly Bloom: the father, an average man whose life is incomplete because his only son died in infancy and whom no one will honor or remember after his death; the son, a young poet who finds no spiritual sustenance in

art or religion, and who is looki symbolic father—a certainty on can base his life; the wife, wh earthly element, a parody of Penelo inconstancy, her bawdiness, her anin ence. The theme of the Odyssey has be "the dominance of mind over circu and the theme of Ulysses, "the dom circumstance over mind."

Each of the characters in Ulysses three different planes of reality. First, alistic which involves the adventures o and Leopold during one day in Dublin the classical which concerns the paral tween Ulysses and the Odyssey in resp characters, events, and pattern; third, bolic which brings in the allusions to p and to Irish history which have given special esoteric significance to a few readers. Here Joyce makes every chap sent a color, a science or art, a symbol, of the body, and a literary technique. things need not concern the general rea enjoyment of Ulysses depends on its h wisdom, and its essential humanity. Be esoteric significance of parts of the b beyond the tremendous wealth of detail about manners, morals, customs, thou tures, and speech, the the solid basis of it on most exciting stories o modern fiction: the unexpurgated record o uninhibited adventures and physical, during t of one full day.

To better underst action of Ulysses and tion of the characters real life as well as counterparts in the the following list of characters will be hel

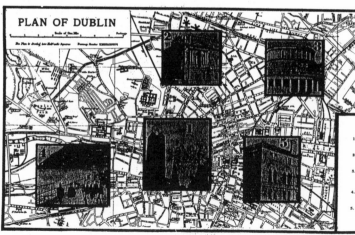

PLAN OF DUBLIN

The Plan is drawn into Half-with Square

From *Saturday Review of Literature* 10 Feb. 1934: 474–75.

from his day's wanderings. Gerty romanticizes Bloom as a hero, and day-dreams a love-affair with him. Bloom's thoughts and actions in regard to Gerty are more direct and realistic.

14 THIS is the culminating chapter of parodies, more or less summarizing the outstanding prose styles of English literature from the mediaeval to the present. The medical students are at dinner in the Lying-In-Hospital, Dublin, while Mrs. Purefoy is being delivered of a child upstairs. It ends in a mixture of dialect and slang, as Stephen and the students, followed by Bloom, go to a barroom and get drunk. Homeric parallel: The Oxen of the Sun.

15 PROBABLY the most famous chapter of *Ulysses* —the Circe episode in the brothel, and all of it in dramatic dialogue. Many new characters are involved— soldiers, prostitutes, an idiot; and various characters in Bloom's and Stephen's imaginations, as these are worked upon by alcohol. This scene is a magnificent orgy, which outlines all the significant events of Stephen's and Bloom's lives.

PART THREE

THE MEETING of Odysseus and Telemachus; the return to Penelope.

16 BLOOM takes Stephen to the shelter of the cabman, Skin-the-Goat, to recuperate. (In the *Odyssey*, Telemachus meets Odysseus in the cave of Eumaeus, the goat-herd, but does not recognize him.)

17 BLOOM takes Stephen home with him. (The return to Ithaca.) The style is that of a theological catechism. Stephen departs, and Bloom goes to Molly.

18 IN the final chapter the story returns to earth, in the Gargantuan coda of the earthly Penelope —Molly Bloom's soliloquy in bed. The story comes down to the terms of the animal as we see what Molly thinks of Bloom and Boylan, of herself and her life. The triumph of circumstance over mind is complete.

READ WHAT THE CRITICS SAY:

"For readers to whom books are an important means of learning about life, *Ulysses* stands preeminent above modern rivals as one of the most monumental works of the human intelligence."—*Time.*

"To my mind one of the most significant and beautiful books of our time."—*Gilbert Seldes, in The Nation.*

"Talk about understanding 'feminine psychology'—I have never read anything to surpass it, and I doubt if I have read anything to equal it."—*Arnold Bennett.*

"In the last pages of the ..., Joyce rises to such rhapsodies of beauty as have probably never been equalled in English prose fiction."—*Edmund Wilson, in The New Republic.*

"It comes nearer to being the perfect revelation of a personality than any book in existence."—*New York Times.*

"By what almost amounts to genius, Random House has made *Ulysses* extraordinarily attractive in form."—*Philadelphia Record.*

The RANDOM HOUSE edition of this great work offers the complete and unexpurgated text, with an introductory note by the author, a foreword by Morris Ernst, and a reprint of the historic decision by Judge John M. Woolsey whereby the Federal ban on this book was removed once and for all.

CHARACTERS IN ULYSSES

Ulysses	In Real Life	In The Odyssey
Dedalus	Joyce at 22	Telemachus, son of Odysseus
Bloom	An Irish Jew, the "average man."	Odysseus
Bloom	Wife of Leopold; with Spanish, Jewish and Irish blood.	Penelope and Calypso
Mulligan	Young medical student, friend of Stephen (identified as Dr. Oliver St. John Gogarty, friend of Joyce).	Partly Antinous, in relation to Telemachus.
Boylan	Cheap man-about-town.	Antinous, the suitor of Penelope.
Dignam	Deceased friend of Bloom.	Elpenor
Deasy	Master of school where Stephen teaches.	Nestor
Citizen	A mad patriot, who tries to kill Bloom.	Polyphemus
MacDowell	Romantic girl who attracts Bloom.	Nausicaa
Bohrn	Proprietor of a brothel.	Circe

the deepest pleasure to be derived from reading *Ulysses* is not the artificial one of being able to identify the characters and episodes. That is the recognition only of the framework for a story of vast proportions and microscopic detail.

Here are brief summaries of the eighteen chapters that compose the book:

PART ONE

PRELUDE: Stephen Dedalus' morning. Like Telemachus in the Odyssey, Stephen sets out to find his spiritual father.

1 BREAKFAST in the Round Tower. Stephen and Buck Mulligan, with a young Englishman named Haines in Ireland for "local color." Dedalus, Mulligan talk facetiously, sometimes blasphemously; discuss Irish art and history.

2 STEPHEN teaches history class at boys' school. Talks with Mr. Deasy (Nestor) who doubts if Stephen will remain long in the school.

3 STEPHEN walks on the beach; his thoughts reflect his life. Corresponds to episode in Odyssey where Stephen meets Proteus, the "old man of the sea."

PART TWO

4 BLOOM's day—the wanderings of Ulysses. Bloom is an advertising solicitor; his job is to "make news"—hence his itinerant adventures. Through him we see the whole panorama of Dublin, from the lieutenant to the bum in the pub. He is the *homme sensuel,* with enough intellectual curiosity to discover—as he might say—what life is all about.

Bloom prepares his wife's breakfast. Buys and cooks a kidney for himself. Takes breakfast and Molly in bed; one letter from her suitor, Blazes Boylan, impresario for Molly's concert tour. Episode corresponds to Calypso's island in Odyssey, where Odysseus struggles against his will. Bloom is held in Ireland by

Molly; would prefer to live in the sunny Mediterranean land of his ancestors.

5 BLOOM goes to post-office, receives letter addressed to "Henry Flower," the name he adopted to carry on lonely-hearts correspondence. Goes to mass, reflects on Catholic religion; emerges, buys soap, goes to public baths. Bloom's characterization and lively thoughts are the substance of this episode, which corresponds to that of the Lotus-Eaters in the Odyssey.

6 BLOOM goes with Stephen's father and others to the funeral of Paddy Dignam. They pass Stephen. Theme of Death developed; Bloom recalls his father, who committed suicide, and his son Rudy, who died in infancy.

7 THIS chapter is told in journalese, with sections broken by headlines. Bloom visits newspaper office to insert advertisement. The newspaper men and their work are described. Stephen enters, to arrange for publication of Mr. Deasy's article, but does not meet Bloom. *Evening Telegraph* office corresponds to Cave of the Winds in the Odyssey.

8 BLOOM looks for a place to have lunch; passes various people, including sandwich-men and the poet A. E.; talks with Mrs. Breen of Mrs. Purefoy, who has been in labor three days and whose child is to be born in a later episode. One lunch room reminds him of slaughter house where he once worked; he gets a sandwich elsewhere; sets out for library, where he has to look up ad in back newspapers; stops en route at Museum to look at nude statues.

9 THE scene is the National Library; Stephen Dedalus (Joyce), Mulligan (Gogarty) discuss *Hamlet* with Irish literati including A. E. and John Eglinton. Father-son theme of *Hamlet* predominantly parallels the same theme in *Ulysses.* Opposing points of view represent Scylla and Charybdis of The Odyssey.

10 THIS chapter consists of 18 short episodes, the events befalling various Dublin characters. Blazes Boylan buys fruit for Molly Bloom whom he is to see at 4 o'clock. Mr. Bloom buys novels for his wife. Chapter closes with passage through Dublin of the Lord Lieutenant of Ireland. Homeric parallel: the course of Odysseus at sea.

11 THE scene is the barroom of the Ormond Hotel; the barmaids, Miss Douce and Miss Kennedy, hear the Lord Lieutenant's carriage go by. They flirt with Boylan who then leaves to go to Mrs. Bloom; Bloom enters for a belated lunch. Simon Dedalus (Stephen's father) and two others sing at the piano. Bloom, as "Henry Flower," answers letter from Martha Clifford, received that morning.

12 THE "Cyclops" chapter, the most gorgeously humorous in the book. It is told by a Dublin bum, in racy Irish dialect (perfectly comprehensible), and it tells of the meeting of Bloom and "The Citizen" —a drunken banshee of a Sinn Feiner—in a saloon. Bloom wants to kill Bloom, chases him into the street, throws a biscuit-tin 'at him but misses, because—like Polyphemus—he is blinded by the sun. Bloom and the Citizen are gorgeously taken off in parodies of scientific jargon, cheap journalism, romance: showing the difference between their opinions of themselves and the realities which they represent.

13 ANOTHER extremely humorous chapter, almost entirely a parody of cheap romantic fiction— the self-projection of Gerty MacDowell (Nausicaa) at the beach, Dublin Bay, where Bloom has gone to rest

NOTES

Introduction: Readers in and out of Texts

1. I should make clear at the start that in differentiating the actual reader from the textual reader, I am not making essentialist claims about my ability to access and convey in unmediated fashion the presence of the "real" reader. My rendition of this reader is as much a construct as the textual reader is. What I am interested in exploring is the changes in and the differences among constructions.

2. I am indebted to Molly Rothenberg's explanations of the various conceptions of agency and her psychoanalytic critique of a naive performative notion of agency that implies an unsplit subject that can be fully present to itself in a performance of self that completely accounts for the subject and controls the effect of signification. A full discussion of Rothenberg's argument is forthcoming in her collaborative text with Joseph Valente, *Raising the Unreal: A Post-Lacanian Approach to Cultural Analysis.*

3. My ideas about agency have been informed by Paul Smith's argument in *Discerning the Subject* (1988). Smith engages in an astute critique of several critical theories (including Althusserian Marxism, Derridean deconstruction, and Kristevan semiotics) in regard to their inability to allow for agency, yet he himself does not construct a theory of agency. He suggests that one must turn to cultural studies to discover descriptions of agency.

4. See Dan Sperber and Deirdre Wilson's *Relevance: Communication and Cognition.*

5. Criticizing the *Screen* project from the perspective of psychoanalysis, Joan Copjec points out that Althusserian film theory mistakenly believes itself to have followed directly from Lacanian theory when in actuality it has "Foucauldianized" Lacan by conceptualizing "the screen as a mirror," with the subject recognizing her- or himself as perfectly represented and fully present on the screen. Antithetical to the conclusions of psychoanalysis, this conception of the film screen ignores, in Copjec's words, "Lacan's more radical insight, whereby the mirror is conceived as a screen" or a "veil of representation" that seems to be hiding some reality about the subject but that "actually conceals nothing; there is nothing behind representation," no way by which the subject can confirm the truth of its being (15–16, 35–36).

6. Radway's study was well received and seemed to signal an impending change in reader/audience research. But this change did not occur in literary criticism dealing with the reader. The question is, why have theories of structural determinism held such currency for so long? First of all, as a result of trenchant critiques of modernity, there is among literary critical theorists a profound distrust of any claims that appear to champion an atavistic individualism. One can also point to the arrogance of theorists and critics who feel that the benighted public is incapable of reading and actively appropriating on its own. In this scenario only theoreticians/critics can be the right kind of readers, using deterministic theories but themselves not

subject to the determinism. Closely related to this assumption about a benighted public is what Richard Grusin calls "the technological fallacy," which involves the granting of agency to technology, for example the belief (indeed, the faith) that advertising and visual media in general possess the power to transfix audiences and transform them into the right kind of consumers. Then there are the problems inherent in any empirical project: in focusing on the responses of real readers, one encounters the difficulty informants have in articulating what they actually do as they read, the deep-seated and often overlooked assumptions of informants, and the tendency of the researcher's questions to determine the informants' responses (Mills 5). Also, film and literary theories are still modernist—tied to the notion of the work of genius and the text as a work, so that the text remains the ground. Cultural studies' ethnography of the viewer/spectator of popular culture is threatening to those literary scholars who are committed to holding the line against the encroachment of nonliterary culture and against empirically oriented (as opposed to formal) theories. But I want to argue that formal theory and cultural studies empiricism need each other, with each questioning the other's warrants and conclusions.

7. Because his theories are also materialist/sociological, Pierre Bourdieu is often put in the same theoretical camp with de Certeau. This is a mistake. Like Althusser before him, Bourdieu has developed a model of cultural reproduction that features subjects as caught in a feedback loop in which they internalize and reproduce dominant norms and values, a process that allows for no social change, no agency. Despite his radical intentions, Bourdieu's model is static and monocultural.

8. At bottom, de Certeau's theories work against the master logocentric theory of geometric determinism. Ilya Prigogine and Isabelle Stengers have uncovered and analyzed pervasive epistemological assumptions in the physical sciences that reveal an ideological bias toward a mechanistic model. Based on the assumptions of geometry, this model claims that physical events are reversible in temporal terms and that all events can be reduced to simple, immutable laws that transcend natural events. This model derives from the perspective of *being*. Prigogine and Stengers, who perceive serious flaws in this model, point to an opposing model derived from the perspective of *becoming*, in which, because of the inconstancy of time, laws governing its behavior cannot be immutable (Rosenberg 279–83). Yet geometry seduces through the promise of transcendence, with this seduction extending well beyond the physical sciences to numerous systems of thinking, including computer languages. See Prigogine's *From Being to Becoming* and Prigogine and Stengers's *Order out of Chaos*.

9. It is this making rather than discovering that differentiates hyperrhetorical creativity from the *inventio* of classical rhetoric, which involved recovery but not invention. In the Aristotelian scheme, one extracted ready-made forms from *topoi*, or places, and in the hands of the Sophists, the topics became *topoi koinoi*, or commonplaces that were storehouses of stereotype and clichéd propositions. Barthes discerns two sentiments implied by *inventio*: "on the one hand, a complete confidence in the power of a method, of a path . . . ; on the other, the conviction that the spontaneous, the unmethodical brings nothing in return" (*Semiotic Challenge* 52).

10. Although Birkerts mourns the loss of "unbroken subjective immersion" in computer-mediated communication, Robert Markley perceives the concept of cyberspace as "shot through with monadological idealism" in which one is offered the promise of becoming self-

present and self-actualizing, efficiently reproducing to oneself the design of a transcendent order (498). In chapter 4, I discuss the opposition between the monadological and the nomadilogical in the conception of hyperspace. My term nomadilogical refers to the characteristics of aimless wandering, with the agent completely detached from a transcendent ordering or a structural determinism.

11. Iser's conclusions about the necessity of continual performance in the construction of self supplement Kendall Walton's important study, *Mimesis as Make-Believe* (1990), by answering the "Why?" question that lies behind Walton's analysis. Examining representational arts, Walton argues that mimesis is collective imagining/make-believe and realism is an effect that cannot be explained completely by claims for the correspondence between object and referent. A work of art serves as a prop in this game, functioning in the same way as dolls, hobbyhorses, and mud pies do. The key to understanding mimesis lies not "in what one sees [representational works] as or sees in them, but rather in the manner in which one sees" (348); the more representational a work is, the more participatory the reader/spectator can be in the game of imagining. In terms of fiction, extensive participation means that the reader is immersed in the text, while diminished participation in the make-believe indicates the more detached response to a metafictional text.

12. Because there are no page numbers in electronic journals, I have cited paragraph numbers.

1. Two Cultures of Reading in the Modernist Period

1. See also DeKoven, DuPlessis, Gilbert and Gubar, and Scott for discussions of gender and modernism.

2. Lisa Tickner suggests that numerous indicators pointed to a crisis of masculinity in England after 1900: the humiliating outcome of the Boer Wars (1899–1902); reports of government commissions attesting to the general physical decline of the English population, the apparent increase in the number of mentally ill persons, and the thirty percent drop in the birth rate between 1875 and 1910; and the growing economic prosperity and military strength of Germany in the face of intellectual and physical decline in Britain. The discourse of social Darwinism informed this debate, with eugenicists calling for "manly" men and "womanly" women to regenerate and revitalize the population of the Empire (Tickner 7).

3. The word *docile* derives from the Latin *docilis*, which in turn comes from *docere*, meaning to teach. Cicero was one of the first thinkers to claim that learning could not occur unless the student was docile, tractable.

4. Brian McHale describes "the repertoire of pattern-making and pattern-interpreting operations" modernist readers used to comprehend the new literary texts they encountered. At the level of narrative, such operations included the reader's ability to "reconstruct the chronology of the *fabula* [raw story-material] from the sometimes drastically displaced order of the *syuzhet* [finished plot]; impart intelligible motivation to sequence and transitions; motivate large-scale parallelisms, doublings, and analogies . . . ; discover narrators and evaluate their knowledgeability and reliability; reconstruct psychological processes, and the external reality which they mediate, from such conventions as interior monologue and [free indirect discourse]"

("Modernist Reading" 88). These operations were not entirely new to literary interpretation, McHale points out, but before the modernist period they were required only in unusual narrative situations, such as that posed by *Tristram Shandy* (88).

5. These modernist texts call into play both primary and secondary processes of experience. In literary theory, primary processes are often referred to as presymbolic processes and include dedifferentiation of the boundary between subject and object and between figure and ground, as well as a perspective characterized by syncretism and the lack of hierarchical ordering. Secondary/symbolic processes include differentiation, analysis, and hierarchizing. In Freud's narrative of the subject's psychogenesis, the relationship between these processes is profoundly agonistic, with the primary processes continually surfacing to subvert the symbolic order. But in the object-relations theory of D. W. Winnicott, the relationship between the processes is described more in terms of a productive interaction in which the primary processes play an important role in creativity. The centered subjectivity of Enlightenment rationalism attempts to bury the primary processes. And by the early twentieth century, all varieties of intellectual inquiry and discourse were feverishly seeking to pattern themselves after the hard sciences and perfect an interpretive method of analyzing, categorizing, and hierarchizing data. The feverishness of the efforts portended an imminent paradigm shift in epistemology. Gabriele Schwab's *Subjects Without Selves: Transitional Texts in Modern Fiction* convinced me of the significance of the interaction between the primary and secondary processes at work in modern literature.

6. See Judith Ryan's *The Vanishing Subject: Early Psychology and Literary Modernism* for an analysis of the considerable influence of radical empiricism—"psychologies without self"—on European intellectual and artistic circles before the circulation of Freud's theories in the 1920s. Ryan points out that Freud's work began as an effort "to consolidate the self" in response to the dissolution of personality that he encountered among his female patients, whom he considered to be the most overwhelmed by rapid social change (20). One suspects that he was also reacting against the alarming tendencies of the early psychologies. Freud's solution was to adapt the Romantic heritage to contemporary life, allowing for both a divided self and the way to reintegrate it (21).

7. Gilbert and the New Critics are part of the critical tradition of holistic interpretation that Steven Mailloux describes in *Interpretive Conventions: The Reader in the Study of American Fiction*: "Most old and new critical approaches specify meanings that are spatial or holistic, whether they look for unities or myths, symbolic systems or allegorical messages, whether they find ethical, psychological, and political themes or generic, structural, and imagistic patterns" (68). Such approaches ignore the reader's temporal reading experience, which involves the adjustments and the succession of responses to the parts of the narrative that occur during the process of reading. Holistic interpretation focuses only on the final totalizing synthesis and completely overlooks the trials that the reader goes through to arrive at that point (68–71).

8. Though in 1920 the defense claimed Joyce's novel to be unthreatening because it was so obscure and unfathomable, Ernst, abetted by Gilbert's interpretation, would argue convincingly in 1933 that the novel was a rational and carefully designed artistic masterpiece.

9. To understand Eliot's need to domesticate *Ulysses*, we should look to *The Waste Land*.

Despite the fact that these works, both published in 1922, tend to be lumped together as *the* two touchstones of literary modernism, they differ in important ways, the most profound difference resulting from their attitudes toward language. Whereas Joyce plays with language and explores its radical potential, Eliot distrusts his own lyrical gift. At the end of *The Waste Land*, Eliot offers up a silence that can deliver us from a corrupted language, turning to the Upanishad *shantih*, "the peace which passeth understanding." Just as he struggles to transcend a sexuality inextricably bound up with death, so does he struggle to transcend the condition of loss and absence that the use of language makes apparent. Eliot's nostalgia implies a belief in an original essential plenitude that can make whole the fragmented condition of existence. In spite of its brilliant formal experimentation, *The Waste Land* is anything but revolutionary in terms of the writer's and reader's subjectivity.

Michael Levenson argues that in the signification of British modernism, perhaps the single most representative event of that memorable year, 1922, was not the publication of *Ulysses* or the publication of *The Waste Land* but Eliot's establishment of the journal *Criterion*, a far cry from *Blast*, which had been published just eight years earlier (213). As the editor of *Criterion*, Eliot made modernism traditional, integrating the avant-gardist aspects of the movement into general intellectual life and securing for modernism a place in intellectual history (219–20).

10. Like Stein, Joyce was influenced by cubism, which in turn was informed by relativity theory. Cubism meant the end of the Renaissance perspective that had reigned for hundreds of years in Western art. The Renaissance perspective implies a static universe, with the spectator anchored to one particular vantage point and the potentially mobile objects in the painting arrested. But in cubist art, time is added to spatial dimensions, because objects are not frozen at one moment but rendered in a temporal sequence that moves the object through space and that implies the observer's movements necessitated by the object's movements.

11. Lydia at the beerpull is a representative scene in a chapter that calls attention to gender differences in reading response and demonstrates that Joyce's implied reader is male. As Judith Fetterley makes clear, female readers of patriarchal texts have always had to read against themselves in order to take up the subject position implied by masculinist texts that objectify woman. Although I argue that *Ulysses* as a whole undermines the notion of the subject sponsored by liberal humanism and agree that this also is a necessary project for feminism, I would not argue that *Ulysses* can be recuperated as a feminist text, rather that it is alternately, and perhaps even simultaneously, oppressive and liberatory. Patriarchalism/masculinism (displaying the resilience and staying power of the cockroach) long preceded the Enlightenment movement and survives handily in posthumanist theories.

12. Harry Levin in *James Joyce: A Critical Introduction* observes that the extreme difficulty of *Ulysses* prompted critics to adopt the exegetical mode, continuing in the pattern established by Gilbert's authorized commentary (237). Through Gilbert's agency, the holistic interpretation came to resemble the holy interpretation.

13. Janet Flanner discovered that T. E. Lawrence (of Arabia) ordered two copies of the most expensive versions of the 1922 edition, at 350 francs apiece, while W. B. Yeats and André Gide both chose the least expensive version, 150 francs (*Paris Journal* 415).

14. By late 1920, Pound was objecting to the serialization of *Ulysses*, but his objections did

not derive from aesthetics. Instead, he felt that serial publication would damage Joyce's chances of publishing the manuscript in book form. John Quinn, who had hoped to publish an expensive private edition, shared Pound's concern. Pound warned Joyce that Anderson and Heap were exploiting him financially: "in general the editrices have merely messed and muddled, NEVER to their own loss" (qtd. in Scott and Friedman xxxi).

15. In 1915 Anderson and her living companions—a group that included her divorced sister Lois and Lois's two young sons, an unpaid office assistant, Harriet Dean, a cook-nursemaid, Clara Crane, and Clara's son Johnny—set up tents on the beach of Lake Michigan because they did not have money to pay rent. The intrepid band of seven (described by various new reporters as "a back-to-nature-colony," "a Hellenistic revival," "a freak art group," and "a Nietzschean stronghold") had dwindled to just Anderson and Dean, who left camp when the weather of mid-November became too forbidding (*My Thirty Years' War* 88–91). My point in mentioning this episode is to draw attention to Anderson's financial struggle to keep the *Little Review* afloat, but I want also to include the fact that Anderson considered this the most lyrically beautiful six months of her life, with only one aspect of her fantasy unrealized: a plan to have her Mason and Hamlin piano shipped to the beach site. And it is this last piece of the picture that perhaps best explains Anderson's philosophy of living and her indomitable efforts to *make* a place for her art magazine in a world that seemed unsuited to such art.

16. Thanks to the theorizing of the Frankfurt School—especially the work of Max Horkheimer, Theodor Adorno, and Herbert Marcuse—and to that of later theorists influenced by it (for example, Peter Bürger and Fredric Jameson), we now recognize that *any* form of anarchy can be packaged and commodified in a late modern or postmodern culture. Nihilistic punk/industrial rock music and gangsta rap, to name only two recent examples, have proved infinitely bankable. I discuss this phenomenon in chapter 2 in relation to the fiction of Kathy Acker.

17. Although refusing to compromise, the *Little Review* established "The Reader Critic" column, which allowed a much more dialogic relationship with readers than was true of other magazines of its kind, such as Harriet Weaver's *The Egoist* and Eugene Jolas's *transition* (Benstock 376–78). Because Anderson was interested in promoting an exchange of ideas rather than in imposing her own program, she provided a forum for twenty-three systems of art and for artists representing nineteen countries. Explaining this (anti-) position in an advertisement on the inside back cover of an issue, Anderson wrote, "My idea of a magazine which makes any claims to artistic value is that . . . it should suggest, not conclude; that it should stimulate to thinking rather than dictate thought" (qtd. in Hoffman, Allen, and Ulrich 60).

18. This same lament over the loss of depth is being replayed in a new key in current critiques of hypertext. I discuss this lament at length in chapter 4.

19. This collocation of vital peasant and enervated middlebrow is evident in much of modernist literature and criticism, which makes one wonder why D. H. Lawrence is still considered excessive and iconoclastic in this regard. He was in a large company. This idealization of the peasant is one of the features of what Umberto Eco calls "eternal fascism," and in the particular form of Nazi fascism it derived from the *Blut und Boden* (blood and earth) ideology (58).

20. Scherman was also the mastermind of the Little Leather Library in the 1920s. He proposed including a miniature copy of Shakespeare's *Romeo and Juliet*, bound in sheepskin,

with a pound of Whitman candy in a combination called "The Library Package." Woolworth's alone sold a million copies of the package in the first year of marketing. Up to 1925, when the mail-order cost became prohibitively expensive, the Little Leather Library sold forty million copies of a hundred literary titles (Cerf 17).

21. In the August 1926 issues, the formidable Lamberton Becker managed to answer questions that ranged from "Which contemporary works of fiction are suitable for reading clubs?" and "Would you please suggest a travel book suitable for reading aloud?" to "Where might I find a history of the Paisley shawl?" and finally "[W]hat American authors of fiction are in a position to write with authority about negroes[?]" (61). The balanced ration that she offered in the August 21 issue included Edna Ferber's *Show-Boat*, Ford Madox Ford's *A Mirror to France*, and Walter Damrosch's *My Musical Life*.

2. Sexing the Text: Postmodern Reading, Feminist Theory, and Ironic Agency

1. See Judith Butler's *Bodies That Matter* for a cogent discussion of the limits of agency in a theory of constructivism.

2. See Inderpal Grewal and Caren Kaplan's *Scattered Hegemonies: Postmodernity and Transnational Feminist Practices* for an excellent collection of essays that expands the bounds of postmodern theory by considering how feminist postmodernism is conceptualized and practiced differently across cultural and national boundaries.

3. Although feminists would resist the traditional scopophilic perspective, there are lesbian feminists whose tastes in erotic and pornographic objects resemble those of straight men. But though the objects might be the same or similar, lesbian desire is not masculine desire.

4. Some of these paintings reproduced in Kate Flint's study are Edward Ward's *Girl Reclining on a Sofa* (1854), Robert Martineau's *The Last Chapter* (1863), Thomas Brooks's *Tales of the Sea* (1867), Alexander Rossi's *Forbidden Books* (1897), and Gwen John's *A Lady Reading* (1910–1911). These paintings show the female object becoming increasingly more active and independent through the course of the nineteenth century.

5. Richard Rambuss's essay "Christ's Ganymede" reminded me of the corporeal nature of the spiritual poetry of Crashaw, Donne, and Herbert.

6. I am grateful to Cindy Scurria for making this connection for me.

7. Recently, when I read a conference paper extolling the wit and transgressiveness of Carter's carnivalesque excesses, a member of the audience vigorously disagreed with my thesis and criticized me for having taught Carter's texts to undergraduate students, who she was sure would have read Carter without catching the inflections. Without a sufficient knowledge of theory, these students could not have grasped the excesses in Carter's work as excesses, and thus for these readers her work would have simply perpetuated the ideological effects of sexism and racism. Though surprised at the anger that my paper prompted and miffed by the implied charge of elitism, I had to admit that this criticism reflected my own conclusions about reception. A text, no matter how politically empowering, does not necessarily interpellate the reader as the writer intends.

8. This sense of irony also characterizes the (anti-) discipline of cultural studies. Recently, Peter Brooks has argued that the New Historical turn in literary studies, which has led

146 ▼   Notes to Pages 68–69

to the creation of various kinds of cultural studies, has derailed the practice of what he calls "an exemplary deconstruction," a term that denotes an interrogation of language and literary discourse that is grounded in philosophy and poetics ("Aesthetics and Ideology" 512). Evident in Brooks's complaint is the often repeated charge that cultural studies have sacrificed rigorous textual analysis of literary and philosophical texts for the bricolage (making use of all kinds of diverse texts/materials) of cultural context, with this process of bricolage leveling or obscuring the cornerstones of High Culture. The critique of cultural studies that finds them to be guilty of shallowness and of promiscuously mixing methodologies and theories ignores cultural theorists' attempts to provide "thick description" of textured synchronic analysis and a self-reflective ethnography that is sensitive to differences among meanings and identities. As a marxian discourse, cultural studies have learned from the mistakes of Marxists who believed that they could get beyond the distorted ideological perspective of the camera obscure and outside the effect of language. I heartily concur with the conviction that although we are never free of ideology, we are able to actively or passively resist the call or interpellation of some ideologies. A cultural studies methodology is characterized by ideological critique qualified by insights from poststructuralist linguistics but holding on to the belief in self-reflection—a syncretist position constructed from bourgeois humanism, Marxism, and poststructuralism. Furthermore, this position entails the goal of critical engagement and political intervention in cultural practices. By constructing a reading agency from a combination of feuding if not mutually exclusive metanarratives arising from different historical situations and temporalities, cultural studies reading is postmodern reading par excellence.

3. Beloved *and* Middle Passage*: Race, Narrative, and the Critic's Essentialism*

1. Since Weixlmann made this comment in his review of Henry Louis Gates's *Black Literature and Literary Theory* (1984), Gates has published an edited work called *Reading Black, Reading Feminist: A Critical Anthology* (1990). The anthology focuses not on black feminist readers but on the rereading of early and contemporary writing by black women, with the stress placed on the writer and the text, not on the reader.

2. It is interesting to note the similarities between Ellison's position and Zora Neale Hurston's position more than twenty years earlier. Owing in large part to Richard Wright's damning assessment of *Their Eyes Were Watching God* as a book having "no theme, no message, no thought," Hurston's novel stayed out of print during the thirty years that Wright's perspective dominated the black literary scene (Washington 35). In calling Hurston's novel substanceless, Wright obscures the real reason for his objections: Hurston's theme, message, and thought do not derive from an aesthetics devoted to forcing social change. Unlike Wright's, Hurston's was not a literature of protest against racism; rather, she looked to the black folk culture and celebrated the inner vitality and strength of that culture. In "What White Publishers Won't Print," Hurston anticipates Ellison's remarks about Howe when she claims that "the average, struggling, non-morbid Negro is the best kept secret in America" (89). Amiri Baraka's accusing Ellison of acting as an agent of the ruling ideology to subvert the issue of race in America echoes Wright's complaints about Hurston. See Baraka's "Afro-American Literature and Class Struggle" in his *Daggers and Javelins: Essays, 1974–1979.*

3. A close analysis of Ellison's and Howe's beliefs about the relationship between art and politics reveals that the two positions are not as opposed as they seem, for they trace back to the same philosophical father—Schiller—and his privileging of the faculty of the aesthetic so that it functions as ontology and ideology. Ellison's and Howe's positions both represent a recourse to the aesthetic realm to deal with complex political questions and problems. See Norris for a provocative discussion of Schiller's misreading of Kant.

4. The jury of the National Book Award does include some nonwhite members; indeed, Charles Johnson has served as a judge.

5. The situation of a white male jury judging the value of an African American woman's narrative brings to mind the Anita Hill–Clarence Thomas hearings. And how much did those distinguished members of the Senate Judiciary Committee really hear? For an excellent, multifaceted analysis of the Hill-Thomas hearings, see *Race-ing Justice, En-gendering Power: Essays on Anita Hill, Clarence Thomas, and the Construction of Social Reality*, edited by Toni Morrison.

6. I have arrived at these generalizations about the historical evolution of the slave narrative after reading many individual narratives, with examples chosen to cover the expanse of a century.

7. My version of the relationship between nineteenth-century slave narrator and reader stresses the *rhetorical* effect of the genre on actual readers but does not delve into the narrative relationship between the implied writer and implied reader. Robert Stepto claims that to understand the complexity of the relationship between African American writers and their readers, we need to recognize the mutual suspicion involved in the narrative transaction. He points to "the requisite presence, and frequently active role, of the distrusting reader—thinly guised as an unreliable story listener—in storytelling texts" (304). Nineteenth- and twentieth-century African American literature abounds in storytelling texts that "coerce authors and readers (or, if you will, texts and readers) into teller-hearer relationships" (306), relationships that reader-response analysis has ignored. Contemporary theories of creative or active reading usually offer scenarios of devious texts inciting the aggressive responses of resisting readers. Stepto observes that African American storytelling texts seek to construct "acts of communication . . . not when the text is assaulted but when the reader gets 'told' or 'told off'—in such a way that he or she finally begins to *hear*" (309). The competent reader will face the necessity of submitting to this model of listening or, alternatively, of resisting it to occupy a detached position outside the frame of the narrative.

8. See Morrison's "Unspeakable Things Unspoken: The Afro-American Presence in American Literature" and her interview with Claudia Tate in *Black Women Writers at Work* for discussions about her readers.

9. By "rhetorical-authorial audience," I refer to that part of the authorial audience involved in an agonistic relationship with the writer. Rhetoric always implies difference, so the rhetorical audience would be at odds with or at a distance from the writer's fictional or metafictional propositions—unlike the narrative audience, which is contained within the narrative logic. See Peter Rabinowitz's *Before Reading: Narrative Convention and the Politics of Interpretation* for a helpful discussion of authorial audience.

10. Stanley Fish's social model of reading is actually a neopragmatic theory of reading,

concerned with interpretive strategies learned from one's membership in a specific discourse community. Fish's hermetic hermeneutic "community" undercuts the dialogism that one would expect in a social model of reading.

11. This and all subsequent citations from *Beloved* refer to the New American Library edition (1987).

12. Calvin Hernton points out that this obligation has applied to black female writers as well. In "The Sexual Mountain and Black Women Writers," he details the sexist resentment that contemporary black male writers have shown toward their female counterparts—and especially toward Morrison—with some of the harshest critics claiming that "black women should be about the all-important business of exposing and fighting racism and capitalism so that the successful struggle of black men rising to their rightful position of power and dominance in their families, in their communities, and in America in general would be hastened" (201).

13. Sethe's character is based on the actual case of Margaret Garner, a fugitive slave from Kentucky who killed one of her children and vowed to kill the other three rather than have them imprisoned again in slavery. Unlike Sethe, Margaret Garner was never freed. She was tried not for killing her child but for the "real crime" of escaping and thus robbing her owner of his property. Found guilty, she was sent back into slavery. See Lerner's *Black Women in White America: A Documentary History* for an account of Garner and other women written out of traditional historical narratives.

14. Of course, there are some readers such as Elizabeth House who insist that Beloved is not a haint but an actual woman, a survivor of the middle passage whom Sethe takes in as a surrogate for the daughter she killed. In this reading, the related desires and delusions of Beloved, Sethe, and Denver lock them in a terrible bond/bind. To maintain this interpretation of the novel, one has to overlook a multitude of signs indicating that Beloved is indeed Sethe's daughter. See House's "Toni Morrison's Ghost: The Beloved Who Is Not Beloved."

15. These page numbers and all subsequent citations from *Middle Passage* refer to the 1990 Atheneum edition.

16. *In My Father's House*, a beautifully written book, was chosen as a 1992 *New York Times* Notable Book of the Year, so Johnson's prediction that the work would reach only a small number of academics may prove to have underestimated its influence. Then again, perhaps not— notability rarely guarantees wide cultural circulation.

17. The impulse to eradicate race through rational assertion is not limited to American writers and critics. Some members of the African National Congress presently are committed to the construction of a raceless society. Baker's critique notwithstanding, in *In My Father's House* Appiah makes clear that African identity and political unity in a continent of diverse cultures and languages must derive from foundations more secure than race.

18. In a letter to Elizabeth Abel, Morrison explains that in "Recitatif," the only short story she has ever written, her project was to remove the racial codes and substitute class codes in order to differentiate two categories that are always conflated. In an essay in *Critical Inquiry*, Abel candidly discusses her own misreading of the story, a reading that "installs the (racialized) body at the center of a text that deliberately withholds conventional racial iconography" ("Black Writing" 474).

19. Morrison's project of "re-memory" indicates that she does not accept the Baudrillardian picture of the world in which memory and history are eroded through the leveling and homogenization of a postmodern process of techno-capitalist simulation that produces the real from a model. See Baudrillard's *Simulations*.

20. See Michael Awkward for a cogent analysis of the delimiting effects of an experientially based politics of interpretation in feminist and African American criticism.

4. Reading (in) Cyberspace: Cybernetic Aesthetics, Hypertext, and the Virtual Public Space

1. Though the terms *informatics* and *cybernetics* are often used interchangeably, they are not synonymous: *cybernetics* is the broader term, concerned with systems of communication and control, and includes information technologies and their effects in its theory and application. I have chosen to concentrate on cybernetics not only because it is the more capacious term but also because it foregrounds the tension between the human and the machine that is often elided in discussions of informatics.

2. Consider, for example, this pitch from Theodore Nelson: "Our objective at the Xanadu project . . . has been the only proper objective: to make a new world. Don't think of the universal electronic docuverse, of open hypertextual publishing with transclusion, as my dream; it's your dream too, if you will only feel it. I want you to see, to feel in your gut, what open hypertextual publishing can do for the life of the mind, and perhaps for the life of the planet. Open hypertext publishing is the manifest destiny of free society. It is fair, it is powerful, and it is coming" ("Opening Hypertext" 56–57). The anaphoric final line reminds me of one of the pitches for the nuclear power industry in the 1960s: "It's clean, it's efficient, and its time has come."

3. Richard Lanham points out that the demand for computers preceded the marketing of the first computer kits in the mid-1970s; there were hundreds of prepaid orders for the 1975 Altair 8800 (*Electronic Word* ix).

4. Despite Wiener's aspirations, many computational questions remain unanswered in physics. For the inaugural lecture in 1980 marking his appointment as Lucasian Professor of Mathematics at Cambridge University, Stephen Hawking (a perfect example of a cyborgian fusion of human cerebral function and machines that enable bodily functioning) read a paper entitled, "Is the End in Sight for Theoretical Physics?" He ended the lecture with a warning: "[I]f one extrapolates their recent rapid rate of development, it would seem quite possible that [computers] will take over altogether in theoretical physics. So maybe the end is in sight for theoretical physicists, if not for theoretical physics" (qtd. in Boslough sec. 7). Hawking claimed that much of the work left to do in arriving at a unified theory or in conclusively disproving the possibility of a unified theory would depend on exceeding the present computational limits in theoretical physics. Thus, computers become increasingly more necessary to augment human intellectual capacity. Hawking's claim prompts a reexamination of Wiener's conviction that he could mathematically master even the most resistant of processes; as the founder of cybernetics and the father of the computer, Wiener can be credited with solving, at least indirectly, the most complex cosmological problems.

5. See David Porush's "Cybernetic Fiction and Postmodern Science" for an excellent discussion of the impulses behind and the reactions to cybernetic theories.

6. We can add that at a time when the modern conception of the nation-state is dying out, the response is an American sublime or some other version of a nationalist sublime that temporarily denies the shift to multinationalism, with its decentering and diffusion of power and deconstruction of politicocultural identity.

7. Klaus Theweleit describes a version of this sublimation in the practices of the proto-fascist German *Freikorps* between the world wars: "The new man is a man whose physique has been machinized, his psyche eliminated" (162)—the phallic man of steel who achieves his apotheosis as a machine of destruction, part of the totality-machine of the *Korps* (xix).

8. Another explanation for the anachronisms that result from the juxtaposing of the futuristic and the atavistic in science fiction has to do with the narrative concessions necessary to connect with an audience unable to imagine the future unless it is drawn in the shapes and shades of the familiar present or past. As Pam Rosenthal humorously observes, *Star Trek* features a futuristic control cabin where Sulu effortlessly presses buttons to accelerate the *Enterprise* to warp speed, "while Scotty wrestles with the clanking engines below deck, in an engine room that looks like a twentieth-century boiler room; one expects him to hit the pipes with a wrench" (91).

9. Mark Dery points to the misogynism that permeates the *Alien* films and *Terminator 2*, the loathful representation of a monstrous female sexuality as an engulfing viscosity and the female genitalia as "a noisome, pestilent sinkhole" (505). Thus, the cyborg is not so much a machine as it is a symbol for an overdetermined and armored masculinity besieged by that which would infiltrate it. The cloacal images of female goo and liquid filth also feature prominently in the *Freikorps* imagination that Theweleit uncovers. Woman—the soft, liquid, warm, gooey—was connected with terrifying libidinal energies, the flood that threatened to deluge the rational, the other that the *Freikorps* soldier had to dam within and steel himself against from the outside. The soldier was disgusted by the "heavy mass" of the internal organs and sought to become the machine-body without organs (Theweleit 3). The female miasma is associated with "the mass," otherwise known as the "Red Flood": "the face of the mass, rolling sluggishly onward, prepared to suck anything that offered no resistance into its mucous whirlpool" (4). As the reader will recall, this is the exact imagery Wyndham Lewis used in his scathing attacks on the work of Gertrude Stein, James Joyce, and other writers who manifested naturalist or feminine traits.

10. I do not mean to imply that all university students find Haraway's postgender cyborg a reasonable or comforting model for material socialist feminism. Some undergraduates in my feminist theory course react vehemently in opposition to Haraway's speculations. But I think the opposition stems from anxiety about gender as much as about an interface between the human and the machine. These students, for whom gender identification has not gelled or for whom gender does not feel oppressive, oppose Haraway's effort to get beyond gender.

11. Robert Markley argues that none of us should feel threatened by the concept of cyberspace, for it represents the age-old metaphysical attempt to transcend the problems of materiality and embodiment. In his critique of the "largely unchallenged discourses of the metaphysics of cyberspace—the philosophizing that ignores or mystifies the theoretical and historical underpinnings of this hallucinatory realm," Markley calls cyberspace "a consensual cliché"

(486). Markley claims that the reason cyberspace seems so inevitable and "irresistible" is that "it reproduces the sexualized oppositions—mind/body, form/content, idea/matter, male/female . . . that have characterized Western thought since (at least) Plato" (488).

12. See Shoshanna Zuboff's *In the Age of the Smart Machine: The Future of Work and Power.*

13. De Certeau's description of Brownian motions of innumerable and indeterminable effect sounds much like the butterfly effect posited in chaos theory, a microeffect that sets in motion a chain of effects that results in a macrotransformation (that is, the beating of the wings of a butterfly $\rightarrow$ X $\rightarrow$ . . . $\rightarrow$ alteration of wind currents $\rightarrow$ major change in the weather pattern). The butterfly effect is an appealing concept to those thinkers looking for a way to explain a postmodern agency in the face of all the forms of structural determinism to which we are heir.

14. Michael Heim says that when Gerritt Schroeder and Tim Murphy of UCLA began computerizing *Finnegans Wake* in 1987, they discovered that its hermeneutic structure perfectly represented hypertext (31). Mapped as a hypertext, the *Wake* might finally find a wider audience.

15. There being no established citation conventions for hypertext (which does not have page or paragraph numbers), I have decided to use the title of the screen on which the cited material appears. This quote comes from the "read at depth" screen in *Afternoon.*

16. It is interesting to imagine the changes in the shape of academic argument when the scholarly paper is rendered in hypertext or hypermedia form, which would not only allow but obligate the scholar to provide either the entire text or a generous portion of the cited text for the reader to see or hear (in the case of a hypermedia audio text file). The reader will be able to more easily judge whether the writer has fairly and skillfully cited and used the texts of others and will have the other texts in the intertextual web to allow for a thicker understanding of the author's paper.

17. In 1994, Visions of Reality (backed by several astronauts and other military personnel) began selling its Cybergate space battle team game to amusement parks, starting in Anaheim, California. Arcades such as Virtual Gaming in Austin, Texas, offer virtual reality versions of computer games such as Doom.

18. In *Listening to Prozac,* Peter Kramer explains the shortcomings of psychoanalysis by using an argument similar to Hayles's critique of late Cartesianism that ignores embodiment: "Modern biology attacks the centrality of mind altogether, highlighting the roles of brain and body. Psychiatrists used to concede that the mind and the brain were one, where the concession entailed letting a little biology creep into the mind-dominated discussion. Today, an exclusively mind-centered psychology would have trouble finding a seat at the table. . . . Now we are faced with the likelihood that introspection alone will not explain us to ourselves" (297–99).

19. Digitized films are now available, with viewers given the opportunity to piece a film together and to choose among various endings (Lanham, *Electronic Word* 7).

20. One repeatedly encounters the claim that in computer mediated communication what counts is idea and not personality, with the content of the message becoming all-important once the sender is virtualized. But what gets ignored in the idea/personality dichotomy is language. I would argue that a charismatic (or morbid) personality can be, and often is, embodied in the style of writing. Precisely because of the lack of material, kinetic, parasymbolic

cues and inflections, electronic language—like other *dialogic* forms of writing—must emote, pose, and perform (for) the user.

5. Cultural Production and the Teaching of Reading

1. Arjun Appadurai compellingly argues that this tension within global culture should not be conceived in simple mechanical terms of force and counterforce but arises from the growing disjunctures between and among "different streams or flows along which cultural material . . . mov[es] across national boundaries" (290); he designates these five flows as ethnoscape, finanscape, technoscape, mediascape, and ideoscape (275).

2. In his analysis of the process of canonization in U.S. fiction, Richard Ohmann admits that his conclusions about the levels of cultural gatekeeping involved in canonization (such as the power of the New York market) apply with certainty only until 1975 (220, n. 2).

3. Perhaps the most regressive teaching practice to result from computer technology is instructors' use of software style checks, which "analyze" a student's prose style according to the hoariest and most superficial of maxims, such as: "It is best to avoid beginning a sentence with *and* or *but.*" Or "The frequent use of passive voice can result in unclear writing." Such pearls of wisdom, devoid of any accompanying explanation, evoke in me the eerie sensation of encountering the ghost of my ninth-grade English teacher in the machine. (Into cyberspace their scattered bodies go.) The spelling checker and thesaurus, software companions to the style/ grammar checker, dispense such advice as "*Episteme*—not in dictionary. Consider changing to *epistle.*"

4. In the textbook canon of U.S. literature, there are only five fictional works by women: Willa Cather's "Wagner Matinee," Kate Chopin's "Story of an Hour," Katherine Anne Porter's "Jilting of Granny Weatherall," Flannery O'Connor's "The Life You Save May Be Your Own," and Eudora Welty's "A Worn Path" (Pace 35). As Barbara Pace rightly claims, all of the female characters in these stories are victimized in negative experiences with men, and they are silenced as well (35). Though Welty, for example, obviously means for the reader to admire old Phoenix Jackson's resourcefulness, resilience, and love for her grandson, Phoenix also comes across as being childishly dependent on unkind white people. Though we are to credit love for the rebirth that impels her on the long journey to get the medicine, there is also something of the Energizer bunny about her: wind her up and watch her go and go and go.

5. Bruce McLeod makes the interesting point that the architect who designed the University of California at Irvine was Walt Disney's first choice to design Disneyland (90).

6. Numerous educational networks have been established to link students and classrooms across the United States and internationally: for example, BreadNet (Bread Loaf School, Middlebury College) which connects students from Native American reservation schools, rural public schools, urban public schools, and private schools; and International Learning Network in San Diego, which links university students in California, Mexico, Israel, and Japan (Schwartz 17).

7. Of course, a lengthy response does not always indicate a student is reading carefully and participating in discussion; flaming can occur, which means that the lack of face-to-face confrontation has given a student the perfect opportunity to indulge in an emotion-laden, sometimes hateful diatribe. In this case, the frictionless ease of producing and disseminating

one's text results in extreme social friction. Anyone who has experienced electronic logorrhea on a computer network understands that this is an effective way to kill debate and jam the system. If the multicultural classroom is to serve as an intermediate space for the discussion and debate of multicultural issues, the instructor will have to anticipate the possibility of flaming and find ways to deal with it. The most obvious solution would be to "teach the conflict." Unlike the meaning of conflict in Graff's sense, in which professors incorporate critical debates into their teaching, this conflict actually emerges from the classroom exchange in the antagonism between kinds of discourse and between ideological positions. As a hollow pocket, the electronic multicultural classroom can be both a safe space and a contact zone.

8. Knowledgeable proponents of virtual reality foresee its offering the potential experience of other forms, objects, and modes of the self (Lanier and Biocca 161). Jaron Lanier predicts a proliferation "of games that have to do with merging bodies. . . . [producing] sensory feedback from the world that is a merger of the input from multiple people" (Lanier and Biocca 162). I am reminded of the concept of "simstim" (simulated stimulus) in Gibson's *Neuromancer.* Case wires into Molly's senses, gaining intimate proprioceptive knowledge of her, but little else. Fluidly assuming the proprioception of another object, animal, or human will be startling and enlightening in itself, but multicultural awareness also will require the social and political friction and ethical weight of performed embodied differences.

WORKS CITED

Abel, Elizabeth. "Black Writing, White Reading: Race and the Politics of Feminist Interpretation." *Critical Inquiry* 19 (1993): 470–98.

Acker, Kathy. *Empire of the Senseless.* New York: Grove Weidenfeld, 1988.

Adams, Henry. "The Dynamo and the Virgin." *The Education of Henry Adams: An Autobiography.* Ed. Henry Cabot Lodge. Boston: Houghton, 1918. 379–90.

Anderson, Margaret. *My Thirty Years' War.* New York: Horizon, 1969.

———. " 'Ulysses' " in Court. *Little Review* 7 (1921): 22–25.

Anderson, Perry. "Modernity and Revolution." *New Left Review* 144 (1984): 96–113.

Appadurai, Arjun. "Disjuncture and Difference in the Global Cultural Economy." Robbins 269–95.

Appiah, Anthony. *In My Father's House: Africa in the Philosophy of Culture.* New York: Oxford UP, 1992.

———. "Is the Post- in Postmodernism the Post- in Postcolonial?" *Critical Inquiry* 17 (1991): 336–57.

Applebee, Arthur. "Stability and Change in the High-School Canon." *English Journal* 81.5 (1992): 27–32.

Awkward, Michael. "Race, Gender, and the Politics of Reading." *Black American Literature Forum* 22.1 (1988): 5–27.

Baker, Houston. "Caliban's Triple Play." Gates, *"Race"* 381–95.

Bakhtin, M. M. *The Dialogic Imagination.* Trans. Caryl Emerson and Michael Holquist. Ed. Michael Holquist. Austin: U of Texas P, 1981.

———. *Problems of Dostoevsky's Poetics.* Trans. Caryl Emerson. Minneapolis: U of Minnesota P, 1984.

———. *Rabelais and His World.* Trans. Helen Iswolsky. Bloomington: Indiana UP, 1984.

Baraka, Amiri. "Afro-American Literature and Class Struggle." *Daggers and Javelins: Essays, 1974–1979.* New York: Quill, 1984.

Barth, John. "The Literature of Exhaustion." *The Friday Book: Essays and Other Nonfiction.* New York: Putnam's, 1984. 62–76.

Barthes, Roland. *The Pleasure of the Text.* Trans. Richard Miller. New York: Hill, 1975.

———. *The Semiotic Challenge.* Trans. Richard Howard. Berkeley: U of California P, 1994.

———. *S/Z.* Trans. Richard Miller. New York: Hill, 1974.

Baudrillard, Jean. *The Ecstasy of Communication.* Trans. Bernard Schutze and Caroline Schutze. New York: Semiotext(e), 1988.

———. *Simulations.* New York: Semiotext(e), 1983.

Bauman, Zygmunt. *Legislators and Interpreters: On Modernity, Postmodernity and Intellectuals.* Ithaca: Cornell UP, 1987.

Becker, May Lamberton. "The Reader's Guide." *Saturday Review of Literature* 21 Aug. 1926: 61.

Benhabib, Seyla, Judith Butler, and Drucilla Cornell. *Feminist Contentions: A Philosophical Exchange.* New York: Routledge, 1995.

Benstock, Shari. *Textualizing the Feminine: On the Limits of Genre.* Norman: U of Oklahoma P, 1991.

Berry, Ellen E. *Curved Thought and Textual Wandering: Gertrude Stein's Postmodernism.* Ann Arbor: U of Michigan P, 1992.

Bhabha, Homi. "Of Mimicry and Man: The Ambivalence of Colonial Discourse." *October* 28 (1984): 125–33.

Birkerts, Sven. *The Gutenberg Elegies: The Fate of Reading in an Electronic Age.* Boston: Faber, 1994.

Blackmur, R. P. *The Lion and the Honeycomb.* New York: Harcourt, 1955.

Boehm, Beth. "Readers Lost in the Funhouse." *Reading Narrative: Form, Ethics, Ideology.* Ed. James Phelan. Columbus: Ohio State UP, 1989. 102–19.

Booker, M. Keith. *Techniques of Subversion in Modern Literature: Transgression, Abjection, and the Carnivalesque.* Gainesville: U of Florida P, 1991.

Booth, Wayne. *The Rhetoric of Fiction.* Chicago: U of Chicago P, 1961.

Boslough, John. *Stephen Hawking's Universe.* Audiocassette. Dove Audio, 1991.

Bourdieu, Pierre. *The Field of Cultural Production: Essays on Art and Literature.* Ed. and intro. Randal Johnson. New York: Columbia UP, 1993.

Braxton, Joanne M., and Andree Nicola McLaughlin, eds. *Wild Women in the Whirlwind: Afra-American Culture and the Contemporary Renaissance.* New Brunswick: Rutgers UP, 1990.

Brooks, Peter. "Aesthetics and Ideology: What Happened to Poetics?" *Critical Inquiry* 20 (1994): 509–23.

———. *Reading for the Plot.* New York: Knopf, 1984.

Bukatman, Scott. *Terminal Identity: The Virtual Subject in Post-modern Science Fiction.* Durham: Duke UP, 1994.

Bump, Jerome. "Radical Changes in Class Discussion Using Networked Computers." *Computers and the Humanities* 24 (1990): 49–65.

Bürger, Peter. *The Decline of Modernism.* University Park: Pennsylvania State UP, 1992.

Burke, Kenneth. *Counterstatement.* 2nd ed. Berkeley: U of California P, 1984.

Bush, Vannevar. "As We May Think." *Atlantic Monthly* 176 (1945): 101–8.

Butler, Judith. Bodies That Matter: On the Discursive Limits of "Sex." New York: Routledge, 1993.

———. "For a Careful Reading." Benhabib 127–44.

Caillois, Roger. *Man, Play, and Games.* Trans. Meyer Barash. New York: Free Press of Glencoe, 1961.

Calinescu, Matei. *Rereading.* New Haven: Yale UP, 1993.

Calvino, Italo. *If on a Winter's Night a Traveler.* New York: Harcourt, 1981.

Canby, Henry Seidel, et al. *Designed for Reading: An Anthology Drawn from the Saturday Review of Literature 1924–1934.* New York: Macmillan, 1934.

Carey, John. *The Intellectuals and the Masses: Pride and Prejudice among the Literary Intelligentsia, 1880–1939*. New York: St. Martin's, 1993.

Carroll, David. "Community After Devastation: Culture, Politics, and the 'Public Space.'" *Politics, Theory, and Contemporary Culture*. Ed. Mark Poster. New York: Columbia UP, 1993. 159–96.

Carter, Angela. "Black Venus." *Saints and Strangers*. New York: Viking, 1986.

——. *Nights at the Circus*. New York: Viking, 1985.

——. "Notes from the Front Line." *On Gender and Writing*. Ed. Michele Wandor. London: Pandora Press, 1983. 69–77.

——. *The Passion of New Eve*. London: Virago, 1977.

——. *The Sadeian Woman and the Ideology of Pornography*. New York: Pantheon, 1988.

Cerf, Bennett A. "200,000 Customers: Harry Scherman and His Book-of-the-Month Club." *Saturday Review of Literature* 4 Dec. 1937: 17+.

Chartier, Roger. *Forms and Meanings: Texts, Performances, and Audiences from Codex to Computer*. Philadelphia: U of Pennsylvania P, 1995.

Christian, Barbara. "Somebody Forgot to Tell Somebody Something: African-American Women's Novels." Braxton and McLaughlin 326–41.

Christie, Chris. "Theories of Textual Determination and Audience Agency: An Empirical Contribution to the Debate." Mills, *Gendering the Reader* 47–66.

Cixous, Hélène. "The Laugh of the Medusa." *Critical Theory since 1965*. Ed. Hazard Adams and Leroy Searle. Gainesville: U of Florida P, 1992. 309–20.

Cooper, Marilyn M., and Cynthia L. Selfe. "Computer Conferences and Learning: Authority, Resistance, and Internally Persuasive Discourse." *College English* 52 (1990): 847–69.

Coover, Robert. "The End of Books." *New York Times Book Review* 21 June 1992, 1+.

Copjec, Joan. "The Orthopsychic Subject: Film Theory and the Reception of Lacan." *Read My Desire: Lacan Against the Historicists*. Cambridge: MIT Press, 1994. 15–38.

Cornell, Drucilla. "What Is Ethical Feminism?" Benhabib 75–106.

Crouch, Stanley. *Notes of a Hanging Judge: Essays and Reviews 1979–1989*. New York: Oxford UP, 1990.

Debord, Guy. *Society of the Spectacle*. Detroit: Black and Red, 1983.

de Certeau, Michel. *The Practice of Everyday Life*. Trans. Steven Rendall. Berkeley: U of California P, 1984.

DeKoven, Marianne. *Rich and Strange: Gender, History, Modernism*. Princeton: Princeton UP, 1991.

Delaney, Paul, and George P. Landow, eds. *Hypermedia and Literary Studies*. Cambridge: MIT Press, 1991.

de Lauretis, Teresa, ed. *Feminist Studies/Critical Studies*. Bloomington: Indiana UP, 1987.

Deleuze, Gilles, and Félix Guattari. *A Thousand Plateaus: Capitalism and Schizophrenia*. Trans. Brian Massumi. Minneapolis: U of Minnesota P, 1987.

Deming, Robert H., ed. *James Joyce: The Critical Heritage*. 2 vols. New York: Barnes, 1970.

Dery, Mark. "Cyberculture." *South Atlantic Quarterly* 91 (1992): 501–23.

Douglas, J. Yellowlees. "What Hypertext Can Do That Print Narratives Cannot." *Reader: Essays in Reader-Oriented Theory, Criticism, and Pedagogy* 28 (1992): 1–22.

DuPlessis, Rachel Blau. *The Pink Guitar: Writing as Feminist Practice*. New York: Routledge, 1990.

Eagleton, Terry. *The Ideology of the Aesthetic*. Oxford, UK: Basil Blackwell, 1990.

Eco, Umberto. "Eternal Fascism." *Utne Reader* 72 (1995): 57–59.

Edmondson, Belinda. "Black Aesthetics, Feminist Aesthetics, and the Problems of Oppositional Discourse." *Cultural Critique* 22 (1992): 75–98.

Elam, Diane. *Romancing the Postmodern*. New York: Routledge, 1992.

Eliot, T. S. " 'Ulysses,' Order and Myth." *Selected Prose*. Ed. Frank Kermode. New York: Harcourt, 1975. 157–78.

Ellison, Ralph. "The World and the Jug." *Shadow and Act*. New York: Random, 1964. 107–43.

Ellmann, Richard. *James Joyce*. New York: Oxford UP, 1982.

———. Preface. Joyce, *Ulysses* ix–xiv.

Emerson, Caryl. Preface. Bakhtin, *Problems* xxix–xliii.

Ess, Charles. "The Political Computer: Hypertext, Democracy, and Habermas." Landow, *Hyper/Text/Theory* 225–67.

Fetterley, Judith. *The Resisting Reader: A Feminist Approach to American Literature*. Bloomington: Indiana UP, 1978.

Flanner, Janet. "A Life on a Cloud." *New Yorker* 3 June 1974: 44–65.

———. *Paris Journal: 1944–1965*. Ed. William Shawn. New York: Harcourt, 1977.

Flint, Kate. *The Woman Reader 1837–1914*. New York: Oxford UP, 1993.

Flynn, Elizabeth, and Patrocinio Schweickart, eds. *Gender and Reading: Essays on Readers, Texts, and Contexts*. Baltimore: Johns Hopkins UP, 1986.

Foster, Hal, ed. *The Anti-Aesthetic: Essays on Postmodern Culture*. Seattle: Bay, 1983.

Foucault, Michel. *Discipline and Punish: The Birth of the Prison*. Trans. Alan Sheridan. New York: Vintage, 1979.

Frank, Joseph: "Spatial Form in Modern Literature." *The Idea of Spatial Form*. New Brunswick: Rutgers UP, 1991. 5–66.

Fraser, Nancy. "Rethinking the Public Sphere: A Contribution to the Critique of Actually Existing Democracy." Robbins 1–32.

Freund, Elizabeth. *The Return of the Reader: Reader-Response Criticism*. London: Methuen, 1987.

Gates, Henry Louis, Jr. "Beyond the Culture Wars: Identities in Dialogue." *Profession 93*: 6–11.

———. "Critical Fanonism." *Critical Inquiry* 17 (1991): 457–70.

———, ed. *"Race," Writing, and Difference*. Chicago: U of Chicago P, 1986.

———, ed. *Reading Black, Reading Feminist: A Critical Anthology*. New York: Meridian, 1990.

Gelley, Alexander. "City Texts: Representation, Semiology, and Urbanism." *Politics, Theory, and Contemporary Culture*. Ed. Mark Poster. New York: Columbia UP, 1993. 237–60.

Gibson, William. *Neuromancer*. New York: Ace, 1984.

Gilbert, Sandra, and Susan Gubar. *No Man's Land: The Place of the Woman Writer in the Twentieth Century*. 2 vols. New Haven: Yale UP, 1988.

Gilbert, Stuart. *James Joyce's "Ulysses": A Study*. New York: Vintage, 1955.

Giroux, Henry. "Post-Colonial Ruptures and Democratic Possibilities: Multiculturalism as Anti-Racist Pedagogy." *Cultural Critique* 21 (1992): 5–39.

———. *Teachers as Intellectuals: Toward a Critical Pedagogy of Learning*. South Hadley, MA: Bergin, 1988.

Graff, Gerald. "The Pedagogical Turn." *Journal of the Midwest Modern Language Association* 27 (1994): 65–70.

Grewal, Inderpal, and Caren Kaplan, eds. *Scattered Hegemonies: Postmodernity and Transnational Feminist Practices*. Minneapolis: U of Minnnesota P, 1994.

Grusin, Richard. "What Is an Electronic Author? Theory and the Technological Fallacy." *Configurations* 2 (1994): 469–83.

Guyer, Carolyn. *Quibbling*. Cambridge, MA: Eastgate, 1993.

Hacker, Andrew. *Two Nations: Black and White, Separate, Hostile, Unequal*. New York: Scribner's, 1992.

Haraway, Donna. "A Manifesto for Cyborgs: Science, Technology, and Socialist Feminism in the 1980s." *Socialist Review* 80 (1985): 65–107.

Hawisher, Gail, and Cynthia L. Selfe. "The Rhetoric of Technology and the Electronic Writing Class." *College Composition and Communication* 42 (1991): 55–65.

Hayles, N. Katherine. *The Cosmic Web: Scientific Field Models and Literary Strategies in the Twentieth Century*. Ithaca: Cornell UP, 1984.

———. "The Materiality of Informatics." *Configurations* 1 (1992): 147–70.

Hayman, David. *Ulysses: The Mechanics of Meaning*. Madison: U of Wisconsin P, 1982.

Heap, Jane. "Ulysses." *Little Review* 9 (1922): 34–35.

Heath, Stephen. "Ambiviolences: Notes for Reading Joyce." *Post-structuralist Joyce: Essays from the French*. Ed. Derek Attridge and Daniel Ferrer. New York: Cambridge UP, 1984. 31–68.

Heim, Michael. *The Metaphysics of Virtual Reality*. New York: Oxford UP, 1993.

Hernton, Calvin. "The Sexual Mountain and Black Women Writers." Braxton and McLaughlin 195–212.

Hoffman, Frederick, Charles Allen, and Carolyn F. Ulrich. *The Little Magazine: A History and a Bibliography*. Princeton: Princeton UP, 1947.

House, Elizabeth. "Toni Morrison's Ghost: The Beloved Who Is Not Beloved." *Studies in American Fiction* 18 (1990): 17–26.

Howe, Irving. *The Decline of the New*. New York: Harcourt, 1970.

Hughes, Linda K., and Michael Lund. "Linear Stories and Circular Visions: The Decline of the Victorian Serial." *Chaos and Order: Complex Dynamics in Literature and Science*. Ed. N. Katherine Hayles. Chicago: U of Chicago P, 1991. 167–94.

Hurston, Zora Neale. "What White Publishers Won't Print." *Negro Digest* 8 (1950): 85–89.

Hutcheon, Linda. *The Politics of Postmodernism*. New York: Routledge, 1989.

Huyssen, Andreas. *After the Great Divide*. Bloomington: Indiana UP, 1986.

Iser, Wolfgang. *The Fictive and the Imaginary: Charting Literary Anthropology*. Baltimore: Johns Hopkins UP, 1993.

Jameson, Fredric. Interview with Anders Stephanson. *Flash Art* (internatl. ed.) 131 (1986/1987): 69–73.

———. "Postmodernism, or the Cultural Logic of Late Capitalism." *New Left Review* 146 (1984): 53–92.

Johnson, Barbara. "Thresholds of Difference: Structures of Address in Zora Neal Hurston. Gates, *"Race"* 317–28.

Johnson, Charles. *Being and Race: Black Writing since 1970.* Bloomington: Indiana UP, 1988.

——. "Inventing Africa." *New York Times Book Review* 21 June 1992: 8.

——. *Middle Passage.* New York: Atheneum, 1990.

Johnson, Mark. *The Body in the Mind: The Bodily Basis of Meaning, Imagination, and Reason.* Chicago: U of Chicago P, 1987.

Joyce, James. *Ulysses.* Ed. Hans Walter Gabler. New York: Random House, 1986.

Joyce, Joyce A. "Black Woman Scholar, Critic, and Teacher: The Inextricable Relationship among Race, Sex, and Class." *(En)Gendering Knowledge: Feminists in Academe.* Ed. Joan E. Hartman and Ellen Messer-Davidow. Knoxville: U of Tennessee P, 1991. 159–78.

Joyce, Michael. *Afternoon, a Story.* Cambridge, MA: Eastgate, 1987.

——. "Notes Toward an Unwritten Non-Linear Electronic Text, 'The Ends of Print Culture.'" *Postmodern Culture* 2.1 (1991): 45 pars. Online. BITNET. 10 Aug. 1994.

Keenan, Thomas. "Windows: Of Vulnerability." Robbins 121–41.

Kenner, Hugh. *Joyce's Voices.* Berkeley: U of California P, 1956.

Kramer, Peter. *Listening to Prozac: A Psychiatrist Explores Antidepressant Drugs and the Remaking of the Self.* New York: Viking, 1993.

Landon, Brooks. "No Slipping Out." *American Book Review* 13.4 (1991): 7.

Landow, George P. *Hypertext: The Convergence of Contemporary Critical Theory and Technology.* Baltimore: Johns Hopkins UP, 1992.

——, ed. *Hyper/Text/Theory.* Baltimore: Johns Hopkins UP, 1994.

Landow, George P., and Paul Delaney. "Hypertext, Hypermedia and Literary Studies: The State of the Art." Delaney and Landow 3–50.

Lanham, Richard A. *The Electronic Word: Democracy, Technology, and the Arts.* Chicago: U of Chicago P, 1993.

——. "The Extraordinary Convergence: Democracy, Technology, Theory, and the University Curriculum." *South Atlantic Quarterly* 89 (1990): 28–50.

Lanier, Jaron, and Frank Biocca. "An Insider's View of the Future of Virtual Reality." *Journal of Communication* 42 (1992): 150–72.

Larsen, Deena, *Marble Springs.* Cambridge, MA: Eastgate, 1995.

Larson, Susan. "Back to the Future: Sci-fi Writer William Gibson Returns to the Cyberpunk World in 'Virtual Light.'" *Times-Picayune* 29 Aug. 1993: D-1+.

Lefevbre, Henri. *The Production of Space.* Trans. Donald Nicholson-Smith. Oxford, UK: Blackwell, 1991.

Lerner, Gerda, ed. *Black Women in White America: A Documentary History.* New York: Vintage, 1973.

Levenson, Michael. *The Genealogy of Modernism: A Study of English Literary Doctrine, 1908–1922.* New York: Cambridge UP, 1984.

Levin, Harry. *James Joyce: A Critical Introduction.* Rev. ed. New York: New Directions, 1960.

Levine, Lawrence. *Highbrow/Lowbrow: The Emergence of Cultural Hierarchy in America.* Cambridge: Harvard UP, 1988.

Lewis, Wyndham. *Time and Western Man.* London: Chatto, 1927.

Lorando, Mark. "Talking with Your T.V." *Times-Picayune* 29 June 1994: E1–E2.

Lyotard, Jean-François. *The Postmodern Condition: A Report on Knowledge.* Trans. Geoff Bennington and Brian Massumi. Minneapolis: U of Minnesota P, 1984.

MacCabe, Colin. *James Joyce and the Revolution of the Word.* New York: Barnes, 1979.

Madison, G. B. *The Hermeneutics of Postmodernity: Figures and Themes.* Bloomington: Indiana UP, 1988.

Mailloux, Steven. *Interpretive Conventions: The Reader in the Study of American Fiction.* Ithaca: Cornell UP, 1982.

Mann, Harveen Sachdeva. "U.S. Multiculturalism, Post-Colonialism, and Indo-Anglian Literature: Some Issues of Critical Pedagogy and Theory." *Journal of the Midwest Modern Language Association* 27 (1994): 94–108.

Marchand, Roland. *Advertising the American Dream: Making Way for Modernity, 1920–1940.* Berkeley: U of California P, 1985.

Marcus, Jane. "Britannia Rules *The Waves.*" *Decolonizing Tradition: New Views of Twentieth-Century "British" Literary Canons.* Ed. Karen R. Lawrence. Urbana: U of Illinois P, 1992. 136–62.

Markley, Robert. "Boundaries: Mathematics, Alienation, and the Metaphysics of Cyberspace." *Configurations* 2 (1994): 485–507.

Max, D. T. "The End of the Book?" *Atlantic Monthly* September 1994: 61–71.

McCaffery, Larry. "The Artists of Hell: Kathy Acker and 'Punk' Aesthetics." *Breaking the Sequence: Women's Experimental Fiction.* Ed. Ellen G. Friedman and Miriam Fuchs. Princeton: Princeton UP, 1989. 215–30.

McCarthy, Patrick. "Stuart Gilbert's Guide to the Perplexed." *Re-viewing Classics of Joyce Criticism.* Ed. Janet Egleson Dunleavy. Urbana: U of Illinois Press, 1991. 23–35.

McDowell, Deborah E. "Negotiating Between Tenses: Witnessing Slavery after Freedom— *Dessa Rose.*" *Slavery and the Literary Imagination.* Ed. Deborah E. McDowell and Arnold Rampersad. Baltimore: Johns Hopkins UP, 1989. 144–63.

McHale, Brian. "Modernist Reading, Post-modern Text: The Case of *Gravity's Rainbow.*" *Poetics Today* 1 (1979): 85–110.

———. *Postmodern Fiction.* New York, Routledge, 1987.

McLeod, Bruce. "Staking Out the University (Or, the Spaced-Out University)." *Journal of the Midwest Modern Language Association* 27 (1994): 85–93.

McMillan, Terry. *Waiting to Exhale.* New York: Viking, 1992.

Michael, Magali Cormier. *Feminism and the Postmodern Impulse: Post-World War II Fiction.* Albany: State U of New York P, 1996.

Mills, Sarah. Introduction. Mills, *Gendering the Reader* 1–21.

———, ed. *Gendering the Reader.* New York: Harvester, 1994.

Moores, Shaun. *Interpreting Audiences: The Ethnography of Media Consumption.* London: Sage, 1993.

Morley, David, and Kevin Robins. *Spaces of Identity: Global Media, Electronic Landscapes, and Cultural Boundaries.* New York: Routledge, 1995.

Morris, Meaghan. "Feminism, Reading, Postmodernism." *Postmodernism: A Reader.* Ed. Thomas Docherty. New York: Columbia UP, 1993. 368–89.

Morrison, Toni. *Beloved.* New York: New American Library, 1987.

———. Interview. *Black Women Writers at Work.* Ed. Claudia Tate. New York: Continuum, 1983. 117–31.

———. *Playing in the Dark: Whiteness and the Literary Imagination.* Cambridge: Harvard UP, 1992.

———, ed. *Race-ing Justice and En-gendering Power: Essays on Anita Hill, Clarence Thomas, and the Construction of Social Reality.* New York: Pantheon, 1992.

———. "Unspeakable Things Unspoken: The Afro-American Presence in American Literature." *Michigan Quarterly Review* 28 (1989): 1–34.

Moulthrop, Stuart. "Deuteronomy Comix." *Postmodern Culture* 3.2 (1993): 25 pars. Online. BITNET. 10 Aug. 1994.

———. "Reading from the Map: Metonymy and Metaphor in the Fiction of 'Forking Paths.' " Delaney and Landow 119–32.

———. "Rhizome and Resistance: Hypertext and the Dreams of a New Culture." Landow, *Hyper/Text/Theory* 299–319.

———. *Victory Garden.* Cambridge, MA: Eastgate, 1991.

Nabokov, Vladimir. *Lolita.* Putnam's, 1955.

———. *Pale Fire.* Putnam's, 1962.

Naremore, James, and Patrick Brantlinger. "Introduction: Six Artistic Cultures." *Modernity and Mass Culture.* Ed. Naremore and Brantlinger. Bloomington: Indiana UP, 1991. 1–23.

Nelson, Cary. "Multiculturalism Without Guarantees: From Anthologies to the Social Text." *Journal of the Midwest Modern Language Association* 26 (1993): 47–57.

Nelson, Theodore Holm. *Literary Machines.* Sausalito, CA: Mindful, 1980.

———. "Opening Hypertext: A Memoir." Tuman 43–57.

Norris, Christopher. *What's Wrong with Postmodernism: Critical Theory and the Ends of Philosophy.* Baltimore: Johns Hopkins UP, 1990.

Nunberg, Geoffrey. "The Places of Books in the Age of Electronic Reproduction." *Representations* 42 (1993): 13–37.

Ohmann, Richard. "The Shaping of a Canon: U.S. Fiction, 1960–1975." *Critical Inquiry* 10 (1983): 199–223.

Olney, James. " 'I Was Born': Slave Narratives, Their Status as Autobiography and as Literature." *The Slave's Narrative.* Ed. Charles T. Davis and Henry Louis Gates, Jr. New York: Oxford UP, 1985. 148–74.

Owens, Craig. "The Discourse of Others: Feminists and Postmodernism." Foster 57–82.

Pace, Barbara. "The Textbook Canon: Genre, Gender, and Race in U.S. Literature." *English Journal* 81.5 (1992): 33–38.

Paulson, William. "Computers, Minds, and Texts: Preliminary Reflections." *New Literary History* 20 (1989): 291–303.

Poirier, Richard. *A World Elsewhere: The Place of Style in American Literature.* New York: Oxford UP, 1986.

Pollitt, Katha. "Why We Read: Canon to the Right of Me. . . ." *Reasonable Creatures: Essays on Women and Feminism.* New York: Knopf, 1994. 16–25.

Porush, David. "Cybernetic Fiction and Postmodern Science." *New Literary History* 20 (1989): 373–96.

———. "Hacking the Brainstem: Postmodern Metaphysics in Stephenson's *Snow Crash*." *Configurations* 2 (1994): 537–71.

Poster, Mark, ed. *Politics, Theory, and Contemporary Culture*. New York: Columbia UP, 1993.

Pratt, Mary Louise. "Arts of the Contact Zone." *Profession* 91: 33–40.

Prigogine, Ilya. *From Being to Becoming: Time and Complexity in the Physical Sciences*. New York: Freeman, 1980.

Prigogine, Ilya, and Isabelle Stengers. *Order out of Chaos: Man's New Dialogue with Nature*. New York: Bantam, 1984.

Rabinowitz, Peter. *Before Reading: Narrative Convention and the Politics of Interpretation*. Ithaca: Cornell UP, 1987.

Radway, Janice. *Reading the Romance: Women, Patriarchy, and Popular Literature*. Chapel Hill: U of North Carolina P, 1984.

———. "The Scandal of the Middlebrow: The Book-of-the-Month Club, Class Fracture, and Cultural Authority." *South Atlantic Quarterly* 89 (1990): 703–36.

Rainey, Lawrence. "The Price of Modernism: Reconsidering the Publication of *The Waste Land*." *Critical Quarterly* 31.4 (1989): 21–47.

Rambuss, Richard. "Christ's Ganymede." *Yale Journal of Law and the Humanities* 7 (1995): 77–96.

Reed, Christopher. "Through Formalism: Feminism and Virginia Woolf's Relation to Bloomsbury Aesthetics." *Twentieth-Century Literature* 38 (1992): 20–43.

Rheingold, Howard. *The Virtual Community: Homesteading on the Electric Frontier*. New York: Addison-Wesley, 1993.

Richter, David. "The Reader as Ironic Victim." *Novel* 14 (1981): 135–51.

Rickels, Laurence A. Interview with Kathy Acker. *Artforum* (February 1994): 61+.

Robbins, Bruce. "Introduction: The Public as Phantom." Robbins viii–xxvi.

———, ed. *The Phantom Public Sphere*. Minneapolis: U of Minnesota P, 1993.

Robinson, Sally. *Engendering the Subject: Gender and Self-Representation in Contemporary Women's Fiction*. Albany: State U of New York P, 1991.

Rosenberg, Martin E. "Physics and Hypertext: Liberation and Complicity in Art and Pedagogy." Landow, *Hyper/Text/Theory* 268–98.

Rosenthal, Pam. "Jacked In: Fordism, Cyberpunk, Marxism." *Socialist Review* 21.1 (1991): 79–103.

Rovit, Earl. "Modernism and Three Magazines: An Editorial Revolution." *Sewanee Review* 93 (1985): 540–53.

Rubin, Joan Shelley. "Self, Culture, and Self-Culture in Modern America: The Early History of the Book-of-the-Month Club." *Journal of American History* 71 (1985): 782–806.

Russo, Mary. "Female Grotesques: Carnival and Theory." De Lauretis 213–29.

Ryan, Judith. *The Vanishing Subject: Early Psychology and Literary Modernism*. Chicago: U of Chicago P, 1991.

Ryan, Marie-Laure. "Immersion vs. Interactivity: Virtual Reality and Literary Theory." *Postmodern Culture* 5.1 (1994): 39 pars. Online. BITNET. 7 Oct. 1994.

Said, Edward. *Culture and Imperialism.* New York: Vintage, 1993.

——. "Opponents, Audiences, Constituencies and Community." Foster 135–59.

Schleifer, Ronald. *Rhetoric and Death: The Language of Modernism and Postmodern Discourse Theory.* Urbana: U of Illinois P, 1990.

Scholes, Robert. *Fabulation and Metafiction.* Urbana: U of Illinois P, 1979.

——. *In Search of James Joyce.* Urbana: U of Illinois P, 1992.

Schwab, Gabriele. *Subjects Without Selves: Transitional Texts in Modern Fiction.* Cambridge: Harvard UP, 1994.

Schwartz, Jeffrey. "Using an Electronic Network to Play the Scales of Discourse." *English Journal* 79 (1990): 16–24.

Schweickart, Patrocinio. "Reading Ourselves: Toward a Feminist Theory of Reading." Flynn and Schweickart 31–62.

Scott, Bonnie Kime, ed. *The Gender of Modernism.* Bloomington: Indiana UP, 1990.

Scott, Thomas L., and Melvin J. Friedman. *Pound/The Little Review: The Letters of Ezra Pound to Margaret Anderson.* New York: New Directions, 1988.

Sekora, John. "Comprehending Slavery: Language and Personal History in the *Narrative.*" *Frederick Douglass's Narrative of the Life of Frederick Douglass.* Ed. and intro. Harold Bloom. New York: Chelsea, 1988. 153–64.

Senn, Fritz. *Joyce's Dislocutions: Essays on Reading as Translation.* Ed. John Paul Riquelme. Baltimore: Johns Hopkins UP, 1984.

Silver, Brenda. " 'Anon' and 'The Reader': Virginia Woolf's Last Essays." *Twentieth Century Literature* 25 (1979): 365–441.

——. "Virginia Woolf: Cultural Critique." B. K. Scott 626–28.

Slusser, George. "The Frankenstein Barrier." Slusser and Shippey 46–71.

Slusser, George, and Tom Shippey, eds. *Fiction 2000: Cyberpunk and the Future of Narrative.* Athens: U of Georgia P, 1992.

Smith, Paul. *Discerning the Subject.* Minneapolis: U of Minnesota P, 1988.

Smith, Valerie. "Black Feminist Theory and the Representation of 'Other.' " *Changing Our Own Words: Essays on Criticism, Theory, and Language by Black Women.* Ed. Cheryl A. Wall. New Brunswick: Rutgers UP, 1989. 38–57.

Sosnoski, James J., and David B. Downing. "A Multivalent Pedagogy for a MultiCultural Time: A Diary of a Course." Unpublished essay, 1993. Forthcoming in *PRETEXT.*

——. "The Protocol of Care in the Cycles Project." *Journal of the Modern Language Association* 27 (1994): 75–84.

——. "Teaching in Electronic Schools: The Cycles Project." Unpublished essay, 1993.

Sperber, Dan, and Deirdre Wilson. *Relevance: Communication and Cognition.* Cambridge: Harvard UP, 1986.

Spillers, Hortense. "A Hateful Passion, a Lost Love." *Feminist Issues in Literary Scholarship.* Ed. Shari Benstock. Bloomington: Indiana UP, 1987. 181–207.

Spivak, Gayatri. "Theory in the Margin: Coetzee's Foe Reading Defoe's *Crusoe/Roxana.*" *Consequences of Theory.* Ed. Jonathan Arac and Barbara Johnson. Baltimore: Johns Hopkins UP, 1991. 154–80.

Sponsler, Claire. "Cyberpunk and the Dilemmas of Postmodern Narrative: The Example of William Gibson." *Contemporary Literature* 33 (1992): 625–44.

Stallybrass, Peter, and Allon White. *The Politics and Poetics of Transgression.* Ithaca: Cornell UP, 1986.

Stepto, Robert B. "Distrust of the Reader in Afro-American Narratives." *Reconstructing American Literary History.* Ed. Sacvan Bercovitch. Cambridge: Harvard UP, 1986. 300–22.

Suleiman, Susan Rubin. *Risking Who One Is: Encounters with Contemporary Art and Literature.* Cambridge: Harvard UP, 1994.

———. *Subversive Intent: Gender, Politics, and the Avant-Garde.* Cambridge: Harvard UP, 1990.

Suleri, Sara. "Multiculturalism and Its Discontents." *Profession 93:* 16–17.

Tamir-Ghez, Nomi. "The Art of Persuasion of Nabokov's *Lolita.*" *Poetics Today* 1 (1979): 65–83.

Theweleit, Klaus. *Male Fantasies.* Vol. 2. *Male Bodies: Psychoanalyzing the White Terror.* Trans. Erica Carter and Chris Turner. Minneapolis: U of Minnesota P, 1989.

Thomas, Brook. "*Ulysses* on Trial: Some Supplementary Reading." *Criticism* 33 (1991): 371–93.

Tickner, Lisa. "Men's Work? Masculinity and Modernism." *differences* 4.3 (1992): 1–37.

Tuman, Myron, ed. *Literacy Online: The Promise (and Peril) of Reading and Writing with Computers.* Pittsburgh: U of Pittsburgh P, 1992.

Ulmer, Gregory L. "Grammatology (in the Stacks) of Hypermedia: A Simulation." Tuman 139–64.

Walker, Alice. *The Color Purple.* New York: Washington Square, 1982.

———. *Possessing the Secret of Joy.* New York: Harcourt, 1992.

Walton, Kendall L. *Mimesis as Make-Believe: On the Foundations of the Representational Arts.* Cambridge: Harvard UP, 1990.

Washington, Mary Helen. " 'The Darkened Eye Restored': Notes Toward a Literary History of Black Women." Gates, *Reading Black* 30–43.

Waugh, Patricia. *Feminine Fictions: Revisiting the Postmodern.* New York: Routledge, 1989.

Weixlmann, Joe. "Black Literary Criticism at the Juncture." *Contemporary Literature* 27.1 (1986): 48–62.

Westfahl, Gary. " 'The Gernsback Continuum': William Gibson in the Context of Science Fiction." Slusser and Shippey 88–108.

Whelehan, Imelda. "Feminism and Trash: Destabilising 'the Reader.' " Mills, *Gendering the Reader* 217–35.

Wilson, Edmund. *The American Earthquake: A Documentary of the Twenties and Thirties.* Garden City, NY: Doubleday, 1958.

Wilson, Rob. "Techno-euphoria and the Discourse of the American Sublime." *boundary 2* 19 (1992): 205–29.

Wines, Michael. "Disney Will 'Recreate' U.S. History Next to a Place Where It Was Made." *New York Times* 12 Nov. 1993: A8.

Winnett, Susan. "Coming Unstrung: Women, Men, Narrative, and Principles of Pleasure." *Publications of the Modern Language Association* 105 (1990): 505–16.

Winnicott, D. W. *Playing and Reality.* New York: Basic, 1971.

Woodmansee, Martha. *The Author, Art, and the Market: Rereading the History of Aesthetics.* New York: Columbia UP, 1994.

Woolf, Virginia. *Between the Acts.* London: Hogarth Press, 1941.

———. *The Letters of Virginia Woolf.* Vols. 1–6. Ed. Nigel Nicholson and Joanne Trautmann. New York: Harcourt, 1975–80.

———. "Middlebrow." *The Death of the Moth and Other Essays.* New York: Harcourt, 1970. 176–86.

———. "Modern Fiction." *The Common Reader.* New York: Harcourt, 1925. 150–58.

Yankelovich, Nicole, Norman Meyrowitz, and Andries van Dam. "Reading and Writing the Electronic Book." Delaney and Landow 53–80.

Ziegfeld, Richard. "Interactive Fiction: A New Literary Genre?" *New Literary History* 20 (1989): 341–72.

Zizek, Slavoj. *The Sublime Object of Ideology.* New York: Verso, 1989.

Zuboff, Shoshanna. *In the Age of the Smart Machine: The Future of Work and Power.* New York: Basic, 1988.

Zwerdling, Alex. "*Between the Acts* and the Coming of War." *Novel* 10 (1977): 220–36.

INDEX

MOLLY ABEL TRAVIS is an associate professor of English at Tulane University who teaches courses on twentieth-century British and American literature, feminist theory, cultural studies, and rhetoric. She has published essays on reader/reception theory, on hypertext, and on gender and race in nineteenth- and twentieth-century literature and culture. She is currently working on a book about feminist irony in contemporary art and theory.